Applied Ethics

21st century problems and perspectives

Preliminary Edition

Emily Kulbacki
Pierce College

Kendall Hunt
publishing company

Cover image courtesy of S. Kulbacki.
Interior illustrations, unless otherwise credited are courtesy of S. Kulbacki.

Kendall Hunt
publishing company

www.kendallhunt.com
Send all inquiries to:
4050 Westmark Drive
Dubuque, IA 52004-1840

ISBN 978-1-4652-3879-5

Printed in the United States of America
10 9 8 7 6 5 4 3 2 1

To Wayne Mann who is and always will be my favorite and most loved challenge.

Contents

Preface

This text represents what I feel are substantial improvements over traditional applied ethics and contemporary moral problems texts that are currently available to instructors. Unlike traditional applied ethics texts that are either subject specific or offer well-worn moral problems, this book offers a diverse range of subjects and relies on the latest developments in science and technology to frame moral issues that are unique to our time in history. Additionally, the voices of contemporary philosophers have been added to reflect the diversity of contemporary thought and to help students to see that ethics as a discipline is not only alive but doing well.

My goals, which have shaped both the content and structure of this text, are to help students (1) see why ethics matters, (2) understand key concepts in applied ethics, (3) become more familiar with the latest scientific and technological advances that shape the ethical challenges we face, and (4) become adept at applying ethical theories, principles, and concepts to a variety of contemporary moral issues.

Features

- An extensive introduction to the moral theories of both traditional and contemporary philosophers that reflects the diversity of 21st-century philosophy
- In-depth discussions on the latest developments in bioethics, neuroscience, and information technology that help students gain a better understanding of the underlying causes of the moral issues to be discussed
- Up-to-date and detailed case studies that allow students to apply what they have learned to real-world issues
- An electronic resources list for instructors featuring primary resource materials that can be easily obtained by students through popular databases such as EBSCO Host and J-STOR
- Illustrations that offer material for further instruction or can serve as discussion-starters for individual and group activities
- A digital test bank that features test questions for each chapter and additional case studies

CHAPTER ONE

Morality and Ethical Theories

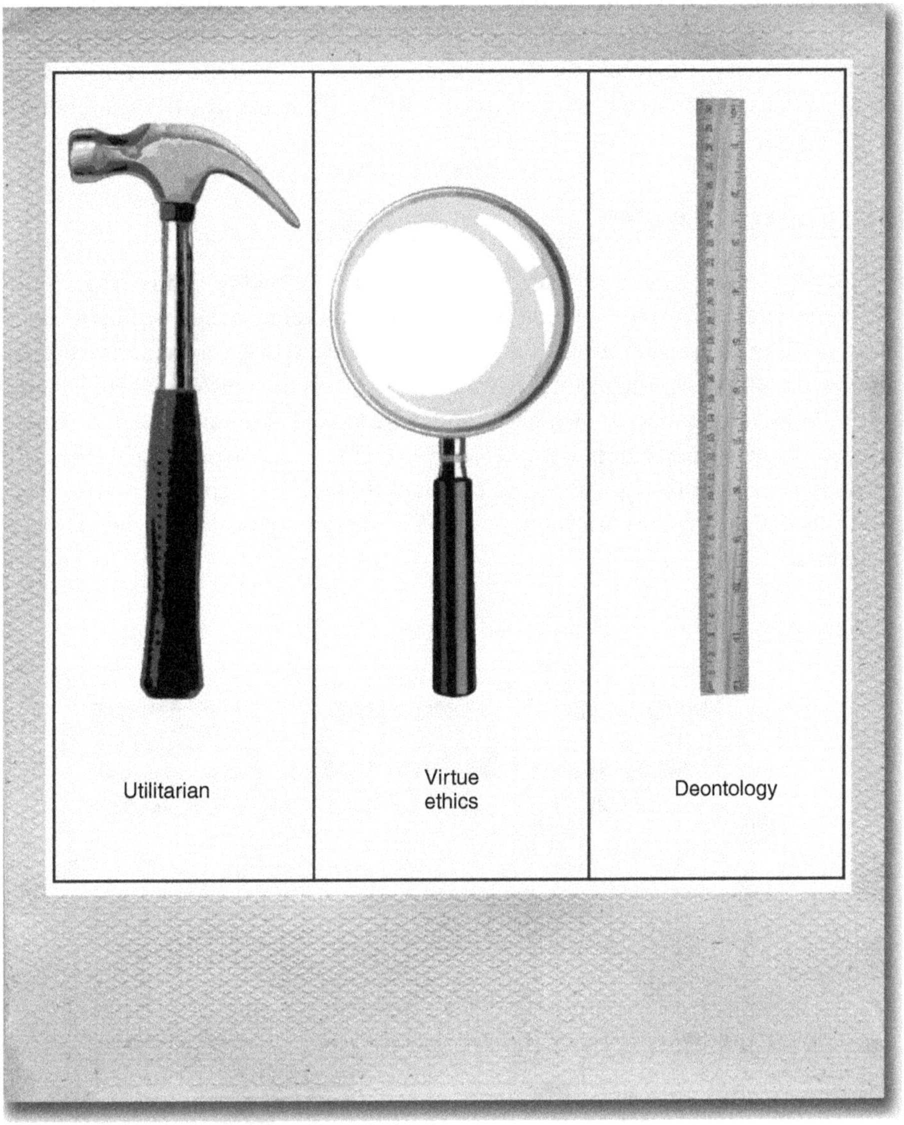

Utilitarian

Virtue ethics

Deontology

Imagine you've recently found out that a cancerous growth had invaded your chest cavity. Now imagine you're out of work and unable to get the medical treatment you need. What would you be willing to do? Lie on your insurance claim? Steal someone else's medical card? Rob a bank? Given your situation, would it be morally wrong to commit these crimes? What if you decided to rob a bank but only took a dollar then waited in the lobby for the police to arrest you? Well, that is exactly what Richard James Verone did on June 20, 2011.[1] Verone was ill and had no medical coverage. He robbed a bank, not for money, but in hopes of going to prison, where healthcare is free. The question on many people's minds following this incident was, "Did Verone do something morally wrong?" Many sympathized with him, stating that he did no harm, and had few other options. Others disagreed; saying that being terminally ill is not an excuse to break the law. So how do we attempt to understand a case like Mr. Verone's? What do we need to know in order to make an appropriate judgment about his actions? To begin with we need to understand exactly what is meant by the term "morality," and how ways of thinking can inform and justify this term. To do this we must first make some distinctions between the term "morality" and the related term "ethics."

Morality and Ethics

Although they are often used interchangeably, the terms "morality" and "ethics" don't mean exactly the same thing. The term "morality" is used to express our beliefs or judgments concerning right and wrong. It usually includes a list of rules that express the values or principles that guide our actions. When we study morality we study a system of commonly held beliefs that link to what we've learned from our parents, peers, and culture. A person can be said to be moral when they act based on what they feel is right or what is endorsed by society. Being moral does not always mean that we have thought about or reasoned through the beliefs that guide our actions; rather, it means that we are conforming to a set of predetermined rules laid out for us to follow in most situations.

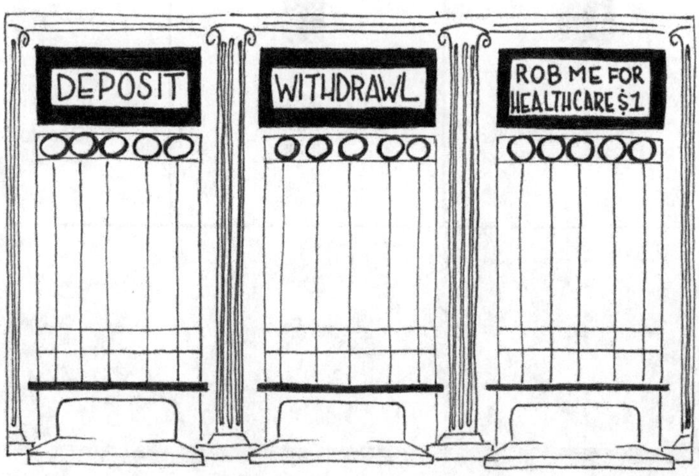

Ethics or moral philosophy is the philosophical study of right and wrong and the reasons that are given to support these judgments. Ethics tends to be an exercise in justification, meaning that we don't just simply say any given act is wrong; rather, we attempt to show why a particular action is wrong or right through the use of a variety of philosophical tools.

So the study of ethics, unlike the study of morality, is directly linked to reflections on our reasoning processes, not just of the end results of the process. For example, you're probably inclined to think that robbing a bank is wrong. I say "inclined" because most of us simply feel this way. But have you actually stopped to think about why robbing a bank is wrong? For many of us the answer is likely to be no. The reason you may not have stopped to ask yourself what is fundamentally wrong with robbing a bank is because there is a general moral rule in our society that tells you taking things without permission is wrong. You have taken this general moral rule and applied it to a number of distinct situations throughout your life without really thinking about exactly why it applies. You just know that taking things that belong to others is wrong and you don't need your parents, teachers, or culture to tell you "Don't take money from the bank." Having never had to justify your moral rule that "taking things that don't belong to you is wrong," you probably haven't thought of reasons why this is a good moral rule. So what would happen if you encountered a person who did not feel that robbing a bank was wrong? What if this person sees stealing as perfectly acceptable when they are low on money? Clearly this view conflicts with the view you hold about stealing, but if this person honestly sees nothing wrong with theft, how can you figure out which one of you holds the correct moral outlook? Well, if you're going to call on morality alone, you could reiterate that in your society, robbing a bank is looked upon unfavorably. Although this is certainly true, this would not be a very convincing reason. In this case, you are only describing what is discouraged by your society and not persuading her to do the same. Using ethics, however, you could explain to this person why you don't steal, why property is important, or why people should be respected. You can do all of this using reasons that go beyond merely describing what is right and wrong in your society. With ethics, you can engage in a dialogue with this person citing the reasons you have for promoting one behavior and discouraging another. If she were to disagree with your reasons, you could encourage her to present her own reasons. Eventually, through detailed discussions the two of you can come to an agreement about the best way to act when faced with an opportunity to steal.

The Benefits of Studying Ethics

Although you'll probably never encounter a situation involving bank robbery, you will encounter no less interesting conflicts about the rightness or wrongness of human actions where you'll be asked to justify your reasons for accepting or rejecting a particular behavior. Studying ethics can help you do this in a number of ways. Let's imagine another, more plausible encounter between friends to illustrate all the ways that ethics can help you resolve a conflict.

Over the last few decades there has been a dramatic decrease in the population of polar bears. Every year, the climate gets warmer and every year the ice floes upon which polar bears rely to obtain their food are not forming properly. The ice is either too thin to support the bears or the floes are breaking up earlier in the year, leaving large expanses of ocean that the bears are forced to traverse to find what little prey they can. Because of this an unusually large number of polar bears are unable to find adequate food and as a result, many die of starvation.[2] Let's suppose you're discussing this with a friend and her response to this issue is, "Who cares about the bears? Let them go extinct!" You, on the other hand, care deeply about the bears and are convinced that we have a moral responsibility to help them. Clearly you both see the situation differently. So what can be done to resolve this disagreement?

As with any disagreement, you are first going to have to discuss the reasons for your moral position. Then you will both need to listen carefully to one another and be open to questions and criticisms. Finally, you will need to respond in turn to the questions and criticisms acknowledging the strengths and weaknesses in both positions. Only then can you start to come to an agreement about which moral attitude toward the polar bears is the best attitude to take.

Now we know the steps involved in resolving our moral disagreements, let's look at some specific ways the study of ethics can help us with this process. Since ethics involves the study of our justifications in addition to our moral beliefs, studying ethics can help us understand what is involved in creating good arguments, presenting sufficient evidence, and making our ideas more clear. If we have to present our reasons in a clear and careful way we are more inclined to see the strengths and weaknesses of our own reasoning process. If after this process you find that your opinion about the polar bears can be supported more consistently than the opinion held by your friend, then your opinion may have merit. If you find yourself struggling to present sufficient evidence, you may need to rethink your position.

Since a large part of ethics consists of exploring the reasons behind our moral judgments before we assert our moral position, we need to be open to the idea of criticism. By studying ethics we can learn to accept the fact that our reasoning may be flawed and as a result we may not always be right in our moral opinions. By being aware of this fact we can learn how to adjust our views, recognizing that our moral beliefs are just one set of beliefs among many and that even the most intelligent people can be misguided in their thinking. Moreover, you will come to see that changing someone's moral view (including your own) is not easy and involves careful research and analysis.

Finally and probably most important, you will understand that views offering us good reasons are simply better than views that don't. At the end of the discussion with your friend it's likely that a dominant view will emerge that simply offers better supports can stand up to critique, and has fewer weaknesses. Whether this theory happens to be your own and you convince your friend to give to the World Wildlife Fund, or her's and she convinces you to cancel your membership, through studying ethics you will learn how to accept the better moral position, even if it's not the one you initially held.

Applied Ethics and Ethical Theory

The polar bear and bank robbery scenarios have given you some insight into the content and focus of this course. Our philosophical inquiry will center on the branch of philosophy known as *applied ethics*. Applied ethics is the practice of applying a variety of ethical theories to real-world situations and seeing how well each particular theory is able to resolve the situation in question. An ethical theory is an attempt by philosophers to justify our actions using a system that can be universally applied to most all situations. These systems tend to assess the way in which a person acts based on many different criteria that not only guide our actions but allow us to evaluate our moral conduct as well. When asked on what grounds we judge a person's actions to be right or wrong, there can be a number of different responses. Some people will say that the action was wrong because it produced bad consequences (i.e., the polar bears become extinct). Others would look at the person motivation and say that the action was wrong because the person was motivated in the wrong way (i.e., by peer pressure instead of duty or greed instead of love). Finally, there are those who judge an action to be wrong because the person performing the action had a flawed or corrupted character (i.e., they behaved selfishly, cowardly, or irresponsibly). Almost without thinking about it we tend to judge a person based on one or more of these reasons at any one time. However, philosophers who study applied ethics tend to concentrate their focus on only one judgment criterion in an attempt to make our thoughts about moral right and wrong more coherent and clear. Theories that focus on the consequences of an action are known as *consequentialist theories*. Those theories that focus on the motivations are called *deontological theories* and the theories that focus on the character traits of a person are known as *virtue-based theories*.

Although each type of ethical theory may require a different justification for why an action is right or wrong, different justifications don't always lead to different overall judgments. Any type of ethical theory is capable of being either compatible or incompatible with the other types of theories. Much of this depends on the situation to which they are applied and what action we are attempting to judge. To illustrate how these types of theories may align in their specific judgments of a situation, let's pretend you're walking through the park on a sunny day. You're in a part of the park that is a bit shady and wooded when you decide to text a friend. As you're concentrating on the text you hear someone shout. You look up to see a stranger yelling and running straight toward you. Without pause he knocks you to the ground. Though badly bruised and shaken, you're not seriously injured. You brush yourself off and yell "Hey! What gives?!" You're angry and frightened and your first impression is that this person is trying to harm you. A few minutes later, however, you discover that the stranger was pushing you out of harm's way. While you were distracted by your phone, you failed to notice you were walking right into a bee's nest.

Of course most of us at that point would be grateful to the stranger and would no doubt feel that what he did was morally good. But how can we justify our sense that this act was morally good? As consequentialists we could justify our belief by looking at the consequences of his act, which would lead us to say that it was good because it spared us the pain and suffering that certainly would have resulted had we stepped on the nest. Or we could look at the stranger's motivation and after asking him what motivated him to help you, say that what the stranger did was good because his motivation was good. Finally, we could look at his character traits and decide that what he did was good because he acted kindly and courageously.

So, it would seem that despite the fact that we looked at the situation from three different points of view, we arrived at the same conclusion about the stranger's action: what he did was morally good.

In the remainder of this chapter we look more closely at specific examples of each general type of ethical theory using a variety of scenarios to increase our understanding about how each theory works in practice. Since ethical theories, like scientific theories, are constantly evolving and adapting to new facts about the world, both a historical and a contemporary version of the theories are presented in each section. This allows you to see how these theories were initially proposed and how they have responded to the dynamic intellectual environment of the 21st century

Now some of you may be wondering why, if the theories have been modified to express contemporary sensibilities, we are looking at the historical versions in the first place. Aren't the original ideas outdated? Wouldn't it be easier to simply study just the contemporary versions? The answer to both of these questions is "no." Much of what the historical versions have to offer us is still relevant today, as they form the bedrock upon which contemporary philosophers have constructed their own views. The historical accounts not only offer us the best way to obtain a general understanding of how all these theories work, but they also offer us insight into why modifications to the theories was seen as necessary to more contemporary thinkers. That said, let's examine these three preliminary theories in more detail and look at some of the historical and contemporary philosophers who influenced them.

Consequentialism: Historical Influences

As you may recall in the bee example, a consequentialist theory is one that takes consequences to be the morally relevant part of any action and are what is assessed to determine whether an action is morally right or wrong. Possibly the most well-known consequentialist theory is utilitarianism. Proposed by Jeremy Bentham in the 1800s, the basic principle of his version of utilitarian theory is what he called the "principle of utility."[3] This principle states that the way we measure moral goodness is by measuring the overall happiness or pleasure of all those beings involved in our decision. The more happiness or pleasure that is derived from the consequences of our actions, the more morally good the action should be considered. On the other hand, the more unhappiness or pain a particular consequence causes, the more morally wrong the action should be considered.

In essence, if we are to use utilitarianism to solve a moral problem, we need only to look at the consequences of our actions and then determine how much pleasure or pain has been derived from them. If there is more pain than pleasure for the majority of beings affected, we can say that the consequences were morally wrong. Likewise, if we were to say that there is more pleasure for the majority, then the consequences created were morally good. Bentham's idea of the good is derived from the biological fact that all sentient beings given the choice will pursue pleasure and avoid pain. Since pleasure and pain are the most fundamental ways for any creature to make decisions, it seemed natural to him to create a theory that was so intuitive. So in this sense we could say that utilitarianism is based on a factual theory, a fact about the nature of sentient beings. Ultimately, Bentham hoped to not only ground his theory in the facts of the world, but also to reduce our moral problems to simple mathematical calculations. He attempted to do this by introducing a tool called the *hedonic* or *hedonistic calculus*. This tool consists of a number of categories that can be used to determine the overall pleasure or pain derived from any given action. Bentham's idea was that his calculus could be used when a person was encountering a new situation or was acting in a way where the potential for pleasure or pain was unknown. For many everyday decisions, one could use the outcomes from previous calculations as a guide to one's future actions.[4]

Aside from this advice and a brief mention of some categories Bentham felt would be useful for our calculations, he doesn't give us much in the way of examples, so it isn't surprising that there are many variations and interpretations of his calculus. Below is one example of how Bentham might have suggested we employ the hedonic calculus to solve a moral problem. The categories are defined by Bentham but how we complete the remainder of the calculus is left to our imagination.

For some familiar moral content let's return to our strange encounter in the park. Only this time, imagine yourself not as the preoccupied person texting, but as the person who has to make a decision about whether or not to knock a stranger over to save him or her from walking into a bee's nest. To make it a bit more challenging we will attempt to measure the pleasure and pain of the person texting, and not ourselves.

The hedonistic calculus

Situation: I see a person who is unaware that he is about to walk into a bee's nest. There is no doubt that the bees will feel threatened and attempt to sting him. But I don't have much time and I will have to knock him out of the way, potentially harming him and myself.
What should I do?

Using a scale from 1 to 10 (one being the lowest) to represent pleasure points and –1 to –10 (–10 being the lowest) to represent pain points, measure the anticipated pleasure/pains of the person you are thinking of helping if you:

Alternative A: Do nothing and let the person walk into the bee's nest

Alternative B: Tackle the person, sending them away from the bees but onto the ground

Categories to Measure	Alternative A Person's pleasure/pain if I don't help	Alternative B Person's pleasure/pain if I tackle them
Intensity—How intense the prospective pleasure or pain will be	Multiple bee stings really hurt –9	Being thrown to the ground hurts –5
Duration—How long the prospective pleasure or pain will last	Stings can hurt for a long time –9	Bumps and bruises hurt for just a few minutes –4
Certainty—How certain you are that this prospective pleasure/pain will happen	–10	–8
Propinquity or Remoteness—How far away in time from this moment the prospective pleasure or pain will occur	Immediately –10	Immediately –10
Fecundity—The chance that the pleasure will be followed by pleasure or the pain by pain	Pain will follow directly for many days or weeks, person may have an allergy that will make the pain even worse –10	Pain will follow directly but will only last a few hours or days –4
Purity—The chance that the opposite sensation will not follow	No pleasure will follow –10	Pleasure might follow after they realize their narrow escape +5
Extent—The number of people who are affected by your action	Two, but in this case only one will suffer greatly because of my decision –10	Two, but in this case we will both suffer a small amount because of my decision –5
Totals	**–68 pain points**	**–31 pain points**

You will notice that at least two alternative courses of action present themselves so we need to account for both of them. Considering all the possible consequences is a vital part of the calculus process as you need to know which of the many alternative consequences will create the most pleasure in the end. Once you have finished the other person's calculus, complete with all possible consequences, you will need to repeat this process for all the sentient beings involved before you make your final moral decision. Once you've done this first set of calculations, if there are more pleasure points (or in this case, fewer pain points) involved in one course of action as opposed to the other, then that is the action you should take. A brief glance at our somewhat simplified calculus can tell us that the person would experience fewer pain points and more pleasure points if we actually did run over and tackle them. So according to this moral theory, we know exactly what to do based on a bit of biology and a bit of math: just go knock the person over. Simple, right?

Evaluation of the Historical Theory

Two interesting issues arise from the use of Bentham's calculus. The first is the questionable measurability of pleasure and pain in general. The second is the indescribable nature of pleasure itself. When attempting to measure pleasure and pain with a concrete numerical system, we can see firsthand how difficult it can be. Even our own pleasure or pain experiences, those we can calculate the best seem to elude us when we try to rate them numerically. For example, on a scale of –1 to –10, how intense would your pain be if you had to knock someone down with a great deal of force? How certain are you of this measurement? Now if we were to attempt to measure the pleasure or pain of the other person involved in the scenario, how difficult would it be to calculate his or her pain? Think about some of the challenges we might face when attempting to generate precise numbers for other humans or, since they are sentient and need to also be considered, for nonhuman animals. If we return to the scenario of the bees we can see that it was difficult enough to try and measure the pleasure and pain of the person we didn't know, but what if we had to determine the pleasure or pain the bees may experience? At the present time we aren't entirely certain whether or not bees are sentient creatures,[5] but if they are, we would also have to create a calculus for them, measuring the pain they may experience if they were stepped on or the pleasure they would experience if they were left alone. What would this look like? It's very difficult to even venture a guess. So although on the surface it would seem that the hedonic calculus is both straightforward and efficient, once we really have to think about using it the calculus doesn't seem straightforward or efficient at all. In fact, the more one attempts to use the calculus as a measuring tool, the more one sees that the calculus cannot provide the objective numerical data that Bentham hoped it could.

The second issue involves not just the measurability of pleasure but also the nature of pleasure itself. Thinking in terms of pleasure may lead us astray when attempting to create the best outcomes. Think about it this way: the idea of pleasure itself is a vague one and oftentimes what you thought would create pleasure actually did just the opposite. For example, imagine a group of voters in a large city who have just supported a proposal for a new sports stadium to be built downtown. The people who vote for this building are no doubt thinking about how having a new sports facility will bring them pleasure. New facilities are always fun to frequent; a new facility will attract better teams, making the games more exciting. The downtown area will enjoy more prosperity as there will be more potential customers filtered into the area and potential customers mean potential profits. But as has been shown time and again, the pleasures voters think a new stadium will bring are actually outweighed by the unintended pains produced. More traffic in the downtown area on game days now results in traffic congestion that makes getting to and from work difficult. The taxes needed to pay for the building is leaving less income for fans to spend on tickets. The downtown area is packed but people aren't spending as much as the local merchants hoped. In the end, what voters thought would bring them intense pleasure actually brought them intense pain. Just like these voters we can be led astray by our best efforts to bring pleasurable outcomes, producing pain instead. Contemporary utilitarians have acknowledged both this and the aforementioned problems with the calculus and have proposed alternatives to Bentham's utilitarianism. Although Bentham's core ideas are still viable and utilitarianism remains both a useful and popular theory, neither the calculus nor the focus on pleasure has remained a part of mainstream utilitarian theories.

Contemporary Formulations: Consequentialism

One of the most well-known contemporary utilitarians is Peter Singer. Born in Melbourne, Australia, Singer has taught at many renowned universities in the United States and Europe and is a frequent guest on popular programs such as *The Colbert Report*. Although Singer agrees with Bentham on a number of points, he refers to himself as a preference utilitarian in order to distinguish his view from Bentham's in a number of significant ways.

Singer recognized the difficulties with the hedonistic calculus and Bentham's use of pleasure as moral goodness, and offers his own version of utilitarianism as a response to these issues. To begin with, preference utilitarianism does not employ anything that resembles a strict calculus. In contrast to Bentham, Singer argues that having the ability to measure pain or pleasure precisely is not essential for us to rationally decide which actions will produce the best outcomes. You can, with a great deal of precision, assert that if something is painful to you, it is probably equally painful to another human being. When dealing with decisions involving nonhuman animals we can look both at their behaviors and advances in neuroscience to make the educated generalization that if a nonhuman animal has a nervous system similar to ours, it can experience pain similar to our own. That said, if a being resembles us closely and we understand what can and does cause us pain, there is no need for a precise numerical calculation to determine pain in another, similar being. According to Singer we can make very reasonable guesses about pain and these guesses will be sufficient enough to assure us that calculations made using them will be correct.[6]

Another distinct split between Singer and Bentham has to do with the problems surrounding the measurability of pleasure itself. Singer is going to reject the use of pleasure or happiness and substitute it with the idea of increasing the number of overall preferences that are satisfied for any being involved in our moral actions. As we mentioned before, Singer makes this change because of the problems created when we attempt to accurately measure pleasure. He insists that by moving our focus away from what makes us happy to what we would prefer in a given situation we are in a better position to make more accurate predictions both for ourselves and for others.

Let's look at a few examples to highlight the distinction between measuring pleasure and measuring preferences more clearly. Imagine you are trying to determine how much food you should give to your classmates in order to provide them with the most pleasure possible. If you don't know them well, you probably don't know how much food they typically consume or what amount above and beyond this would make them happy. Now consider the same question about your classmates, only this time you are trying to determine the particular preferences they may have regarding food. In terms of food preferences you could argue with some certainty that they would prefer to be full as opposed to hungry or nourished as opposed to malnourished. This is really the essence of preference utilitarianism and as you can see it is much easier to assert something about what a being would prefer when given a variety of options. This approach, according to Singer, solves the issues surrounding the measurement of pleasures as we are no longer having to guess what things would be pleasurable. Rather, we are put in a position where we can make educated assumptions based on basic preferences.

Thus far it would seem that Singer has solved many of the problems created by Bentham's use of pleasure. But there is one more concept that Singer introduces to help us formulate an even clearer picture of which consequences truly reflect the most preferences satisfied. Suppose you're in a situation where you find yourself faced with a moral problem involving two strangers. You've just eaten lunch and are on your way to the train station. You've packed a cheese sandwich just in case you get hungry on the journey but for now you are stuffed. On your way to the station, you encounter two people, one has just eaten a few hours ago but is getting hungry for lunch and the other has not eaten in a week. Both could certainly benefit from your sandwich and giving your sandwich away would certainly satisfy the preferences of these two people. So who do you offer your sandwich to and why? Just calculating the numbers in this situation won't help since we are deciding between two people and it is clear that if I satisfy the preferences of one person, I will frustrate the preferences of the other. In a strict sense it would seem that determining the preferences that need to be satisfied doesn't help much either since both would prefer to have the sandwich as opposed to going without. To help us decide in these difficult cases Singer introduces the principle of diminishing marginal utility. This principle states that once certain preferences have been satisfied for a particular being, further increase of satisfaction does not increase their overall satisfaction or, put another way, the increase in satisfaction is so infinitesimal that once your preferences are met more satisfaction is not necessarily better.

In the example of the sandwich, the satisfaction for the first person is marginal since there is only a modest gain to be had in eating at the moment while the person who is starving would have a great deal of satisfaction because it has been so long since they've eaten anything. Using this principle in addition to calculating preferences and considering those involved, Singer would suggest that you give your sandwich to the person who would reap the most satisfaction from it and that would be the person who has not eaten in some time.

The sandwich example also offers us insight into the utilitarian principle of equal consideration and how it differs from equal treatment. To consider two beings equally is to take their preferences into account equally. The treatment a being receives, however, may be different as treatment is determined by need and biological, emotional, and psychological capabilities beyond simple suffering. To return to our sandwich dilemma, since the two people have different needs but the same capabilities, these needs are taken into account by using the principle of diminishing marginal utility. But if the two beings have both different needs and different capabilities, both need to be taken into account. For the sake of illustration let's say that you need to decide between giving your sandwich to a starving human and giving it to a starving housefly. Though both beings are clearly in need, the human being's capacity to suffer not only physically but also emotionally and psychologically are well documented, where the capacity for suffering experienced by the fly is debatable. Given the distinct differences in their capacities for certain experiences, the sandwich should go to the human. Not because they are human and not because the fly doesn't count in our calculation, but because humans have more relevant capabilities than does the fly.

Deontology: Historical Influences

When thinking about what makes our actions morally commendable deontologists reject consequences, instead choosing to focus on our motivations. A classic example of this focus can be found in the works of Immanuel Kant. Kant will introduce us to an ethical system that is a bit abstract and full of new terms and ideas. Remember that deontologies focus on the motivation of the person and not the consequences, so Kant's theory requires that we get inside the mind of a person, so to speak, in order to make moral judgments about his or her behavior. How can we begin to make an assessment of someone's motivation? It would seem that we need to do more than make the kinds of external observations either Singer or Bentham would make and it's with this in mind that we turn to a description of what constitutes a proper motivation for Immanuel Kant.

A person is properly motivated if that person is motivated to follow what Kant refers to as a moral rule or moral law. When a person does this, they can be said to have a good will. Another way of saying that a person has a good will is to simply say that a person is motived to follow the moral rules because they *are* the moral rules. This may sound strange at the outset so it might be helpful to look at some of the many motivations a person can have for doing something and then look carefully at a motivation that expresses good will.

Imagine a situation where three people—James, Mindy, and Carl—are faced with a similar moral dilemma. All of them work in the same office building and all of them have just received some bad news about their grandmothers. It seems that all three of their grandmothers have become seriously ill and need someone to care for them. This will require each of them to inform their bosses, take several days off of work, redistribute their workload to coworkers, and make a long journey out of town.

James, who loves his grandmother, acts quickly and leaves work that afternoon. Mindy likes her grandmother just fine, but sees this situation as less than ideal since she is in line for a promotion and fears that taking too many days off will make her look bad. At the same time she doesn't want to seem cold and selfish, so she also takes the time off work. Carl, however, dislikes his grandmother. They have never been close and the times they've spent together have been unpleasant. Nevertheless, Carl leaves work quickly and makes arrangements to care for his grandmother because he understands that it is his moral duty to be beneficent since this is a universal moral law.

Assessing the situation as a deontologist, we don't rely on the consequences good or bad that may result from the actions of these three people. Instead, we must look at what motivated them to do what they did. In the first instance, James was motivated by love. Love and other emotions are common motivations for many of us, so it probably seems natural to assume that it was James who acted from good will. But according to Kant good will can't be motivated by how we feel about someone since good will is connected to moral law and if moral laws were motivated by emotions they would be constantly changing since our emotions constantly change. Mindy's motivation is also quite common in that we all want people to think well of us. Here again, Kant would say that this motivation is not expressive of good will because, like emotions, what people think of us and our actions is constantly changing, which again means our moral rules would have to constantly change. Now we turn to Carl and his motivation. Despite his negative feelings toward his grandmother, Carl acknowledged that there was a moral rule that instructs us to be beneficent and recognized his duty to follow this rule. He was not influenced by emotions or peer pressure. Instead, his motivation was simply to do his moral duty and that duty was to follow the moral law. Of all the motivations only Carl's is expressive of what Kant means by good will and as a result is the only one that Kant would say is praiseworthy. So if acting in accordance to the moral law is the only morally praiseworthy thing to do in

Kant's eyes, it would seem that he needs to provide us with a way to find or create these moral laws. After all, how did Carl know that "being beneficent" was the moral law he should follow? Why not choose "never help anyone in need" as your guiding law instead? In other words, if our motivation to adhere to the moral laws is the only morally correct thing to do, how can we be sure we are adhering to the appropriate laws in the first place?

For Kant, these laws are the result of our ability to reason. Human beings have the unique capability to reason and Kant feels that it is this ability that lies at the heart of our moral nature. In addition to rationality, Kant also introduces the idea of autonomy or the ability for a being to act freely and determine his or her own actions. It is this combination of rationality and autonomy that equips us to not only formulate moral laws but also to follow them. So we arrive at moral laws such as "help others in need" through what Kant refers to as moral imperatives or moral commands, formulated using our reason.

We have already encountered the two types of moral imperatives that Kant sees we can formulate depending on our motivations: hypothetical imperatives and categorical imperatives. The latter of the two is a universal and unconditional imperative that should form the basis of all our morality. Categorical imperatives are not formulated from a need or desire, nor are they formulated based on situations or events. Rather, they are formulated using only our reasoning abilities and followed only from a sense of duty. As the name suggests, a categorical imperative is a command that has no exceptions. It applies to all rational beings, at all times and in all situations. No rational being, regardless of their situation or standing, can reasonably break a categorical imperative. It is this type of law that we have a duty to uphold in all situations and under all circumstances. This is the type of categorical imperative that Carl used when determining whether or not he should help his grandmother. We will look at two of the most influential formulations of the categorical imperatives momentarily, but first we need to look at the other type of categorical imperative Kant recognized as available to us: hypothetical imperatives.

Hypothetical imperatives are employed by James and Mindy in the grandmother scenario. They are formulated based on desires, needs, or the perceptions of others. Moral laws can also be created using hypothetical imperatives but the moral laws they create are not self-evident, universal, or absolute. It is easy to see this in the case of James and Mindy. For James, love was his motivation. If we were to formulate a moral rule based on this emotion we would be setting up a rule that only applies to those one loves. Making a law that only applies to a small group of people is certainly not applying it universally or absolutely as your feelings about people can change over time. Likewise, in the case of Mindy, her rule was to help those in need only if it makes you look like a good person. Again, this rule would only apply to situations where there are others who are aware of your situation and are in a position to judge it. For all of those times when no one is watching, this rule simply wouldn't apply.

So in the grandmother scenario it was the fact that James and Mindy were not following a categorical imperative that made their motivations less than praiseworthy. Carl, on the other hand, was motived by categorical imperatives and it is this fact and this fact alone that made his action praiseworthy.

Through a bit of reflection both on the grandmother example and on our own motivations it becomes easy to distinguish between the kind of motivations that warrant moral praise (following a moral law created through categorical imperatives) and those that don't (being motivated by external factors, created through hypothetical imperatives). Having made this distinction, we now turn to two formulations of the only imperatives Kant felt warranted praise, the categorical imperatives.

Kant offers us a number of categorical imperatives, each thought to reflect the same general idea in a number of distinct forms, or formulations as philosophers call them. For our purposes we look at two of his most famous, the first and second categorical imperatives.

The first formulation of the categorical imperative states that one should always "Act in such a way that you could will your action to be universal."[7] This means that whenever a person acts in a particular way they are essentially advocating the same type of actions for all other persons. This is what philosophers refer to as "universalization," which simply means that if it's good for me to behave in this way, then it's good for all other rational beings to behave exactly the same way. This idea is not entirely new as most of us would like to think that if an action is right or wrong for us, it's also wrong for everyone else as well. One of Kant's most famous examples of this categorical imperative involves the idea of promise-keeping. In this particular situation, Kant asks us to imagine a person who desperately needs to borrow some money, but already knows they will be unable to repay it. Now this person knows that if they don't promise to pay back the loan, no one will be willing to give them the money they need. So they do what Kant refers to as making a "lying promise," which amounts to making a promise to pay back a loan fully knowing it won't be repaid. According to the first categorical imperative if one chooses to make a lying promise, one is really advocating that everyone should make a lying promise.

Let's pretend that we are the person about to make a lying promise but also want to apply the first categorical imperative to our action. How would we proceed? First, we would need to look at what we intend to do and from that action create a general moral rule for everyone. Our general rule could amount to something like: "Whenever you need money, you can lie in order to borrow some." Now if we were to universalize this law so that everyone should do the same, what would be the outcome? Well, one of the first things we might notice is that something very interesting happens to the idea of promise-keeping in general. Why, after all, does making a "false promise" (i.e., lying) work as an effective way to get money? Well, promises tend to work because most people assume that when someone makes a promise they have every intention of keeping it—promise-keeping is the rule, not the exception. But if we were to universalize a moral law that stated it was acceptable to lie or make false promises, the idea of a promise would no longer carry any weight. Think about it this way: if someone made a promise to return borrowed money and you knew that it was entirely possible and morally permissible for this person to be lying, on what grounds would we offer him or her the money? If lying was permitted one could never be sure if a promise was an actual promise or simply a ruse to get what you want. So, the idea of promising to return money could no longer be taken seriously and the whole idea of promising would lose its validity.

With the meaning of a promise now lost, people would simply stop giving other people loans. But it's not the fact that there would be no more loans that troubled Kant. Remember, he does not look to consequences to determine the correctness of our actions. Think about the effect that universalizing a law involving promise-breaking would have on the idea of promising itself. It would seem that if we universalize promise-breaking, we essentially do away with promises altogether. If there are no more promises, then there is no way to secure your loan since there is nothing to assure the person loaning you the money that you will repay. Of course that means you won't get your loan and through universalizing lying promises you have created a situation where it is not possible for you to get what you wanted in the first place.

Kant recognized that this would be the result and referred to it as creating a "self-defeating" situation or a situation where you actually thwart your own efforts by universalizing your behavior. So to universalize lying, the whole reason why lying is effective goes away, thus making the act of lying ineffective and self-defeating. Now no one would be behaving very rationally if their actions led to a self-defeating situation, since we actually wanted to get the money, not create a situation where getting the money was impossible. So Kant asserts that through the use of the first categorical imperative a rational being will see that the lying promise is self-evidently wrong because it is irrational and therefore would never "will" the moral law of promise-breaking. That said, if it can't be reasonably universalized, it shouldn't be done. To behave this way one is working from motivations that stem from hypothetical imperatives (such as need or desire) and thus one is not doing something morally praiseworthy as their motivations are not reflective of the good will.

It would seem that if we remain consistent in our application of the first categorical imperative, we can know what to do in all situations, regardless of our needs and desires. But is this always true? Are there situations where it seems that moral rules, when universalized, don't create a self-defeating outcome? Take, for example, the morally praiseworthy idea of giving to charity. If you were opposed to anything charitable and wanted to universalize this action you may create a law that goes something like this: "One should never be charitable with one's money." Unlike the example of the lying promise, if you were to universalize this law it doesn't seem to create a self-defeating situation. One could easily envision a world where no one ever gives and no one is morally obligated to give. Your purpose, which was to keep all the money for yourself, can be achieved with no self-defeating situation arising.

So according to the first categorical imperative, it seems like advocating that no one give to charity is a law that could and should be universalized. But is a life without charity really something that a rational person would want to advocate? A person who does not want to be charitable is probably in a good position financially and presently doesn't need help from anyone else. But as we all know financial situations can always change. What you had today you could lose tomorrow. So what if the day after you created your universal moral rule against being charitable you found yourself penniless? You'd probably be wishing you hadn't universalized that moral law after all.

The point here is that even though there are some laws that could be created without negative logical consequences, as rational beings we probably wouldn't want to advocate their universalization. We all know that our financial luck can change in an instant and we probably wouldn't want to live in a world where no charity was available if and when we needed it. In situations like this, Kant would say that giving money to a charity should still be a moral law that is considered something we are obligated to do; however, it's not the same kind of obligation as keeping a promise. Kant refers to obligations of the promise-keeping type as perfect duties and those that are like giving to charity as imperfect duties. Perfect duties are those duties whose opposite generates moral laws that are self-defeating. The imperfect duties are moral duties that may not create self-defeating situations but would leave us wishing we didn't advocate them.

The second categorical imperative proved to be very influential in Kant's own time and remains so to this day. This imperative states that we should treat persons as having inherent value and because of this we should never treat them as a means to an end, but as ends in themselves. Although written in the same straightforward manner as the first categorical imperative, Kant uses many unfamiliar terms in this formulation so it may be helpful to begin our discussion of this imperative by exploring some of the terms Kant uses and the meanings behind them. The first terms we need to familiarize ourselves with are two that Kant mentions with regard to his first imperative. They are the ideas of rationality and autonomy. From our earlier discussion we know that rationality is simply our ability to reason and autonomy is our freedom to make choices. In his second categorical imperative Kant is specifically addressing beings that possess both of these characteristics and he is going to make a distinction between those beings who are autonomous and those who aren't. In contemporary philosophy we also recognize this distinction and make it clear by separating the term "human" from the term "person." Where the term "human" simply describes a being with a certain DNA sequence, the term "person" specifically refers to any being that possesses both rationality and autonomy.

Of course, at this point in time the only being that is known to possess both rationality and autonomy just happens to also possess human DNA. However, for Kant and other philosophers it wouldn't be out of the question to assume that in some distant galaxy persons who are not humans could exist. Moreover, some philosophers are currently arguing that here on Earth there are a select few nonhuman animals (apes and dolphins in particular) who could also qualify as persons.

The second term that would be helpful to understand is what is known as *inherent value*. Something can be said to have this property when it is considered valuable in its own right, that is to say it has a value that was not assigned to it by other beings. In the second categorical imperative, Kant explains that a person must be treated as an end and not as a means to an end. In this context being treated as an end means that one is treated as a being in possession of inherent value; in other words, you as a person are valuable just because you are a person.

We already know that a person is a being that is rational and autonomous. But what is it about rationality and autonomy that grants us inherent value? Being rational and autonomous gives you the exclusive ability to look out onto the world and give all other objects and nonhuman animals a value.

An object or being that can be assigned a value is said to have instrumental value since, as a general rule, we tend to value things that are useful or can act as instruments to further our goals or projects. All value-makers have the ability to assign instrumental value to objects or nonhuman animals, but no value-maker can assign this type of value to another inherently valuable being. So when we encounter other persons we need to realize that each person, just like us, is a value-maker and therefore cannot be assigned a value since they are already endowed with the inherent value that stems directly from their rationality and autonomy.

To make the inherent/instrumental value distinction more clear, let's use the example of a forest. When we look at a forest landscape we as value makers decide how valuable this forest is and what it is that makes it so. Is it the resources it can provide us? The beauty and serenity it affords? We identify the value of the forest with what it can do for us. In this way, the forest can be seen as instrumentally valuable since its only value lies in what we as value makers assign to it.

Now consider another rational being, your best friend for example. If you were to value your friend in the same way you valued the forest, you would look at her and ask yourself what valuable resources she could provide or what goals she could help you achieve. There seems to be something fundamentally misguided in our thinking when we look at a person in this way. After all, isn't there more to a friendship than getting what you need and want? The reason that seeing a best friend as a resource seems so strange is that when we think of other people instrumentally we are in some sense reducing them to an object, such as a tree or a flower. The result of this devaluation not only has detrimental effects on our relationships with other people, but according to Kant it has a detrimental effect on all relationships with all persons, including our relationships with ourselves. Remember that Kant encourages us to universalize all of our moral rules, thus encouraging everyone to act the same way we do. If we were to act as though a person were merely an object, we are in essence not only devaluing one specific person but devaluing all persons, including ourselves. Our friend is just as valuable as we are and if we choose to devalue her, we have also chosen to devalue ourselves.

This brings us to the final term of Kant's that we need to clarify and that is the term "end-in-itself" or "end-in-themselves." By stating that a person should be thought of as an end-in-themselves, Kant is merely emphasizing the inherent value we have been discussing. To be an end simply means you must not be used instrumentally, that is, you should not be used as an instrument or a tool to further the ends or goals of other persons. Rather, you should be treated as an inherently valuable being whose worth cannot be calculated or conferred upon you by others.

Evaluation of the Theory

Kant's use of categorical imperatives and the absolute moral laws they create leaves us with some very interesting challenges when it comes to how we view morality. Although the idea of absolute, universal moral laws seems to conform to what most of us view as the proper moral attitude, the absolute nature of Kant's laws go further than simply asserting that what is good for person A should also be good for person B. He is asserting that moral laws are applicable to all persons at all times in all situations. Kant's moral philosophy suggests that moral laws once created are absolute and universal and as such can never be overridden regardless of the situation (remember consideration of situations would make the imperative hypothetical and not categorical and Kant would not approve of these as moral laws).

Regardless of what our common sense seems to suggest, Kant's promotion of moral laws that have no exceptions creates a challenge to our commonsense morality in a number of situations. Let's take another famous moral dilemma that attempts to show us just how challenging a system with absolute moral laws would be. Remember the lying promise? Well, this time, instead of lying to get a loan, you are faced with the possibility of having to lie to save a good friend. Imagine that one night you hear a frantic knock on your door. You open it to find your friend, visibly shaken and afraid. She relates to you that she is being stalked by a person who intends to murder her. She has come to your house hoping you will help her stay safe. Of course, you assist her and she is now safe and sound hiding in a closet in your basement. She has described the murderer to you so you will know him if he shows up asking questions. The doorbell rings again and upon opening the door you find yourself face to face with the person your friend just described. It's the murderer and he's asking if you know the whereabouts of your friend. As a Kantian, what should you do? Remember, we've already seen that by universalizing the act of lying we create a self-defeating situation. From this we know that we have a perfect duty not to lie. We also know that for Kant it's not the consequences that determine moral goodness but your moral motivation. It would seem the only way you can maintain good will in this situation and do the right thing would be to tell the truth and expose your friend's whereabouts. If you tell the truth that will surely be the death of your friend, but if you lie you aren't doing the morally praiseworthy thing. It would seem that in this situation Kant would urge you to tell the truth since the consequences won't count against you, but breaking an absolute moral law surely will. For most people, telling the murderer the truth and endangering a person's life seems like a bit of moral insanity. Common sense tells us that Kant's response is not moral at all and the thought of exposing someone to harm and death simply to adhere to a moral rule runs completely counter to what a moral person should do. From this example, the problem that comes from asserting absolute moral laws becomes quite clear as it would seem that causing someone harm or death is much worse than breaking a moral rule. The problem with absolutes has vexed Kant scholars for hundreds of years, and it will be this challenge among others that leads to contemporary interpretations and applications of Kant.

Contemporary Formulations: Deontology

As you can see one of the most fundamental aspects of Kant's theory, that of absolute moral laws, creates unique challenges for his followers. Contemporary Kantians have attempted to address this particular challenge in a variety of ways. One philosopher, Christine Korsgaard, responds directly to the murderer at the door problem through a reinterpretation of Kant's remarks concerning the creation of moral laws. Through this reinterpretation, Korsgaard gives us a plausible way to deal with this famous problem, also giving us additional insight into what she feels is the appropriate application of both the first and second categorical imperatives.

You recall that the situation involving your friend and the murderer at the door left us in a moral quandary that seemed to obligate us both to not tell a lie and to help our friend stay safe from harm. We know that Kant would say that since not lying is a perfect duty, we can't lie under any circumstances but we also know that our friend will surely meet her end if we don't lie. Given the situation you know that you have a duty to tell the truth, but wouldn't intentionally putting someone in harm's way be morally wrong? Maybe even more morally wrong than telling a lie? Korsgaard agrees with our commonsense understanding of the situation and states that putting someone in harm's way is indeed morally wrong.[8] So how does she reconcile Kant's insistence that we must obey the moral law with the fact that we also shouldn't put someone in harm's way, especially in a situation that seems to require that we do both things at once? For Korsgaard, setting up a hypothetical situation like this is not as straightforward as it seems. On the surface it appears as if the universal moral law to not lie is set up in such a way that all those who recognize it as a perfect duty are obligated to follow it blindly. If this were the case, our response to the murderer situation would simply be to tell the truth. But consider the application of this particular moral law more carefully. In situations such as those involving the procurement of a loan, the people we are involved with have the expectation that we will be truthful with them. But in the case of the murderer at the door we don't find ourselves in that same situation. When there is a murderer at your door, you certainly wouldn't expect him to tell you the truth about his intentions. Given this you can be pretty certain that this murderous person is entirely unaware that you know he intends to kill your friend. So whatever this person says to you would be suspect and you can assume that he is attempting to deceive you about his intentions toward your friend. This fact, according to Korsgaard, is critical if we are going to formulate our universal law about lying properly. Instead of the straightforward and simplistic formulation "Don't lie," Korsgaard suggests we formulate our moral law as something like "It is permissible to lie to a deceiver." Stated this way we can see that our moral law can be quite easily universalizable and not self-defeating. The key to successfully formulating absolute moral laws seems to lie in recognizing the complexities of life and creating universal laws that reflect these complexities instead of creating overly simplistic rules that create situations that are morally counterintuitive.

Further confirmation that we can reconcile the murder scenario using Kant's moral theory comes in the application of the second categorical imperative. The second formulation has to do with how we are to treat people. It is clear that one shouldn't purposefully put another person in harm's way, so this seems to suggest that one shouldn't tell the murderer the truth about your friend. However, isn't lying to a person in order to obtain a favorable outcome a way of using them as a means to an end? Again, Korsgaard suggests that we are not presented with a situation where we are deceiving an innocent person. The murderer is certainly going to attempt to deceive us about his intentions so it would seem that we would actually be deceiving a deceiver. Is deception used to counter deception morally wrong? Does it suggest that we are devaluing the murderer by lying to him? Korsgaard's response to both of these questions is certainly not. We can all assume that the murder would arrive at our door expressing good intentions toward our friend; after all, this is the only way he is going to get us to reveal where she is hiding. So in a very real sense, he is attempting to appeal to our good nature and our honesty in hopes of using us as a tool to locate our friend. If it is not permissible for one person to use another as a means to their own end, it would seem that the murder has clearly violated this by lying to me to get vital information. When we are in a situation where we know that another person is attempting to use us as a means to their own ends, according to Kant we are under no obligation to allow someone to do this. Korsgaard points out that Kant was clear about a person's ability to defend themselves against exactly this type of treatment. He suggests that we are perfectly within our right to defend ourselves from abuse and disrespect and may use a variety of moral "weapons" to ensure that our own inherent worth is not devalued.[9] These careful analyses of Kant's work through Korsgaard's interpretative lens show us that although a historical theory may appear irretrievably flawed, analysis and interpretation can show us otherwise.

Historical Influences: Virtue Ethics

The third and final ethical theory we discuss was actually formulated thousands of years prior to both utilitarianism and Kantian deontology. Aristotle's virtue ethic is one of the earliest intact texts on ethics in the Western tradition. His theory is quite distinct from modern or contemporary theories for two reasons. First, a virtue ethic does not judge an action as right or wrong based on the consequences it produces nor does it focus on our motivations; rather, it judges an act based on the character of the individual who performs it. Second, any theory that is concerned with the character or virtue of an individual is not particularly concerned with abstract sets of moral rules. For Aristotle and the ancient Greeks morality was not a question of "what should I do?" but a question of "who should I be?" For a virtue ethicist, morality is not about formulating but about cultivating. This is why the fundamental questions about which rules we should follow no longer apply if we are discussing morality with a virtue ethicist.

Aristotle's ideas stem from ideas about the world that are not as familiar to us as they would have been to his peers, so we begin our discussion of Aristotle by looking at what he thought the world was like and how this line of thinking led him to assert the ethical system he did. For ancient philosophers such as Aristotle, humans were just one being in a long line of beings that had a very specific goal or purpose. For the Greeks in general all things that exist were thought to have a specific purpose or a specific goal; the Greek word for this is *telos*. A being's *telos* could be discovered by looking at what that being tended to do well or do better than other beings. For example, the purpose or *telos* of a race horse is to run fast and win races. The *telos* of a flower is to bloom at the time appropriate for fertilization by bees. Human beings also have a *telos* or purpose according to Aristotle and that purpose is a reflection of what humans do best, or rather what they are capable of doing better than any other beings. Our *telos* was to reason well. The ability to reason seems to be unique to us so it's fitting that the ancients felt that this was our goal or purpose. But remember we are talking about an ethical theory that makes judgments based on our character, so it can't just be about using our reason. There must be something about how a person uses his or her reason that can help us distinguish between character traits that are desirable and those that aren't. This is where Aristotle introduces the idea of virtue along with another Greek term, *arête.*

To contemporary ears, the words *virtue* and *vice* can sound pretty old-fashioned and strangely out of context, but for Aristotle and those who follow a virtue ethic the word *virtue* is simply a shorthand way to talk about how a person feels and acts in any particular situation. Describing a person as honest, hard-working, greedy, or vain is simply describing their virtues and vices.

It is also describing their character or the character traits they express by what they do and how they feel about doing it. We have all experienced a situation where we described someone we knew as "acting out of character" and if you think about this simple statement in terms of a virtue ethic you can get a clear picture of what Aristotle was trying to show us about virtue and vice. Imagine that a good friend of yours, who is usually very generous with her money, suddenly stops giving to charity and paying her share of the lunch tab or refuses to help a mutual friend through their financial difficulties. When you describe her as acting out of character, what exactly do you mean? Well, most of us mean that this person typically responds to money situations in a particular way and generally feels a particular way about the value of money. In the above situations it seems as if both her actions in certain situations and the way she seems to value money have changed in a way that makes what she is currently doing seem strange. Our virtues and vices are expressions of our character and the choices we make and can influence who we are as a person. Shown in this light the idea of virtues and vices may not seem so outdated or odd to us since many of us use the idea of character to describe both our own actions and the actions of others within a specific context. But what makes the character traits that our friend normally expresses so different from those she is expressing when she is behaving out of character? Why might the character trait of being generous be morally praiseworthy while being miserly isn't?

Aristotle felt that we tend to see some actions and feelings as virtues while we see others as vices because certain feelings and actions are more reasonable than others, or, put another way, they are the most appropriate feelings and actions to exhibit within a given context. When our actions and feelings closely accord with our reason, Aristotle refers to this as obtaining an *arête* or an excellence in that particular virtue. A person who excels in honesty (i.e., has obtained *arête* with regard to honesty) is one who is able to reason well and to act and feel as an honest person would in any given situation that requires it. So how exactly do you know if you've obtained excellence in a virtue? Since a virtue ethic doesn't ask the question "What should I do?", as a theory it can't give us a list of hard and fast rules to follow in order to ensure we're doing the right or virtuous thing. Remember, a virtue ethic is about feeling and acting in a way that is appropriate to a virtue and that way can change in light of the situation. So to say that one should be courageous doesn't give us any specific direction about how to act. Courage is a character trait that can be expressed in a number of ways; it isn't a word that reflects a moral rule such as "Don't lie."

Since there are no rules that dictate what our behaviors should be, Aristotle offers us a guide by way of a tool. He refers to this tool as "The Golden Mean" and it can be used as an informal way to track how well our proposed feelings and actions align with the dictates of reason. Aristotle refers to this tool as a "mean" specifically because the term "mean" expresses the midway point between two things and it is the midway point between an excess and a deficit where Aristotle felt we were at our most reasonable. Let's illustrate this idea of a midway point between excess and deficit by using one of Aristotle's favorite virtues: courage.[10]

If we were to ask what we mean when we tell someone to act courageously, we know that this is not very helpful since a person may act courageously in a number of ways, depending on the situation. For example, if a person is a member of the armed forces and she is facing down an enemy, she may show courage by shooting in the direction of the enemy in order to help her and her fellow soldiers get away. But courage may also be a small gesture such as telling your friend the truth when you know that this truth will cause discomfort or hurt or speaking out in someone's defense when they are not there to defend themselves. So we can't readily define courage by pointing to a specific act nor can we define it completely by what we should feel since we can be certain that the soldier will feel something very differently in her situation than the person telling her friend the truth will. We can, however, define it by comparing it to what it's not. If we understand that in addition to a person acting courageously a person can also act cowardly (with too little courage, a deficit) or rashly (with too much courage, an excess), we can then gauge our action, using our reason to make sure that whatever we do, we hold to the midway point between either the deficit or the excess.

Images © Shutterstock, Inc.

For Aristotle, the most reasonable course of action for us to take is the action that is expressive of this midway point that it's neither cowardly nor rash in its nature. The Golden Mean marks this place between excess and deficit of any particular character trait. A person who expresses courage does the right thing, at the right time, toward the right person, in the right amount. In other words, this person's actions and feelings align with their reason and what aligns with reason is what is virtuous.

To modern readers, courage certainly would seem virtuous, but does it seem moral? For most contemporary readers to say that a good person must be courageous to be moral would be a strange statement. Certainly it's good to be courageous but most modern moral systems don't consider it either a duty (deontologist) or something that is measurable such as pleasure and pain (utilitarians) though the outcomes might be. This points to another unique feature of Aristotle's moral theory, in that morality is not a distinct and separate facet of life.

Aristotle recognizes two types of virtues: the intellectual virtues and the moral virtues. Courage is one of the moral virtues, as is honesty and fairness. Wisdom, prudence, and being good with money are examples of intellectual virtues. Just about everything that we can do either well or poorly will be recognized by Aristotle as falling into one of these two categories, making this ethical system actually more of a life system. Now the distinction Aristotle makes between types of virtues is made only because he felt that different virtues were obtained in different ways. The moral virtues couldn't be learned but were acquired through practice and habit. The intellectual virtues, on the other hand, could be learned in much the same way we learn how to add and subtract. Both sets of virtues were cultivated through action and choice over time and required that we perform them in a way that is characteristic of a virtuous person.

Some examples of virtues

Deficit	Virtue	Excess	Moral or Intellectual?
Cowardly	Courage	Rash	M
Laziness	Sufficient studying to be successful	Workaholism	I
Dishonesty	Honesty	Rudeness	M

Evaluation of the Theory

Unlike the other two ethical theories, virtue ethics have been dismissed by many contemporary philosophers as not only too vague but entirely unhelpful in solving our moral problems. The first criticism stems from the fact that over the centuries the character traits that have been taken to be virtues has changed substantially and somewhat contradictory character traits have been offered simultaneously by different philosophers. The second criticism is based on the fact that a virtue ethics does not offer us hard and fast moral rules that we can turn to solve our moral problems. Some argue that without rules, there can't be helpful guidance.

It's certainly true that the character traits that have counted as virtues are numerous and have changed over time and from culture to culture. For example, in Aristotle's day pride was considered a virtue and humility a deficiency. If we move forward in time to the virtue ethicist St. Thomas Aquinas we find that humility is now regarded as a virtue and pride an excess.[11] So who is correct in their assessment? Is pride a virtue or is it humility that we should cultivate? The virtue that we choose will affect what we do and how we judge the actions of others. It would seem that if we can't identify the appropriate virtue there is no way to know what we should be and thus no real way to know if we are behaving morally or not.

The second challenge to this theory is one that seems equally difficult to resolve. As you recall, both utilitarian and deontological systems give us a set of rules to follow. These rules act as guidelines for our behavior in any particular situation. So as a utilitarian I only need to do that which creates the most pleasure or satisfies the most preferences for the most number of beings to know that I have done the right thing. If my action causes more pain or frustrates more preferences, then I know my action was morally wrong. Likewise, if I am using Kant's deontology as a guide, all I need to do is use the categorical imperatives to formulate universal moral laws. I fulfill my moral duty when I follow these laws for their own sake and not out of a sense of desire or personal need. Both of these systems presents us with an easy to follow protocol that sets out very clearly what we are and are not supposed to do in any given situation. But a virtue ethic doesn't contain any hard and fast rules that can guide our actions in this way. With Aristotle's theory it doesn't even make sense to ask what we should do, since it is what we become that counts.

This lack of rules and inability to formulate rules has been seen by some as a good reason to dismiss virtue ethics altogether since it would seem that if there are no moral rules there can be no moral guidance. But should virtue ethics be so easily dismissed in light of these eccentricities? Contemporary philosopher Rosalind Hursthouse thinks not.

Contemporary Formulations: Virtue Ethics

Rosalind Hursthouse is very familiar with the two criticisms of Aristotle's ethics and she is going to address both of them in her account of virtue ethics. She approaches these criticisms in a unique way, that is, she is not going to attempt to "fix" the theory as we have seen contemporary consequentialists and deontologists do earlier in this chapter. Instead, she is going to create logical comparisons between virtue ethics and both utilitarianism and deontology to show us that the challenges faced by a virtue ethic are not exclusive to this theory; rather, they are inherent challenges in all ethical theories. So, by her reasoning, if Aristotle's virtue ethic is unfit to serve as a legitimate moral theory, then by default the other two theories are also unfit. Her hope is that by showing us that these challenges can be found in all ethical theories that we will not abandon ethical theory altogether, but will acknowledge virtue ethics as a moral theory that is just as legitimate as are deontologies and utilitarian theories.

In response to the criticism that a virtue ethic is simply too vague since there are so many often contradictory character traits from which to choose, Hursthouse claims that a virtue ethic is no more or less vague than a utilitarian ethic or a deontological ethic. She begins by asking us to compare the utilitarian rule of creating the greatest happiness or pleasure with any seemingly contradictory virtues such as Aristotle's pride and Aquinas's humility.

For Hursthouse, a list of virtues works in the same fundamental way that a list of moral rules would work for Kant or a list of best consequences would work for a utilitarian. When working with the virtues we would frame our moral statement like this:

> "A virtue is a character trait that can be found on the following list: [refer to Aristotle's list of virtues for an example]"

or we may formulate it like this:

> "A virtue is a character trait that human beings need to do well in life or to flourish."

At first glance, it may still look like describing virtues in this way is still much too vague to be of any use. But Hursthouse argues that this isn't because they truly are too vague, but rather it's because we're used to following standard moral rules and taking for granted that rules that tell us what to do are essentially less vague than advice that tells us what we should be.

To illustrate what Hursthouse means by this, let's look at Bentham's response to moral questions and see if a utilitarian theory is really any more concrete. As a utilitarian, an action is right for Bentham if it creates the best consequences for the most number of beings. But how do we determine what the best consequences might be? Remember the example of the stadium? What we thought would bring the best consequences and thus the most happiness actually did just the opposite. So even knowing that the best consequences means creating the most happiness or pleasure for the most number of beings doesn't help us accurately determine which of our actions will amount to this happiness or pleasure. So although we do have a specific moral rule that we must follow if we are a utilitarian, it would seem that following this rule only gets us so far in terms of knowing exactly what we should do.

The same is true of a virtue ethic. The idea that we can define a virtue ethic as a character trait that allows us to do well in life is no more vague an idea than is the utilitarian definition of the good as that which brings about happiness or pleasure. So in the case of Aristotle and Aquinas if we find that the character trait of humility allows us to do well in life, then we should certainly advocate for it. Likewise, if pride assists us in doing well, we should advocate for it. The bottom line is that having a series of virtues that seem mutually exclusive is no more or less damaging to an ethical theory than is the fact that we are constantly faced with a number of potential actions we can take to promote the good, many of which are also mutually exclusive.

But what about Kant's deontology? Perhaps it is only the utilitarian and the virtue ethicist that face the problem of generating vague and potentially contradictory moral advice. Again, Hursthouse is going to look at the way deontologies presumably work and then see if a theory like Kant's can offer a clearer moral picture about what one should do in a given moral situation. Recall that Kant felt that the categorical imperatives ensured us that we would create a list of moral rules that were both universal and absolute. These rules would be the moral rules that all rational beings were bound by reason to follow. But consider what happens when we use the imperatives to formulate our rules. All too often we begin our formulations with general moral rules that we are already not only familiar with but are also confident in the fact that they are morally correct. General moral rules that prohibit lying, stealing, cheating, and killing are often formulated without reflection. Now Kant felt that it was our reason that informed us of the correctness of such moral rules, but could it also be our predisposition toward these rules that makes them seem like rules that rational people will hold? If reason truly is our guide when formulating moral laws, we need to keep in mind that there are a whole host of moral rules that don't make our list but that have been formulated by many rational people throughout history Absolute moral rules such as "Keep women in their proper place" or "Kill all infidels" may seem misguided or just plain wrong by our rational standards but by the standards of those who advocated them they were as self-evident and reason-reliant as "Don't lie" is to us. For those who may balk at the inclusion of rules like Keep women in their place," it is interesting to note that neither this rule nor "Kill all infidels" creates a self-defeating situation, nor do either of them suggest that it is acceptable to use a person as a means to an end (it may be helpful to note that historically, both women and those who did not share your same religious beliefs were not considered persons, which is still true in some parts of our contemporary world).

So does Kant's theory actually offer us any more concrete moral advice than does either the utilitarian or the virtue ethicist when it comes to our moral decisions? When considered carefully it seems that like the supposed concrete nature of utilitarianism, the strength of Kant's deontology seems like an illusion influenced by our familiarity and comfort with the idea of moral rules. With her comparison model of argumentation, Hursthouse seems to have at least created a case for a logical similarity between all three ethical theories and this may be enough to show critics that despite what they think, a virtue ethic is not substantially different from either utilitarianism or deontology on this count.

The last criticism centers around what some perceive as a virtue ethic's inability to give us any moral guidance. This inability has been attributed to a virtue ethics lack of moral rules. Since both utilitarianism and deontology respond to questions about doing or acting, it's natural that these theories will require a list of action-guiding rules. But with an ethical theory that focuses on character traits there is no need or use for an overarching rule or a list of rules. Does this mean that a virtue ethic has absolutely no rules to guide our conduct? If this is true, how can we know what we should do? Hursthouse thinks that the claim that a virtue ethic lacks rules is entirely mistaken. She argues that there are rules of conduct built into this system but the rules are not overt rules that directly tell us what to do; rather, the rules offered by a virtue ethic are couched in the terms "virtue" and "vice." She refers to these implied rules as the "v-rules" to distinguish them from the kinds of rules offered by utilitarians and deontologists.

To explain what she means by a "v-rule," we can choose a virtue we are all familiar with: honesty. When a virtue ethicist such as Hursthouse says that a person should strive to be honest, the idea of being honest entails the unstated moral rule "Don't lie." This can certainly work the other way too as a person who adhered to the moral rule "Don't lie" could certainly be said to be honest. Many character traits contain unspoken moral rules that need to be articulate. That said, it would seem that the difference between a deontologist and a virtue ethicist seems to be not one of arguing over rules but rather about arguing over how our moral conduct is framed. In the case of a deontologist one shouldn't lie because "Don't lie" is the appropriate moral rule to follow. For a virtue ethicist one shouldn't lie because dishonesty is a vice.[12] Honesty is just one example in a long list of virtues and vices that can be transcribed into a language that stresses moral rules. "Don't be lazy" or "Don't cheat" are other examples that would seem quite acceptable to a person who was more comfortable with a rule-based system.

Hursthouse seems to create compelling arguments that show us a virtue ethic is a viable alternative to utilitarianism and deontologies. This leaves us with three types of ethical theory that can guide our thinking as we move into our contemporary moral problems. As we will see in subsequent chapters, these theories are used as a framework by philosophers to formulate solutions to some of the most important issues we face in the 21st century.

Notes

1. Moisse Katie, "N.C. Man Allegedly Robs Bank of $1 To Get Health Care in Jail." *ABC News*. June 20, 2011. http://abcnews.go.com/Health/Wellness/nc-0man-allegedly-robs-bank-health-care-jail/story?id=13887040.
2. Fong, Jocelyn. "Scientist Responds to Misleading Polar Bear Coverage." *Media Matters for America.* http://mediamatters.org/blog/2012/04/09/ scientist-responds-to-misleading-polar-bear-cov/185580.
3. Bentham, Jeremy. "An introduction to the principles of morals and legislation." http://www.utilitarianism.com/jeremy-bentham/index.html#one.
4. Ibid.
5. Keim, Brandon. "Honeybees Might Have Emotions." *Wired*, June 17, 2011. http://wiredscience.com/wiredscience/2011/06/honeybee-pessimism/.

6. Singer, Peter. *Animal Liberation* (New York: Avon Books Inc., 1990), 7–17.
7. Kant, Immanuel. *Grounding for the Metaphysics of Morals*, trans. James W. Ellington (Indianapolis, IN: Hackett, 1993), 32.
8. Korsgaard, Christine. *Creating the Kingdom of Ends* (Cambridge, UK: Cambridge University Press, 2000), chap. 5.
9. Ibid., 144.
10. Aristotle, *The Nicomaechan Ethics*, trans. Martin Ostwald (New York: Macmillan, 1962), 70–77.
11. Saunders, William. Catholic Education Resource Center, "What are the Capital Sins?." http://catholiceducation.org/articles/religion/re0465.html.
12. Hursthouse Rosalind, *On Virtue Ethics* (New York: Oxford University Press, 2001), 42–47.

Name:______________________________ Date:______________

Review Questions

1. What is the difference between morality and ethics?

2. How would a consequentialist determine whether an action is morally good? How would a deontologist? A virtue ethicist?

3. What tool does Bentham use to measure pleasure/pain?

4. What types of beings do utilitarians consider when making their moral decisions? Why must they do this?

5. What is the "principle of diminishing marginal utility" and how does Singer suggest we use it to calculate the most preferences satisfied?

6. What does the first formulation of the categorical imperative state?

7. What does the second formulation of the categorical imperative state?

8. For Korsgaard, if someone is lying to us, is it morally permissible to lie to them? Explain.

9. What is The Golden Mean and how does it work?

10. According to Hursthouse, can a virtue ethic provide us with moral guidance? Explain.

Name:________________________________ Date:______________

For Further Discussion

1. Research the plight of the polar bear and then apply one of the ethical theories discussed in this chapter to the problem. What solutions did you arrive at? Would they be the same solutions if you were to use another ethical theory from this chapter? Why or why not?
2. Consider Richard Varone's act of robbing a bank to save his own life. What might a deontologist like Kant say about such an action? Would Peter Singer come to the same conclusions about Mr. Varone's actions? Why or why not?
3. Try to determine what a virtue ethicist might do in the beehive situation. How would someone like Aristotle go about determining the best solution to this issue?

CHAPTER TWO

Claims and Arguments

All philosophical inquiry is conducted through argumentation and ethics is no exception. The fact that philosophers argue about moral situations just like everyone else does should come as no surprise. What may surprise you, however, is that the way a philosopher defines an argument may not be how you define an argument. For philosophers an argument is not a fight, doesn't involve yelling, and, contrary to what some undersea creatures may say, doesn't start with a clam. An argument is a special kind of reasoning process that helps us to determine whether a particular line of thought is any good. Technically, an argument is a group of statements, one of which is supported by the rest. You'll notice that the term "statement" is used here and not "sentence." That's because a statement is a special kind of sentence.

We use sentences to communicate a variety of things. For example, some sentences ask questions such as "Where are my keys?" Other sentences command us to do something such as "Shut the door." Still other sentences attempt to show us that something is or is not the case such as "My cat is brown." This last sentence, "My cat is brown," conveys an idea that can be checked against a fact in the world, that is, it can either be shown to be true (the cat happens to be brown) or it can be shown to be false (the cat is black and white); this is the special quality that can only be expressed in a statement. Notice that if we were to ask whether or not "Where are my keys?" is true or false, we would certainly get some puzzled looks. That's because sentences that ask questions can't be checked against facts in the world and thus can't be shown to be either true or false like a statement can. This ability to be either true or false is known as the ability to hold a *truth value*. So, simply put, any sentence that can hold a truth value is a statement. Although other types of sentences are important to communication, statements form the backbone of all argumentation and argumentation is the focus of this chapter.

Now that you know all arguments contain statements, let's discuss the parts of an argument. As mentioned before, in order for a group of statements to be considered an argument it must contain two parts: the part that is supported and the supports. The part of the argument that is supported by the rest of the statements is called the *claim* or *conclusion*. The claim is the statement philosophers are trying to prove, make you believe, or know to be true. Claims can be found at the beginning, in the middle, or at the end of an argumentative paper. For each argument you encounter, there will be one claim. In more complex philosophical works, many smaller arguments may be used to support one overarching claim. When reading any philosophical work, it's a good idea to ask: "What is the author claiming here?" If you can answer this question, then you know what the argument is about, regardless of how long or confusing the work may seem.

Once you know what an argument is about (you know what the philosopher is claiming), you need to know how the author is going to support his or her claim. The supports in an argument are called the *premises* and they too can be found at the beginning, in the middle, or at the end of an argument. Unlike a claim, there can be any number of premises in an argument; there may also be premises that support smaller arguments in the work but do not support the larger claim directly.

If you're new to philosophy it's sometimes difficult to tell a premise from a claim in a complex argument. Philosophers can sometimes guide our reading by trying to indicate what parts of the argument are the premises and which part is the claim. They can use what are known as *indicator words* to guide us in this way. Indicator words are terms that often appear in arguments and can signal that a claim or a premise is nearby. Some common indicator worlds for claims are *therefore*, *consequently, hence, it follows that, thus,* and *as a result.* Common premise indicator words are *because, since, given that,* and *for that reason.* Although these are good to keep in mind, don't plan on always being able to find them in an argument. Many times the author implies these terms and doesn't use them outright. The best way to find the claim of an argument and the premises that support the claim is to perform a thought experiment. First, find the statement or statements that you think are the author's main claim. Then try to find what you think are one or two of the premises. Now ask, Do the premises seem to support the claim? If they don't seem to fully support the claim, chances are you may need to choose another statement as you may have the claim marked as one of the premises. Let's look at some simple arguments and see if we can distinguish the claim from the premises:

Example 1: We can conclude that we should preserve the mountain gorilla's habitat because it is a critical part of the jungle ecosystem and there are only about 700 left in the wild.

Example 2: Gorillas are a critical part of the jungle ecosystem and there are only about 700 mountain gorillas left in the wild, so it follows that we should preserve more of their habitat

Example 3: Because they are a critical part of the jungle ecosystem and there are no more than 700 mountain gorillas left in the world, we should preserve their habitat.

In the first example, the opening statement "We can conclude" is using the word *conclusion* to indicate this is the claim that is being supported. In the second example, "it follows that" also indicates the conclusion. In example 3, the word *because* at the beginning of the statement suggests that this is a support or premise for our preserving the gorilla's habitat. Now that you understand the makeup of arguments in general, you'll need additional information to determine whether the arguments in question are good arguments or poor arguments. Consider again one of the arguments about the gorilla's habitat:

We can conclude that we should preserve the mountain gorilla's habitat because gorillas are a critical part of the jungle ecosystem and there are only about 700 left in the wild.

If you were asked to determine if this was a good argument, how would go about making this determination? Certainly, you would need some criteria by which to judge this argument. The most obvious criterion would be to look at the statements presented and determine whether or not they are true. Are gorillas a critical part of the ecosystem? Are there only about 700 left? Since the arguments are constructed with statements that can be checked using scientific data, you can do this quite easily. This kind of check is called a *truth value check* and it can be performed on all statements in our gorilla example. This is normally the first and may be the only check you are used to doing as a way to determine whether or not an argument is any good. As a general rule, if you find false statements or if you find statements where the truth value is unknown, you may assess this argument as either no good or seriously flawed. This assessment is true to a point, but as you'll see determining whether or not the statements in an argument are true or false is only one test you need to perform on arguments, and although it may be the most common, it may not be the most critical.

Deduction and Induction

Determining the truth value of the statements used to create arguments is only one of two parts of any argument that must be analyzed to determine whether or not an argument is good. The second part of an argument that must be analyzed before you can determine whether or not an argument is "good" is the inferential strength that the argument exhibits. The inferential strength of an argument is essentially how much support the premises provide for the conclusion. Arguments will generally fit into one of two categories, based on their inferential strength: (1) deductive arguments, which are the strongest inferentially, and (2) inductive arguments, which are probabilistic in nature.

What makes deductive arguments so strong is their certainty. In deduction, if the premises of the argument are true then the claim must follow with 100% certainty. The strength of a deductive argument can be derived from its form, or from its reliance on the definition of terms, or by the fact that it is mathematical or sequential in nature. A deductive argument that is formulated properly is referred to as a valid deductive argument or simply as a valid argument. Consider the following example:

Example 1: My dad is taller than I am. My brother is taller than my dad. So, it follows that my brother is taller than me.

The claim "my brother is taller than me" is supported by the premises: "My dad is taller than I am" and "My brother is taller than my dad."

Think about this argument for a moment and ask yourself whether you could deny the claim if both of the premises are true. The strength of this example rests on the definition of a commonly used word: *taller*. By definition, if something is taller than something else it cannot also be shorter than that thing at the same time. So, if my brother is taller than someone who is taller than I am, it must follow that he is taller than me. One could also say that this argument was based on what we know about sequences. Again, if a series of things is increasing in size, the last item in the list can't be the shortest. This is a good example of the 100% certainty rule. The argument is a valid argument because if the premises are true the conclusion must follow.

Since you've determined that the "dad" argument is valid, can we say that it is a good argument based on this information alone? Not exactly. Remember from the gorilla argument that there are two things we need to consider when looking at any argument; we have looked at the inferential strength but we have yet to look at the truth value of the statements. For an argument to be considered good, it must pass not only the inferential strength test, it must also pass the truth value test. So, if you were to try to determine whether or not the "dad" argument was a good argument, you'd have to consider both the inferential strength and the truth value of the statements. Let's look at the argument again, this time focusing on the truth value of the statements (since we already know that it is valid). Since you don't know much about my family, the truth values of each statement have been assigned for you.

Example 1:
My dad is taller than I am. (True)
My brother is taller than my dad. (True)
So it follows that my brother is taller than me. (True)

In this argument, all the statements are true, that is all of these statements match facts in the world. So we can now say that the argument is not only valid but all the statements contained in it are true. We refer to arguments that pass both the inference test and the truth test as sound arguments, so this argument about my family is sound.

Now there are some arguments that just seem obviously flawed. For example, if I were to change some of the information in the dad argument I might say:

Example 2:

My dad is shorter than I am. (True)

My brother is shorter than my dad. (True)

So it follows that my brother is taller than me. (False)

Notice that all the premise statements are still true, but now we have a sequencing problem. If my brother is shorter than both my dad and me, then how can he be taller than me at the same time? This kind of flaw is one that is not reflected in the truth values of our premises but is reflected in the sequence of events that follow. Flaws of this kind create what are known as *invalid arguments*. An invalid argument is simply an argument where if the premises are true the conclusion doesn't follow with 100% certainty. Clearly in the second dad argument the conclusion can't follow at all, so the argument is invalid.

But what about the truth values? Notice that in this case, the conclusion simply can't follow, so although the premises are true, the conclusion is false. Recall that in order for an argument to be sound, you need to have true premises and a true conclusion. Clearly, we can't have this here since our conclusion does not follow from the premises, so the argument is not only invalid but is also unsound.

The second category of arguments is induction or inductive arguments. Unlike deductive arguments, this category of arguments does not rely on absolute certainty. Instead, inductive arguments rely on different levels of probability to determine how good they really are. In the case of an inductive argument, if the premises are true the claim will follow with a high probability. The higher the probability, the stronger the argument; the lower the probability, the weaker the argument. Since we are no longer dealing with absolute certainty, inductive arguments require a slightly different vocabulary to express this fact, so instead of using the words *valid* and *invalid* to describe these arguments, we use words like *strong* and *weak* to express the varying levels of likelihood that the claim follows from the premises. For example, consider a second argument about my family:

Example 3: My dad tells great jokes. My brother tells great jokes too. So it follows that I also tell great jokes.

Although the content of this argument has to do with relationships in a family just like the first argument, you can see that the claim doesn't follow with the same amount of certainty as it did in the first example. Here the argument isn't formulated based on a definitional truth. The theory of biological heredity is supporting my claim here and heredity is causal in nature. We know that many character traits are inherited, so, if you tend to have a strong genetic propensity in your family, it is likely that most members of your family will have that trait. Comedic timing might be one of those genetically inherited traits and, according to this example, I may have inherited it. Example 3, unlike example 1, is probabilistic in nature in that there may be a very good chance I inherited my dad's gift, but it won't be absolutely certain that I did. You can see that this argument doesn't express the same unshakable certainty as did the previous argument. In fact, any causal claim is only probable at best, and as a result we will never claim that such an event can ever be known with certainty.

As with deductive arguments you need to analyze inductive arguments in two ways, only instead of asking whether or not the claim follows with 100% certainty, you need to ask what the likelihood of the claim following from the premises might be. The likelihood can range from a 1% chance to a 99.9% chance and anything in between. The content of the argument often determines what percentage counts as strong or weak and this fact makes inductive arguments the subject of much more debate than you would see with deductive arguments. For example, how likely it is that a trait can be passed on from father to daughter is a matter of understanding what traits are more likely than others to be a part of your DNA. Being able to tell good jokes as an inherited trait may be much less likely than inheriting your father's red hair or his smile, so if we were to create inductive arguments that focused on heredity, we may be faced with a weak argument in the first instance and a much stronger one in the latter instance.

Like deductive arguments, there are also common patterns that can help us identify inductive arguments. These patterns include predictions, generalizations, and arguments that express casual relationships. In example 3, the ability to tell jokes is one that expresses a causal relationship: A father's genetic makeup often determines a child's genetic makeup and so the reason why some people are funny has been caused by the genetic makeup that was passed from father to child.

As is the case in deductive arguments, inductive arguments also have two parts that need to be analyzed before we can determine if the argument is good. An inductive argument where the claim follows the premises with a high degree of probability is referred to as a strong argument. If a strong argument has all true premises and a true conclusion, it's known as a *cogent argument*. So, if the ability to tell a good joke is genetically determined, then the argument could be said to be strong and if it happens to be true that both father and child are funny, then it would also be cogent. Again, it's possible that you will be presented with arguments that are either not very strong or don't have true premises. In cases such as these the arguments turn out to be either weak (when the probability is low) or uncogent (when there are false statements involved). If we were to create a weak, uncogent argument it may look something like this:

Example 4: My dad plays football (True) and my brother plays football (True). So it follows that my two sisters also play football (False).

In this example, there are two problems we can see immediately. The first is generally, just because two men from the same family play football, it is unlikely that the women in the family also play. It is certainly possible, but thinking about this in terms of common sense it would be quite rare. So this argument is probably pretty weak, as the claim doesn't follow the premises with a great deal of probability. Also, you will see that two of the three statements are true. With two true statements, this argument cannot be cogent and so what we have in example 4 is an argument that is inductive and both weak and uncogent.

After learning the distinction between deductive and inductive arguments, some students are inclined to believe that since deductive arguments can give us certain results they are somehow superior to inductive arguments. This assessment is not altogether true. Inductive arguments can be every bit as good as deductive arguments; they are simply dealing with information that can't be known for certain, regardless of how good the argumentation may be. A good example of just how good inductive argumentation can be is displayed nicely in the following argument:

Example: The sun has risen over Earth's horizon for the last 3.5 billion years. Therefore, the sun will rise again tomorrow.

At first glance, many students think this should be a deductive argument since the fact that the sun will rise tomorrow seems 100% certain. However, if you look carefully at this argument you'll see that it's a prediction as we are using a past event to predict a future event and predictions can never be deductive since we can never be 100% certain that what we think will happen actually will. So, as certain as we may be of this event (I would bet my life savings that the sun will rise again tomorrow), any time we are predicting something there is never 100% certainty that what we predict will actually occur. However this fact doesn't mean that inductive arguments can't be incredibly strong, and equally as good as can deductive arguments.

The Structure of Moral Arguments

Now that you understand how arguments work and can identify the two types of arguments you will encounter in ethics, let's have a look at moral arguments and identify some important information specific to them. Like any argument, moral arguments will either be deductive or inductive, sound or cogent depending on their inferential strength and the truth value of their statements. Making these judgments will still be one of the first things you must do when trying to determine whether a moral argument is good or bad. But there are other key elements specific to moral argumentation and knowing them will help you to analyze them and create responses to them.

All moral arguments contain two types of premises: factual premises and moral premises. A factual premise is a premise that expresses a fact about the world. You've already encountered a number of factual premises in this chapter. The statements about gorillas or the members of my family are all examples of factual premises. These statements can readily be checked with information in the world to determine their truth value. All factual claims can be treated in this way though other proclaimed "facts" about the world may not be as clear-cut, and may require more in-depth research to determine their truth value.

For example, many still believe that there are no concrete facts that substantiate the statement, "Human activity is contributing to global climate change." Although there are facts that point to the global climate changing dramatically, the facts that support the claim that climate change is caused by human activities is much less clear. Reports from a 2013 National Oceanic and Atmospheric Administration report verified the summer of 2011 as the hottest in the last 50 years with the summer of 2012 as one of the hottest in the last 10.[1] Despite this clear evidence that the planet is heating up, this fact does not directly point to a human cause. So one set of facts, those that can verify the global climate is changing, can be easily verified but the role that humans are playing in climate change is one of the issues scientists are currently trying to determine.

An ability to determine the truth value of factual premises relating to the contributions of human activity on global warming can help to determine whether an argument blaming the fossil fuel industry for warmer temperatures is sound or cogent. But there may be times when arguments are created using information where the factual nature of some premises is disputed. Creating arguments that reflect disputed facts is a perfectly acceptable thing to do, and you'll see many philosophers who do this. One doesn't need to use only undisputed facts in their arguments; one only needs to acknowledge that the facts in question rests on what is believed to be the best evidence that can be presented at this time. This is called *qualifying* a fact and you will see many examples of this in ethics and philosophy. When a fact is qualified, it simply means that the philosopher is aware of and acknowledges some of the weaknesses in the arguments they are presenting. Qualifying facts is an important part of the philosophical process and you will see that many good arguments that are also full of qualifications to the factual claims they present.

Principles, Judgments, and Theories

In Chapter One you've already encountered the content of what are called our *moral premises*. A moral premise in an argument can consist of an ethical principle, an ethical theory, or an ethical judgment. Ethical principles are those very general statements philosophers use to express the goal they are trying to achieve through their actions. Christine Korsgaard's response to the murderer at the door in Chapter One offers us a good illustration of the ethical principle of beneficence or the idea that we should try to help people as best we can and not harm them if at all possible. This principle can be achieved by lying to the murderer, thus keeping our friend safe from harm.

An ethical judgment, on the other hand, is simply a statement that argues for or against any particular action or activity based on whether or not the author finds the action or activity morally acceptable. Another philosopher you have already encountered, Peter Singer, makes such an ethical judgment about the animal experiments performed by the U.S. Army Medical Bioengineering Research Lab. In these particular experiments, beagles were subjected to intense pain and the results of the experiments remained "inconclusive." Singer understands that this may strike you as particularly wrong in that these experiments use dogs and not rats or pigs, but he is quick to point out that "[with regard to animal experimentation] it is wrong to limit our concern to dogs."[2] Here Singer is preempting the readers' bias toward dogs by making the ethical judgment that it would be wrong for us to be concerned only with the dogs used in experimentation, and not all animals used in experiments. Even though Singer's ethical judgment is applied in this case to a specific situation involving beagles, it's easy to see how particular judgments can lead to the adoption of universal ethical principles that reflect a moral theory, or how particular judgments may be used as evidence for a universal ethical principle or an ethical theory, which in Singer's case points directly to preference utilitarianism.

Finally, you may encounter an ethical theory being used as a premise in an argument. Ethical theories, as you have seen from Chapter One, are a philosopher's attempt to justify actions using a system that can be universally applied to most situations. An example of this would be the use of Rosalind Hursthouse's account of virtues and how they should be used to guide our actions. Both Aristotle and Hursthouse argue that we should use virtues such as courage, honesty, kindness, and prudence to guide our actions in everything from appropriate interactions with the environment, to the way we treat our friends. An ethical theory as opposed to an ethical principle or an ethical judgment is an all-inclusive system that philosophers advocate to guide all of our actions, that is, an ethical system lays out what actions count as morally correct and which will count as morally wrong in any given situation.

So how will an understanding of the component parts specific to moral arguments help you to better understand and respond to the arguments you will encounter in this course? By being able to separate the factual claims from the ethical ones you can more easily understand which claims need to be substantiated with empirical evidence and which claims will need to be defended on theoretical grounds. Additionally, through researching the empirical claims, you can find out for yourself which of these are considered factual and which are still in the process of being verified, allowing you to qualify your arguments when necessary.

Errors in Our Thinking

Argumentation is certainly one of the most important parts of philosophical thinking and plays a large role in how we go about trying to resolve controversial moral issues. But arguing well takes more than simply understanding how argumentation works and applying this understanding to your work. Arguing about controversial topics requires insight into some of the ways our thinking can go wrong despite our best efforts.

Anyone who encounters moral problems is very likely to have strong opinions about them. This is what makes them so difficult to discuss and even more difficult to resolve. One of the first things you may be tempted to do as you read the different viewpoints presented in this book is to simply rely on your current opinion of the topic and restate it in place of well-constructed arguments. Although there's nothing wrong with having an opinion, it's good to remember that there are distinct differences between rational arguments and mere opinions.

Recall that arguments rely on reasons to support their claims. Not only do they rely on reasons but the reasons they rely on need to be good reasons that actually support the claim and do so with a certain amount of inferential strength. Oftentimes, our opinions are not well supported and may even reflect an emotional response to an issue or our personal taste on a topic. As a general rule, to rely on just an opinion means we are relying on a belief we often can't justify. Moreover, opinions are usually viewed as something that everyone is entitled to, implying that one opinion is just as good as the next, which means that opinions need not always be supported with facts. When thinking about certain issues, offering simple opinions can be perfectly acceptable, but when thinking about moral issues your opinions can lead directly to actions that may have a significant impact on your life and the lives of those around you. So, in thinking about moral issues we don't want to be haphazard and careless in our reasoning. Careful thinking involves taking an approach to facts, principles, judgments, and theories that express objective reasoning and an open mind about what a correct response to a moral issue can look like.

There are three ways our thinking can go astray when we are attempting to be objective and open-minded. All three have to do with our natural tendency to prefer certain things over others. They are personal bias, unconscious bias, and confirmation bias. We begin with personal bias as this tends to be the most prevalent of the three types of bias that can prevent us from being open-minded and objective. Personal biases seem a lot like opinions, but they aren't quite the same. While an opinion is something you generally vocalize and make known to others, biases are often unspoken preferences that guide our actions behind the scenes. Although an opinion is not a bias, they are similar in that like an opinion, everyone has a bias about something. In fact, having a bias simply means that you tend to prefer one thing over another, and this is something we all do. Preferring one thing over another can be as simple as preferring pie over cake, which is not really problematic, but it can also be complex and hamper your ability to make reasonable judgments about very important issues that will affect the lives of others around you. If, for example, you are biased toward women and will always hire a woman over a man if the opportunity presents itself, you are being biased in a serious and detrimental way. Whereas being biased toward pie may make you unpopular at a birthday party, being biased against men could seriously harm not only the people who apply for jobs at your company, but also harm the company since there are many qualified men that may, in some instances, do a better job in a particular position than would a woman, all other things being equal.

So, what do you need to do to become more objective and mitigate biases that may have detrimental effects on those around you? First, it's critical to realize that a bias toward or against something is a natural product of being human. That said, you need not attempt to rid yourself of bias altogether, as it simply can't be done. What you can do, however, is attempt to recognize your own biases and then reflect upon how these biases may be affecting your ability to think clearly and argue reasonably, then make adjustments in your thinking to compensate for this. In this way, you can at least partially suspend your bias in order to make the most rational judgments possible. These two strategies work well with personal bias and although they take some practice, many students are able to improve their ability to think objectively and fairly bias-free in just a short period of time.

The second kind of bias is much more difficult for us to recognize in ourselves as it lurks beneath the surface of our thinking and rarely makes itself known to us unless we are faced with a situation that shakes us up a bit. When a person holds a bias that they themselves are unaware of, it is called an *unconscious bias*. For instance, many of you reading this right now may have an unconscious bias against some animal species. You may hold particular attitudes toward an animal that will make some suggestions about them sound laughable or crazy. For example, what would some of your first thoughts be if someone were to say to you, "I feel very strongly that a rat deserves as much moral consideration as a person." Would you laugh? Smirk? Roll your eyes or think what a crazy nut they must be? One could predict that most of you had first reactions similar to the ones just described above. You see, most people have an unconscious bias against animals such as rats because we see them as creepy, nasty, or filthy. Now the idea of animals having the same moral status as humans is strange enough, but giving that moral status to an animal that is considered vile and nasty is more than most people can tolerate.

Most people don't do a lot of thinking about rats so your reaction was probably almost instinctual. Although you didn't know it, you very likely have an unconscious bias against rats. Although many of you think your reaction toward rats stems from facts and not bias, consider what you actually know about them. Did you know that they have a nervous system very similar to ours in its sophistication? They are also very social and have been

scientifically shown to problem-solve, laugh, and even express altruism toward other rats, actions once attributed only to humans.[3] Were these the facts that you were using to make your judgment about whether or not you should agree that they deserve equal consideration? Now that you know something more about them, can you begin to understand why someone might have moral concerns for them? Can you begin to see where your unconscious bias may have blinded you to alternative ways of thinking about these animals? Now take a moment to consider the implications of having an unconscious bias and not exploring other ways of thinking about an issue. If you don't take the capabilities of an animal into account, or you don't give them moral consideration, how might you be willing to treat them? Would this cause undue suffering? Does undue suffering matter morally? These and other questions start to arise when you attempt to see beyond your biases and begin to frame the world objectively.

The third kind of bias we can all fall prey to is called *confirmation bias.* Confirmation bias is where a person tends to seek sources and evidence that agrees with what they currently hold to be true, while at the same time avoiding or ignoring sources or evidence that conflicts with what they hold to be true. Again, we could turn to the rat example. You are no doubt aware that there are many different opinions about how animals are treated. How did you formulate your opinion? Did you start by looking at the arguments on both sides, weighing them carefully, and then deciding? Or did you simply feel one side was most correct and as a result listen to the arguments from that side and use the reasons that side offered to formulate your view? If you are a typical human being (I do this too) you probably listened to the arguments from the side with which you already agree and then discounted the other side as being a bunch of nuts. Perhaps you ignored the other side altogether. This is an example of confirmation bias. We seek what we already believe and ignore what we don't believe.

None of us is immune to the influences of our biases, be they personal, unconscious, or simply a product of our researching habits. There is nothing wrong with holding a bias as long as you are aware of it and you acknowledge that it may be playing a role in how you are thinking about a particular issue. If you follow some of the advice laid out in this section and always stop to check your thinking, you can become a more open-mined and objective thinker through practice.

Paper Writing

So now that you are in a philosophy course you are inevitably going to be faced with the task of writing a philosophy paper. Philosophy papers, like other papers in other courses, have a structure very specific to the content. First and foremost remember all the previous talk about argumentation. Philosophy papers will always contain argumentation of some sort. You know from what you've already read that ethical arguments will contain factual premises and moral premises, moral principles, judgments, or theories. This section looks at how to take these argumentation principles and formulate a philosophy paper. So, what are the basics of writing a good ethics paper? Well, that will depend on what type of ethics paper you are assigned to write.

Generally you can frame a philosophical argument in a number of ways, but since this is an applied ethics course you will most likely be creating theoretical or problem-based papers. When writing a paper on ethical theory you are going to be formulating claims such as "Justice is equal distribution of goods in a society" or "What is pleasurable is what we should call morally good." Theoretical claims are just that, and the previous section discussing theories, moral principles, and moral judgments can help you to clearly understand how to formulate your claim for papers with this emphasis.

When writing about a contemporary moral issue, you will need to understand how to incorporate what you know about the issues (factual claims) with how an issue can be judged (ethical premise: principle, judgment, or theory). Moral papers of this kind tend to make a modest attempt to show the reader that you understand specific parts of the issue. I say "specific parts" because often a moral issue is complex and may contain many issues that need to be covered independently in order for the issue to be made clear. Remember that this is an ethics course so the bulk of your work will focus on the ethical issues presented in the paper and the factual claims will serve to strengthen the argumentation as opposed to being the focal point.

To aid you in your writing, I have provided short outlines of each of the ways one can formulate an ethics paper for this course.[4]

A Problem in Ethical Theory

Paper claim: Food, shelter, and medical care should be considered a natural right and should be given to all humans

Introduction to the theory: Every time you turn on the news it seems like someone, somewhere is going without some fundamental resource. People are starving, are unable to find adequate shelter, or do not have access to basic medical care. Although deontologists tend to think that all persons have rights, not all deontologists feel that food, shelter, and access to basic medical care are part of the rights that all humans should have.

Insight into the problem and my argument strategy for the paper: Can a rights theory really be adequate if it does not include fundamentals that sustain human life? This paper will address this question. I will begin by stating what deontology is as a theory, and then I will examine a deontological viewpoint that does not include the fundamentals of food, shelter, and medical care. I will then refute this position by showing that deontological theories that include these fundamentals are more reasonably justifiable.

An Example of an Applied Ethics Paper

Paper claim: Although I find their treatment problematic, killer whales and dolphins do not fall under the protection of the 13th Amendment of the Constitution of the United States.

Introduction to the problem (factual claims): Over the years, SeaWorld has come under fire from animal rights organizations for holding killer whales in captivity and making them "perform" for a human audience. In 2012, PETA (People for the Ethical Treatment of Animals) filed a legal suit against SeaWorld, arguing that because of their intelligence, whales qualify as "people" and as such their captivity at SeaWorld constituted a form of slavery.

If the designation of "personhood" could be upheld, PETA charged, the actions of SeaWorld violated the 13th Amendment to the Constitution, which states that "Neither slavery nor involuntary servitude except as a punishment for a crime whereof the party shall have been duly convicted shall exist within the United States . . .".[5]

Introduction to the problem (ethical judgment and ethical principle): Although the case was dismissed, the lawsuit again raises questions about both personhood and how we treat highly intelligent animals. I feel that these animals are being poorly treated and their circumstances should be improved, but we should not use the ethical principles about the treatment of persons since whales and dolphins have not been shown to be both rational and autonomous, two fundamental features of personhood.

Notes

1. National Oceanic and Atmospheric Administration. "2012 was one of the ten warmest years on record globally." http://www.noaanews.noaa.gov/stories2013/20130806_stateoftheclimate.html.
2. Peter Singer, *Animal Liberation* (New York: Avon Books, 1990), 30.
3. Gerwin, Virginia. "Rats Free Each Other From Cages." *Nature,* December 8, 2011. http://www.nature.com/news/rats-free-each-other-from-cages-1.9603
4. Vaughn, Lewis, *Writing Philosophy: A Student's Guide to Writing Philosophy Essays* (New York: Oxford University Press, 2005).
5. U.S. Const., Amend. XIII. Print.

Name:____ **Date:**__________________

Review Questions

1. What is the definition of an argument?

2. What is the best way to find the conclusion/claim of any argument?

3. What is the difference between a deductive and an inductive argument?

4. What makes an argument invalid?

5. What makes an argument strong?

6. Cogency and soundness depend on what features of an argument?

7. Why do some people feel that deductive arguments are better than inductive arguments?

8. What is a factual premise and how does it differ from a moral premise?

9. What is an ethical principle? An ethical judgment? An ethical theory?

10. How does unconscious bias differ from confirmation bias?

Name:______________________________________ Date:________________

For Further Discussion

1. Go online and see if you can find an argument about a moral problem. Identify the claim and the premises. After this, determine whether the argument is inductive or deductive.
2. Choose a moral issue you feel very strongly about and then go online for about 10 minutes to research the topic further. Document the following: How many websites did you visit that supported the view you already hold? How many did you go to that argue against your opinion? Of the websites that support your view, how much time did you spend (on average) at each site? Of the websites that oppose your view, how much time did you spend (on average) at each site? Looking at your own research habits, can you conclude that they express some confirmation bias? If not, did you have to work really hard to avoid this tendency?
3. Find at least two different moral issues online. After reading about them assess the following: Does it seem that moral principles, moral judgments, or moral theories are more commonly expressed in the articles? Why do you think this is the case?

CHAPTER THREE

Environmental Ethics

EARTH
DAY
APRIL 22, 1970

On April 22, 1970, the first official Earth Day was celebrated. The celebration was later ratified by the United Nations, who designated April 22 as International Mother Earth Day. What made these events remarkable was that for the first time in human history people were starting to think of the earth not only in scientific and economic terms but also in moral terms.

The implications of this new line of thinking were felt immediately by philosophers who held traditional ethical theories whose focus had been primarily human beings. Utilitarians, deontologists, and virtue ethicists faced many challenges when trying to incorporate this new attitude into their already established ethical systems. Where some philosophers felt that these traditional theories could be modified to fit a more environmentally conscious worldview, many philosophers disagreed and called for new theories to help us understand our moral obligations to the Earth and its many inhabitants. It's from this hotbed of controversy that we've arrived at the diverse ethical ideas surrounding the moral status of the environment we have today.

When thinking about the environment in an ethical context, the central question that needs to be addressed is one of moral standing. A being is said to have moral standing if it fits certain criteria that make it suitable for moral concern. If we're going to include the environment in our moral calculations, what criteria or attributes should we select to determine who or what has moral standing? The question about who deserves our moral concern is not new and answers to that question have changed dramatically over time as our understanding of the natural world has changed. Historically, moral standing was not something that even all human beings possessed. We don't need to go back very far to see that race, religion, and gender have all played a role in determining who counts when it comes to moral concerns and decisions. Prior to 1919, women in America were denied the right to vote, the right to divorce, the right to own property, and the right to work outside the home. Even more recently, a mere 60 years ago, African Americans had to fight for the simple right to eat at the restaurant of their choice or to attend certain universities. Who "counted" in both these instances was determined by gender or race. Certainly it can be said that we've made progress in our understanding of who counts and why but some views about who or what counts when looking at environmental ethics are going to ask us to broaden our worldview substantially when it comes to rights and other moral principles.

Many philosophers are going to ask us to consider nonhuman animals, plants, insects, and even ecosystems as beings worthy of moral consideration and this means a substantial reframing of the question of who counts. Ideas such as counting ecosystems as moral entities not only run counter to many people's commonsense understanding of morality but will also challenge 3,500 years of ethical understanding and tradition because, despite our inconsistent application of moral consideration toward certain human beings, the fact is that only human beings have ever been seen as deserving of moral consideration in the first place (unless you are a utilitarian, but more on that later). So, it should come as no surprise that the most prevalent and overarching response to the question of who should get moral consideration, even within the framework of environmental ethics, has been human beings. The term that expresses the idea that only humans should get moral consideration or that they should at least get more moral consideration than other beings is a view known as *anthropocentrism*.

The anthropocentric outlook fits very nicely with Kant's and Aristotle's view of ethics, both of which you are familiar with from Chapter One. As you may recall, Kant used the idea of rationality to make a distinction between persons, or those with inherent value, and nonpersons, or those who have only instrumental value. Aristotle's view is also anthropocentric as he understood morality as something particular to rational beings (i.e., humans). Although Aristotle didn't place inherent value on humans the same way Kant did, virtue ethics is still focused only on rational beings and the type of characteristics they need to possess in order to be worthy of a good life. Aristotle's theory requires an inward, reflective, and most importantly rational interaction with the world so it is only concern itself with beings that can interact in these fundamental ways.

But how did philosophers such as Aristotle and Kant come to this understanding of moral consideration and how does an anthropocentric viewpoint influence our moral decisions today? The answers lie in three very prominent and influential branches of thought in the West: one of which is attributed directly to Aristotle, the second stemming from Christianity, and the third influenced by another important modern philosopher, Rene Descartes. All three of these sources have created and solidified traditional and contemporary assumptions about human beings and our place in the cosmos and all three still affect the way we view nonhuman animals and the natural world today. We now turn briefly to these historical sources to gain a greater appreciation about how environmental ethics challenges them.

Historical Anthropocentrism

The idea of a human-centered world, human-centered morality, and human-centered values are probably three of the oldest ideas in human thought. Historically, humans have placed themselves above and apart from the natural world based on a number of assumptions about how we came to be and what role we played in the universe. A general focus on reason, our nearness to the Western Christian God, and our ability to use language and solve complex problems have all been seen as unique attributes deserving of considerations that were not afforded to other beings.

Beginning with the Greeks, reason was identified as the property that made a being worthy of moral consideration. If reason was as unique as it appeared to be, argued the Greeks, then it must set humans apart as "special." If a being was special, then certainly it deserved special considerations and special treatment. Thus, early on in the history of Western thought, the idea of humans standing out or above the rest of nature was an integral part of our thinking about the world. As we've already seen, Aristotle would later create an entire ethical system around this idea, with his teleological-centered system asserting that though all things have a purpose, only the human purpose is reflective of something special.

Christianity helped to further solidify the idea of human specialness through their cosmological doctrine of the "great chain of being." Originally conceived by church fathers to denote our relationship to God, this picture of the world would later become the basis for justifying our relationships not only to God but to all other beings on the planet. In essence, the Great Chain of Being shows us that all life on Earth is organized in a linear fashion or, as the name suggests, in a great chain-like structure. With God firmly fixed at the top of the chain, each successive link represented a descent and a removal by one from His perfection. In this scheme we have God, we have the angels, and then we have human beings, existing only once removed from the ultimate perfection. As religious texts tell us, we humans are not only closest to God but are made in His image and endowed with a piece of His perfect nature (in the form of a soul). In essence we are the most perfect beings that exist on Earth. Of course, this meant that the further away a being was from resembling a human either in form or in reasoning ability, the further down it fell on the chain, the further removed it was from God and the less perfect it could be considered. The less perfect the being, the less it counted in the larger scheme of things. This way of thinking resulted in nonhuman animals and the natural world being considered not only imperfect but counting for much less than a human, if they counted at all. We could of course grant them instrumental value, but this simply meant that as perfection on Earth we were permitted to use both nature and nonhuman animals in any way we saw fit and if we had no use for them we were free to dispose of them as we pleased.

Rene Descartes's philosophy was highly influenced by this idea of human perfection and our place on the great chain of being. His philosophy used these ideas as a starting point in order to emphasize rationality in the form of language use as proof of the human soul. He asserted that it was our ability to use language and to solve complex problems that not only separated us from all other beings but illustrated our shared nature with God. Since it was clear to Descartes that these abilities must be a part of that special perfection only a soul could bring, all other beings were not only further removed from human beings and God himself but were declared soulless and basically empty biological shells. Once Descartes established this it was only a short step to asserting that not only were human beings the only beings with souls, but since the mind was part of the soul it must be the case that only humans have minds. Descartes claimed that all other beings were not only incapable of rational thinking but of doing all the things a mind is capable of doing: sensing, feeling pleasure and pain, or experiencing mental states such as emotions. This led him to assert that all other nonhuman animals were merely machines or "autonoma" very similar to today's computers. For Descartes and his adherents an animal appearing to experience pain was merely a misunderstanding on our part. Like a computer that makes a grinding noise, there is no real discomfort for an animal; they are merely reacting to an environmental "glitch" that makes them appear to be in pain, when in actuality, without a soul or mind, this pain is not really possible.

Problems with Traditional Anthropocentrism

After reading the three historical accounts that support the view that humans are the only beings worthy of moral consideration, it's easy to see that there are fundamental, interrelated problems with these ideas. Most of these problems stem from the fact that all three worldviews are simple in terms of their understanding of biology and ecology. Since the writers of their respective times tended to know quite a bit about the human condition but precious little about other beings in the biosphere, it should come as no surprise that their focus was on the human condition and their reasons for excluding other beings were simply misguided.

Today we know that the Cartesian way of thinking about nonanimals as mindless is simply untrue. With advances in biology and neuroscience we now understand that many animals are like us in fundamental ways, including reasoning ability and language acquisition. We also know that they are not only able to experience pleasure and pain but are also capable of complex emotional and psychological states as well.

The idea of a Great Chain of Being that showed sentient life being derived from divine origins has been replaced by the scientifically supported Great Tree of Being, which is a picture of life on Earth where all beings have evolved to adapt to their environments, and are not so much superior or inferior as they are well or ill adapted. Humans on this model are simply one biological variation in a long line of variations, with our staring point not above us, but below us, represented by the microbial common ancestors shared by all beings.

Finally, the idea of a *telos* or a purpose that was so popular with the Greeks has been entirely dismissed by 21st-century science. The idea that the human purpose was to reason makes no more sense than saying a frog's purpose is to jump. Certainly humans and frogs are capable of doing such things, but this fact doesn't speak to an overarching purpose. As we've discovered through biology and ecology, there is no purposeful design in nature. Nature is produced through random variations and as such humans' ability and frogs' ability are both simply random responses to the challenges of existence.

But the simple fact that we must reject the justifications provided by our historical sources doesn't mean that philosophers must reject anthropocentrism completely. It does, however, mean that philosophers will need to use caution to avoid the historical traps that have been set by past philosophers. To do this they will need to provide more plausible justifications to support their anthropocentric views. It's here that we turn our discussion to anthropocentrism in the 21st century and look at how anthropocentric philosophers have attempted to modify their views in light of so many questionable historical justifications.

Contemporary Anthropocentrism

Two 21st-century philosophers who are committed to an anthropocentric viewpoint when it comes to the environment are Wilfred Beckerman and Joanna Pasek. Both of them hold the view that humans are unique in that they are value creators. That is, if the environment is to have a value at all, there must be a person present to place a value on it. Although this sounds a lot like what we've seen in Kant's philosophy, Beckerman and Pasek tend not to view humans as the only beings that have inherent value. Although we're the only beings that can place a value on other things, we have the ability to place either inherent value or instrumental value on objects and nonhuman animals. In some situations, we as value-makers may opt to value a thing having instrumental value, inherent value, or both. The example they use is that of a piece of music. Humans may choose to appreciate a piece of music as inherently valuable or beautiful in itself, while at the same time we may also recognize its instrumental value or the ability it has to put a fussy baby to sleep.[1] For philosophers who adhere to this anthropocentric outlook it's not so much that they are stating that humans are special and important because only they are capable of possessing a certain kind of value; rather, it's the fact that we have the ability to value at all that makes us distinct from other beings. This certainly mirrors the traditional anthropocentric viewpoint that reason is important, but it avoids being linked to any of the historical justifications that have all but been discounted. After all, many philosophers who are anthropocentric in their outlook remind us that as much as we would like to say that humans are nothing special, or that we aren't in a privileged position, the reality of our situation is that we simply don't have a choice. We are in a privileged position by default since we are able to reason at a very high level and have a complex moral system. We are forced to function from this point of view of a rational and moral being whether we like it or not and any attempts to remove this specialness only further supports a distinction between us and other animals as it highlights the fact that we are beings who can either see ourselves as special or we can see ourselves as any other being, a feat only a rational and value-driven being can do. In the end, anthropocentric philosophers such as Beckerman and Pasek are supportive of anthropocentrism simply because they see us as having no other choice. Whether we choose to accept it or deny it, we are value-creators and can't escape this fact.

An environmental example of this may make the idea more clear. Pretend, for instance, that we are looking at a piece of wilderness or a tract of forest and we decide it must be preserved. On what grounds are we making this decision? On what grounds should we leave the area wild as opposed to using it for commercial purposes? It would seem at the outset that we are preserving this land for its own sake (i.e., we are giving it an inherent value). But how did we come to the understanding that it has this value? Anthropocentric philosophers will argue that we come to this understanding through our specifically human view of what matters and why. In other words, we make the decision to leave this land alone based on the same anthropocentric view that we might use to determine that the land should be used for commercial purposes, giving it an instrumental value instead. Regardless of what we choose to do with the land, we will always choose and act from the viewpoint of a human value-maker.

The anthropocentric view has fallen out of favor in recent years as new holistic theories have emerged. This is probably due not to the fact that anthropocentrism is human centered so much as it reflects a rejection of the traditional justifications and unfortunate consequences of them. Contemporary anthropocentrists, unlike their historic counterparts, don't regard the environment as simply a tool or a resource that we may dispose of in any way we choose. Being anthropocentric in the 21st century is not the same as being destructive or "chauvinistic" about our place on the planet. Our unique position does not translate into a need to be apathetic or ruthless toward other species or toward the environment as a whole and contemporary anthropocentrists can hold the same respect for the natural world as can other less anthropocentric views. In the case of both Beckerman and Pasek, both view the natural world with wonder and respect and see that, like human beings, it too can have inherent value. To distinguish themselves from their less-than-enlightened predecessors, anthropocentric philosophers these days prefer the word *anthropocentric* to be translated as "from a human point of view" as opposed to the traditional translation, which amounts to "human-centered" or "human-oriented," to express the ways in which their understanding of our place in the world differs from traditional ways of thinking about our relationship to the environment.

Zoocentrism

Zoocentrism has been a popular historical and contemporary alternative to anthropocentrism. If you hold a zoocentric outlook you recognize that all animals have moral status and deserve moral consideration. You've seen one obvious form of zoocentrism in the first chapter when we discussed the ethical theories of Jeremy Bentham and Peter Singer. Zoocentrism is based on the idea of sentience and similar to utilitarianism argues that if a being is sentient or conscious (has the ability to suffer, or is aware of its surroundings to a high degree), then that being deserves our moral consideration. What kinds of beings count as sentient will ultimately need to be decided by the scientific community, but at this point from their research we know that all mammals, reptiles, amphibians, fish, and birds are sentient. There is even evidence that some mollusks such as squid and octopus are capable of pleasure and pain and therefore must be considered when our decisions affect them adversely. As we move further along the many branches of the life tree, it starts to become unclear as to whether or not a being is sentient. Are spiders, moths, and bees sentient? This is a question that has yet to be answered, but if the answer turns out to be yes, zoocentric philosophers will insist that they deserve our moral consideration too.

It is interesting to note that although many zoocentric philosophers are also utilitarians, these two theories are not identical. There are a number of philosophers that are zoocentric in their views but aren't utilitarians. Christine Korsgaard, who you also met in Chapter One, is a Kantian but holds a zoocentric point of view. For Korsgaard, all sentient beings have goods that they are attempting to pursue and they all seek to promote their own interests. The ability to do those things (similar to the definition of consciousness) gives a being inherent value and this means that like humans it can't be treated as the means-to-an-end for other beings. That said, all sentient animals would qualify as having inherent value and for Korsgaard that means that we owe them moral consideration in addition to owing them a duty not to be treated as tools for our own gain. So zoocentrism as a theory can include many different ethical theories with distinct ways of arriving at the idea that all sentient beings human and nonhuman deserve moral consideration. Considering the zoocentric model in general, it seems to express what many in the 21st century feel is a more realistic and perhaps better model of who should get moral consideration than does the anthropocentric view. It also seems to fit much more closely with what we know about biology and evolution, that is, that we, despite our unique abilities, are simply one animal among many and the relevant similarities outweigh the relevant differences.

The zoocentric model seems to some as a better way to view the world than the traditional anthropocentric model and some would even argue the contemporary anthropocentric model as well. But, like all ethical theories, it isn't without its critics. The main criticisms of zoocentrism come from two very recent schools of thought. Known as *biocentrism* and *ecocentrism*, these two schools go well beyond the zoocentric boundaries of human and nonhuman animals and even beyond the boundaries of individual beings. Both of these ethical theories about the environment are quite new and are considered by some to be quite radical and even eccentric.

Biocentrism

Biocentrism is the view that not just sentient beings are worthy of moral consideration but any being that can be determined as "living" is a being that deserves moral consideration. Ecocentrism, on the other hand, is the view that it is not individual beings that are deserving of our moral consideration; rather, it is a system that extends moral consideration to entire species and whole ecosystems. We return to ecocentrism momentarily, but for now let's focus on the idea that all living individuals are worthy of moral consideration.

Biocentric philosophers are critical of both the zoocentric and anthropocentric views of moral consideration. For them, the anthropocentric and zoocentric views of morality are flawed in a similar way. Recall that the anthropocentrism cites reason and value creation as the relevant attributes separating humans from nonhuman animals. For them, only those beings that are endowed with reason and can assign value to the world are worthy of moral consideration. Now with a zoocentric view, reason and value creation as the ultimate attributes that determine moral consideration are replaced with the attribute of sentience. Although this does widen the circle of moral considerability, many philosophers such as Paul Taylor and James Sterba see the zoocentric focus on sentience as simply another version of anthropocentrism. The zoocentrics, they argue, have simply moved the line of moral considerability from one arbitrary attribute (reason) to another arbitrary attribute (sentience). What, after all, is so special about sentience except of course the fact that we're sentient beings? If zoocentric philosophers can't give us good reasons why sentience is a more valuable or worthy attribute than nonsentience, then philosophers who assert zoocentrism are really no different from those who assert anthropocentrism.

Interestingly, many biocentric theories acquire their justifications by returning to a modified version of the ancient Greek concept of purpose or *telos*. Biocentrists state that the attribute that we should use to determine whether or not a thing receives moral consideration is whether or not the particular being is goal-directed or striving toward its own individual good. To strive toward a good simply means that a being is attempting to achieve what is in its biological makeup to achieve. Trees are biologically programmed to synthesize light and turn nutrients in the soil into food, and bats are biologically constituted in such a way as to seek prey using echolocation. Every being that can be said to be alive is a being with a *telos* and that *telos* needs to be taken into account when we make our moral decisions. If all living things deserve our moral consideration, an interesting question arises, that of how we weigh the interests of so many diverse beings. For example, if I need to decide whether or not to uproot the hedges alongside the road in order to create easier access to food and water for the wildlife, how do I weigh the *telos* or goals of the hedges against the goals of, say, the deer that live in the area?

Fundamentally, there are two schools of thought within biocentrism that attempt to answer the question of how to weigh the interests of diverse species. The first school of thought is known as *egalitarian biocentrism* and the second school of thought is known as *nonegalitarian biocentrism*. Most famously proposed by Paul Taylor and defended further by James Sterba, biocentric egalitarianism is the idea that all living things are in essence equal and should be considered equally when making our moral decisions. Taking the idea of *telos* from Aristotle and the idea of inherent value from Immanuel Kant, Paul Taylor is going to argue for egalitarianism by asserting that all living beings have a *telos* or a life goal and the ability to pursue this life goal represents its good. The good of any being is realized when it's strong and healthy and individuals of any species that are able to sustain themselves over time (reproduce) and function successfully within their given ecosystems are said to be realizing their own particular good. Modifying Kant's philosophy in a way similar to Korsgaard, Taylor argues for the inherent worth of all beings that present themselves as what he refers to as "teleological centers of life."[2] If we can't prove the superiority of human beings and we can't justify what is so valuable about sentience, then for Taylor it has to follow that all beings should be granted inherent worth based on the simple fact that they possess a biological purpose. This seems like the only relevant and nonbiased attribute that we can reasonably take into account when thinking about moral consideration; any other attribute simply can't be justified. But what does it mean to recognize that beings are teleological centers of life? Taylor suggests that we recognize a being as a teleological center when we look at it as an entity that has a goal, whose life can go well or poorly and can be positively or negatively affected by specific actions and situations. In this framework, all entities strive for their own unique good and this striving can either be helped, frustrated, or remain unaffected by the strivings of other beings.

For Taylor, understanding this struggle and acknowledging the uniqueness of individual beings is the first step to acquiring the proper biocentric attitude toward nature. What should follow from the acquisition of this attitude are actions that contribute to the *telos* of all beings, with no being treated as superior to any other. As we begin to understand nature and our place within it through our newfound attitude, what Taylor sees as emerging is the moral idea that each and every living thing has inherent worth. No species is higher or lower, better or worse. No species is to be favored because of arbitrary choices about what should "count" in terms of moral treatment.

All beings that are teleological centers of a life deserve respect for this reason alone and no species preferences should bias us toward or against another species. This notion of equality of species is where the egalitarian part of biocentric egalitarianism comes into play.

When one thinks of all species as having equal inherent worth, one of the first things that come to mind is the challenge presented when one or more species competes with or is faced with a threat from another species. Referring back to the example of the hedges, if all species are equal and have equal inherent worth, how do we go about determining whether or not the hedges should be cut down? If we are using zoocentrism, we could measure the pleasures and pains of the individuals involved and try to create the most pleasure. In this case it would be to cut the hedges since those sentient beings that stand to gain outweigh the nonsentient interests of the hedges. Remember this is just one way a zoocentric theory can be applied and it does not necessarily reflect Korsgaard's idea of inherent value, although the decision would likely be the same. But if we are looking at the inherent value of hedges and the inherent value of deer, we are essentially looking at the equal inherent value of two very different species. We are going to need a way to determine which species or set of species will win in our decision whether to cut the hedge or leave it alone. It seems like a vexing problem when all interests are to be considered equally. We will need the help of egalitarian philosopher James Sterba if we are going to understand how to respond in this situation.

Sterba would start by asking us to compare the idea of universal inherent value to the idea of inherent value that we usually assign solely to human beings. He will then ask that we apply some additional moral principles to the problem, which again are familiar principles used when making assessments about interactions between humans.[3] The idea behind egalitarianism within the strictly human realm involves not equal treatment but equal consideration. We have already seen the distinction between these two concepts earlier in Chapter One of this book. Basically, when we deal with other humans it's not uncommon for some humans to benefit from our actions and for others to be harmed. But the fact that this occurs doesn't mean that we didn't promote the idea of equality, nor does it mean that because some humans benefitted from our actions that we consider them more inherently valuable.

Equal consideration of other human beings amounts to a particular attitude toward them and doesn't designate the kind of treatment they should receive. The same is true for biocentric egalitarianism. Just because one species is harmed by our actions and another benefits from them doesn't reflect an inequality in either consideration or inherent value; it simply means they were treated differently. Even though we have shown that unequal treatment exists, we still need to justify the fact that it occurs. To help us do this, Sterba introduces three general principles that he refers to as "the principle of human preservation," "the principle of disproportionality," and "the principle of human defense."[4] These three principles are not unknown to those who hold both anthropocentric and zoocentric views and for Sterba are perfectly applicable in biocentrism as well.

The principle of human defense is one that can be asserted if/when we are in a position where harm could come to us either from other humans or from animals or plants. Here the idea is that we are able to defend ourselves and other humans from harmful aggression, this aggression being directed either at us or at our property or the property of other human beings. The principle of human defense does not need to be directed at a single individual, there are times when it may need to include entire species or entire ecosystems. To illustrate this principle let's use the example of a very real threat to human livelihood, the disease-carrying flea. For Sterba, the flea certainly represents a teleological center of a life and thus is worthy of our respect (one could even say that the plague bacteria the flea carries is also a teleological center since it is alive and attempts to realize its own good). At the same time, this flea and the bacteria it carries pose a deadly threat to humans and animals. But if all beings have equal inherent worth, on what grounds can we say that it is acceptable to not only kill large numbers of the flea population but also strive to eradicate bubonic plague entirely? For Sterba, if we call on the principle of human defense, we can justify doing these things even if we respect the uniqueness and worth of both the bacteria and the insect.

The other two principles work together and are already routinely applied in ethical situations involving human interactions. The principle of human preservation states that we are entitled to meet our basic needs and the basic needs of other humans even if meeting these needs should end up being detrimental to other species. He justifies this by stating that all beings are goal-directed and life can either go well for us or it can go poorly. To recognize this in other life forms is to recognize this in ourselves and acknowledge that at least in this way we are all alike. We have minimal needs that must be met in order to live, grow, and reproduce and we must have our basic needs fulfilled in order to fulfill our purpose. If our basic needs can only be met to the detriment of other species or ecosystems, then our actions are perfectly permissible. This principle is supposed to be used in concert with the principle of disproportionality, which states that if our actions prevent other species from fulfilling their basic needs and are only fulfilling our wants and not our own basic needs, then our actions are impermissible. Again, this goes back to all beings having equal inherent value: no one's wants or luxury items should be obtained at the cost of another's basic needs. Through these three well-known principles Sterba is attempting to create justifications for our actions that seem to favor some beings or even ourselves at times, putting others at a disadvantage. So what could be said about the hedges and the deer, that ethical problem that was raised at the beginning of this section? Using these three principles we could in good conscience tear out the hedges it they were preventing other beings from realizing their basic needs. A being's ability to forage for food seems to be a basic need, so if we have considered all beings equally we could justify our decision to tear out the hedges. As you can see these three principles can go a long way in helping us to determine what the most moral course of action would be in fairly simple situations, but, like all principles, they are general guidelines and may not be very helpful in the most difficult cases.

Even with the inclusion of these principles, some philosophers don't agree that an egalitarian approach to biocentrism is the best or most useful approach. Although they do agree that all beings are teleological centers of a life, deserving of our respect and our consideration. They don't agree that this simple property of being alive is the only property that we should take into account when making our moral decisions. For the nonegalitarian it seems common sense to think that maple trees, chimpanzees, and humans are very different in a number of important ways. All three are teleological centers of a life but it seems much more reasonable to the nonegalitarian to recognize the fact that the chimpanzee, in addition to having a *telos,* is also a sentient, highly social, and highly intelligent being. Moreover, it would seem that humans, also sentient, social, and intelligent, possess the additional properties of rationality, autonomy, and moral sensibility, over and above both chimpanzees and maple trees.

According to the egalitarian, none of these other attributes should be relevant to our moral decisions, but nonegalitarians question whether this leveling attitude is the best position to take if we are going to truly show our respect for all beings.[5] The following example illustrates quite nicely the deep concern that nonegalitarians are trying to express. Let's pretend that we are biocentric egalitarians and we are trying to decide what to eat for dinner. We have two choices: we can either go out and uproot a turnip or we can go out to the barn and slaughter a pig for our meal. Now we have to eat—which is a basic need—so using Sterba's principles we can justify our having to end the life of another being. But which one should we choose? It would seem that if we took the egalitarian view we would be equally morally responsible for the killing of a turnip as we would the killing of a pig, since both possess the same amount of inherent value. But the idea that killing a plant is just as wrong as killing an animal seems to run counter to what most of us feel would be the appropriate response to taking a life. Whether or not you eat meat, most of us would not be inclined to say that eating a turnip creates as many moral quandaries as eating a pig; after all, we usually recognize and take into account sentience and the ability to feel pleasure and pain when determining whether or not an action is morally acceptable.

It is this kind of moral quandary that a nonegalitarian such as David Schmidtz would ask us to reflect upon and then ask ourselves if biocentric egalitarianism really reflects a respect for the inherent value of beings, or if it actually removes respect from the picture by discounting what may be unique and valuable about individual beings.

Nonegalitarians recognize a hierarchy of valuable capabilities that make each being unique. This hierarchy asserts that though they are distinct, no one trait is superior to any other. Rather, it recognizes that certain attributes bring added value to their possessors. So a nonegalitarian recognizes a sliding scale of inherent value based on a variety of traits. For example, both a maple tree and a monkey are teleological centers of life, but they differ in that one is not only a teleological center but is also sentient. Now sentience is not a superior trait per se, but it does

bring added value to any being who possesses it, according to the nonegalitarian. This differs from anthropocentrism in that humans are not considered superior or the only beings worthy of moral consideration. It also differs from zoocentrism as it recognizes that it's not the attribute of sentience but the attribute of being a teleological center of a life that is the basis for giving moral consideration to a being.

But is nonegalitarianism really that different from anthropocentrism and zoocentrism? That is, if we were to apply biocentric nonegalitarianism to a real-world problem, does it really differ substantially from both anthropocentrism and zoocentrism as it has been claimed?

Schmidtz and other nonegalitarians are well aware of this difficulty and attempt to respond to it by changing their moral focus from the inherent value of a being to our particular capacities to show our respect for other beings as well as recognizing our moral obligation to do so. Schmidtz illustrates these capacities in the form of two principles. The first principle states that we should care about other species because not doing so shows a failure of our own self-respect and, second, if we don't care about other species we have not fully realized our human nature and are stunted in a fundamental way. Both of these reasons for respect point inward, toward our abilities, and not outward, toward the inherent value of the being in question. This strategy allows us to respect beings that may not have a point of view or conscious interests of their own. So, when we consider whether or not to destroy a tree or a plant we can't ask for or advocate from the plant's point of view because it has none. The only thing we can advocate for is our point of view and this should include ideas of what it means to be a responsible, self-reflective, self-respecting human being. Looking at a being in this way should lead us to the conclusion that it would be irresponsible and disrespectful to simply destroy something just for the sake of destruction or just for fun. Whether it's your neighbor's car, your school's gymnasium, or a tree in your own backyard, to break, deface, or destroy something simply because you can or simply because it would give you pleasure is fundamentally wrong in Schmitz's view because it directly reflects what a person thinks of herself and what kind of respect she shows toward her own set of values.

This leads us to Schmidtz's second principle, which highlights a failure to recognize the value of another being and to give it the respect it deserves. This failure in turn leads to a failure on the part of an individual to realize his or her full capacity as a human being. We have a unique ability to put ourselves in the place of other beings, to reflect upon what their existence might be like and to make conscious choices about what actions to take with regard to this existence. This in addition to our ability to think morally about our actions truly defines what it is to be human. When a person fails to do these things, insisting instead on living from a self-interested and human point of view, they fail to achieve what is fundamentally unique about being human. This failure marks an inability on the part of the individual to grow and this results in a person being stunted or not fully human.

At this point in the chapter it seems as if we have covered an immense amount of theoretical ground. We have gone from anthropocentrism to zoocentrism to biocentrism. Although this has taken us far from many of the historical views about the moral status of the environment, there is one more view that moves us even further away from traditional views. We turn now to ecocentrism.

Ecocentrism

Ecocentrism, or *holism* as it is sometimes called, is the view that it is not humans, animals, or teleological centers of life that are worthy of our moral consideration; rather, it is the systems that sustain these and the species that help perpetuate the future existence of these individuals. Of all the moral theories we have covered in this chapter thus far, ecocentrism can be seen as the most radical. Not only is the circle of our moral concerns far wider than it has been with any other moral theory, we are also moving away from a very fundamental idea in ethics, one that places value and moral importance on the individual. An ecocentric viewpoint shifts moral consideration away from the individual entirely and insists that it is systems and species as a whole that are deserving of our moral consideration and not the individuals who comprise these systems. But what does it mean to say that it is a collective system that deserves our moral consideration and not the individual that makes up the system? To see this distinction more clearly it may be useful to reflect on all of the theories we have seen so far. Despite their outward differences, all moral theories we've encountered have directed moral consideration toward the individual. In essence all of them have asserted that moral consideration and/or inherent value was a property to be disputed at the individual level. Whether we are discussing a redwood tree, an ant, or an elephant, the discussion has been about determining which individuals count and why. Even our previous examples involving the forest have been focused on harms and benefits reaped by individuals living in those areas and not the ecological systems to which these individuals belong. For that reason, all of the theories discussed thus far can be thought of as ethically individualistic in nature. An ethically individualistic theory sees the individual as worthy of moral consideration and/or as possessing inherent value. Thus moral respect is asserted for the holder of particular, specific attributes and not for the community of holders or for the system of holders. By way of example, if a zoocentrist asserts that elephants are worthy of moral consideration, she is asserting that each individual elephant is worthy of that consideration and thus all elephants, individually in possession of this property, are worthy of our consideration. The same would be the case for a biocentrist in that if a given redwood tree has inherent value, all redwood trees have that same value and as such we should respect each individual redwood tree as a teleological center of life.

Ecocentrism, on the other hand, states that individuals shouldn't be the focus of our moral consideration; rather, we should focus on the ecosystems and species that sustain these individuals and strive to include them in our moral decisions. This idea emerged along with the "discovery" of ecosystems in the late 1930s and has been popular among many 21st century thinkers as a way to incorporate scientific understanding into our ethical understanding.

When considering ecocentric theories it is important to note that like biocentric systems all ecocentric systems of thought are not created equal. There are many ways of framing this idea and a number of ways to ground this idea of system-centered thinking. For our purposes we look at two ecocentric schools of thought. The first attempts to create an entirely new ethic by breaking all traditional philosophical ties and moving our thoughts about moral considerability away from individuals entirely. The other school of thought attempts to ground ecocentrism in traditional lines of thought, like anthropocentrism.

The first school of thought is best represented by Aldo Leopold's Land Ethic,[6] which can be thought of as the strong version of ecocentrism. The second school of thought has been proposed by contemporary philosopher Brian Norton and is a modified version of traditional anthropocentrism.

Before we move to our examples we need to look at what ecocentrism rejects in traditional philosophy and how this rejection leads to a holistic way of thinking. Ecocentrism is a revolt against the reductionist thinking of both traditional science and traditional philosophy. Reductionism is the view that the whole of any given thing is merely the sum of its parts, that is, what really matters about any given thing is not presented to us on a large scale but, rather, in the details. This can be seen in the biological sciences where the functioning of cells and even the parts of cells are where one looks to determine how a being functions. A good example of this view can be shown through our attempts to understand something familiar to us all: a cat. If we were to look at a cat reductively we would look to the various systems in a cat in order to really understand what is important to know about cats in general.

This is very different from a holistic picture of a cat, which would not be taking the cat down to the cellular level in order to gain understanding of cats; rather, we would look to the cat as a system of biology, psychology, cognition, and behavior to get a true understanding of what it means to be a cat. This example can also be used when looking at ethics. Where a reductionist would argue that the whole is merely the sum of its parts, a holist or ecocentric philosopher would look to the entire ecosystem or species population and then argue that these should be the focus of our moral consideration. Where a reductionist sees a collection of individuals, the holist sees the collection itself as an entity. Where a reductionist sees the trees that populate the forest as the holders of inherent value, the holist sees the ecological system that is the forest as the holder of that value.

When we make this shift the individual no longer has any moral significance; rather, the moral significance attaches to the whole system or species within which the individual functions. That said, as an ecocentrist our moral responsibility is to the communities the individuals inhabit. To see an example of these ideas at work one can look at the common practice of culling. *Culling* is a process where humans strategically reduce the size of a population of animals through killing selected animals, generally the older and weaker of the species. Some wildlife conservationists argue that because of reduced habitat culling is necessary to keep certain animal populations and ecosystems healthy. The focus on ecosystem health and not on individual animals represents what is fundamental about ecocentrism. The loss or death of the individual animal is not morally problematic or even of particular moral concern, just so long as the integrity of the system or species is promoted. For the ecocentrist, keeping the entire system healthy is our moral obligation and we must do what is necessary to ensure this will happen. In contrast, think about the practice of culling through the eyes of a zoocentrist or even a biocentrist. Both zoocentric and biocentric philosophers may take issue with the fact that we are destroying individuals that are entities deserving our moral consideration. Destroying these entities for the good of the community, they would argue, places an inappropriate emphasis on the moral status of the community and reduces entities to mere cogs in wheels, which for some is entirely unacceptable. It is interesting to note here that although a utilitarian may not have a moral quandary about culling, she would certainly not agree that culling individuals from a herd because we have a moral obligation to keep a system or a species healthy is an appropriate justification. Remember that although utilitarians are concerned about the greatest good for the greatest number of beings, the "good" that is measured is individual goods that have been "added" together, so to speak. It is not about the good of the community or the system itself since these entities cannot feel pleasure and pain.

Now that we understand the underlying assumptions of ecocentrism and have a general idea how this theory departs from most mainstream ways of thinking about moral consideration, let's look at the two versions of this theory to get a better understanding of how it functions.

Aldo Leopold's essay "The Land Ethic," while written in 1949, still serves as the fundamental example of traditional ecocentrism. Although not a philosopher (Leopold was an ecologist) he touches on many elements of anthropocentrism, zoocentrism, and reductionism, calling for a shift away from these traditional outlooks. For Leopold, "A thing is [morally] right when it tends to preserve the integrity, stability and beauty of the biotic community. It is [morally] wrong when it tends otherwise."[7] In the past, Leopold explains, we have thought that humans held a privileged place in the world as conquerors of nature and not citizens of the biotic community. From this view we have acquired the misguided understanding that the earth holds only economic value and its resources need to be exploited to be valuable. Our ignorance of the systems that regulate and influence life on the planet has also added to this misguided notion and fueled our destruction of the very biotic systems that sustain us.

As with many of the philosophers we have encountered in this chapter, Leopold challenges our understanding of the relationship humans have with nature. He argues that as much as we would like to think that we are "special" or we live above or outside of nature, things could not be further from the truth. Using examples straight from the theory of evolution, Leopold shows us that not only are we one species among many but that we too have a connection with the land on which we live, as well as the plants and animals that live there too. He offers many examples of how, unknown to us, the land itself and what could be produced on it has steered many events in human history, including what we fought for, what we grew, and how we made use of the land after it was hard won.

Moreover, Leopold shows us that our place within the biotic mechanism or ecosystem is dependent upon the soil, the plants, and the animals. We don't lie outside of this "chain," but are a part of it. Furthermore, this chain, unlike the traditional Great Chain of Being, is not a terminal one, ending in God or even ending with humans, but a chain that forms a loop that turns back into itself with humans, animals, and plants creating waste materials that are subsumed again by the soil, only to be reborn as new plants, animals, and so on.

Situating humans directly within a recursive system allows him to show us that our moral responsibilities as members of a community are much more far reaching than the human communities we immediately recognize. Our real community lies within the holistic chain of life and, as a result, the health of the land that allows for this chain to grow and these cycles to continue should be of the utmost moral concern to each individual.

Morally reaching beyond the human community and even beyond individuals will require a new way of looking at land and the natural world as a whole. This new way must, according to Leopold, incorporate an "…internal change in our intellectual emphasis, loyalties, affections and convictions."[8] Currently, when we look at the land and the ecological systems we approach them with the same anthropocentric viewpoint we have always held. This in turn leads us to value nature instrumentally but not inherently. Recall that when something has merely instrumental value, it can be dispensed of as we the value-makers see fit. So if we don't see a forest or a particular species of bird as having any value, we are free to use it or even destroy it as we please without needing any moral justification. When we couple this attitude with the idea that nature only has an economic value, we need no further justification for destroying a wetland, a forest, or an entire species other than "it had no instrumental or economic value." In many cases the unfortunate reality is that land, plants, and animals tend to have economic value only insofar as they can produce something of use or monetary worth. To allow a plot of land to remain idle or to stay "wild" is to allow it to be "unproductive" in an economic sense. After all, couldn't I clear the land and use it to grow organic veggies to sell at the farmers market? If I don't use the land to make money, what did I buy it for in the first place? Interestingly enough, most of the land, animal, and plant species that inhabit the earth naturally do not have any economic value at all. Song birds, mosses, or insects are of no commercial value and unless we alter the land and remove the species, they are viewed as useless or wasted. If we continue to frame our consideration of the land and species in this way we stand to lose much of the biodiversity of the world, resulting in widespread collapse of the very systems that sustain us.

Finally, Leopold insists that our excessive pride in our human achievements and our ignorance of the complexity of biotic systems leads us to the false assumption that we are conquerors of nature and not a part of an extended community. We are just beginning to understand the fragility and complexity of these systems and have not yet come to terms with the idea that in the end, these systems may be too complex for us to ever fully understand. Again, Leopold attempts to shed light on our true situation and asks us to rethink our mental model of ourselves as conquer. He asks us if it wouldn't be best to take a different approach—a more humble approach—that allows us to become responsible members of a community as opposed to its somewhat ignorant and incompetent rulers.

Viewing ourselves as members of a community as opposed to conquerors would require an added understanding that we are bound by the rules and moral boundaries of the community. As a result, our relationships with the land and the ecological systems would need to change dramatically, as would our actions and activities. But this is Leopold's point entirely: The old anthropocentric system, based on self-interest and individualism, is not only misguided but utterly useless when it comes to ethical questions about the natural world. For Leopold, the only way we can successfully resolve ethical questions about the environment is to reframe the way we look at ourselves and the way we look at the land upon which we live.

Leopold's "land ethic" moves us as far away from traditional ethical concepts as is possible. We move from an anthropocentric view, a reductive view, and an individual view all at once. This total shift in our thinking may account for the reason why so many philosophers attempt to dismiss Leopold and other ecocentrists out of hand. For many philosophers it is simply too radical to fit well with what has been thousands of years of thinking. This might also account for the small number of contemporary philosophers who, like Leopold, feel we need to move to a holistic view of ethics, but who actively try to fit ecocentrism directly into traditional veins of philosophical thinking. Bryan Norton, a more contemporary philosopher, serves as a good example of this type of ecocentrist.

Norton, like Leopold, thinks ecocentrically, but he feels that Leopold was misguided in thinking that an ecocentric outlook required an entirely new ethic. For Norton, ecocentrism can be comfortably grounded in anthropocentrism and need not stand as its polar opposite. It's here we are introduced to his concept of "weak anthropocentrism."

Norton starts by making a clear distinction between what he interprets as traditional or strong anthropocentrism and his version. Strong anthropocentrism is the view that all unquestioned, felt preferences that human beings experience are the determining factor for the value of all other objects. In this view if humans feel strongly that a tract of forest land has no value unless humans are using it for crops or livestock, then the forest literally has no value, except when used for this purpose. The strong version does tend to align with the traditional anthropocentric view in that all objects have mere instrumental value and this value is determined by the wants and desires of human beings.

In Norton's formulation of weak anthropocentrism, it's not the unquestioned, felt preferences of human beings that determine value; rather, value is determined through a rational criticism of our felt preferences and our actions that are purely exploitative in their nature. A weak anthropocentric view does not allow us to make critical decisions based on misinformation or a whim; Norton's view demands that we acquire information about the natural world, which allows us those reflective and critical moments.

Weak anthropocentrism demands that we reevaluate our place in the natural world and this reevaluation then in turn informs us of what an appropriate relationship is with the natural world. For Norton, this relationship is not one of exploitation but one of cooperation. Since the natural world is one of close-knit relationships, it would be logical to assert that humans as a part of the natural world should strive to seek these close-knit relationships. This would require a fundamentally different attitude toward nature, one that commands respect and one that we are told by Norton will become "an important source of inspiration in value formation."[9] He cites the philosophy of Henry David Thoreau as an example of the kind of inspiration nature provides. Thoreau felt that recognizing the value of nature can bring about spiritual experiences that can lead to a more full and healthy set of spiritual values.

Now Thoreau was an anthropocentric philosopher in that he took the experiences presented to us through nature as parts of our human experience. He did not think that the world was human-centered, so much as it was experienced through a human point of view. Granted, concern for the wild was certainly a part of his overall equation, but the emphasis of his concern is strictly one that is human-focused.

With a human-focused view, Norton's philosophy seems to imply a return to not only anthropocentrism but also to the reductive outlook that was so typical of traditional ethical theories. But is this really the case? Norton is going to argue against this idea, stating that it is not possible to argue within an individualist framework and still be said to hold an adequate environmental ethic. One reason for this is that discussions involving resource protection or environmental protection aren't discussions that have an end point or strict end goal in mind. Rather, when we are thinking about the environment we are thinking about it in terms of protection and sustainability over an indefinite amount of time. After all, environmental issues are both intergenerational and cross-generational issues. The individuals involved in our moral decisions regarding the environment may be present at this time, present in the future, or, depending on the choices we make, may never exist at all. So our moral concerns for the preservation of resources are directed not to specific individuals since we don't know exactly who or what will be here over time, but to the overall continued existence of humans, animals, and resources. It would seem illogical to say that an environmental ethic can be individualistic in nature or, put another way, it would be illogical to say that we have any moral obligations that point directly to a morally considerable individual.

That said, even though Norton feels strongly that all ethical concerns must be grounded in anthropocentrism, it cannot be grounded in individualistic or reductive ethical theories. What he suggests is a type of ecocentrism rooted in weak anthropocentrism. It is anthropocentric in nature because humans are still the conscious value-givers and it's holistic because human consciousness can't be aggregated through time. He calls this kind of moral thinking consideration at the "distributional level," asserting that one should not harm human individuals unjustifiably. The second level or the "allocation level" is not based on consideration of the individual at all. This level focuses on the general obligations we have for the continued flow of resources and natural biota. In other words, it is here where our obligations are to the ecosystems and not the individuals who may profit from them. These obligations include a responsibility to inform ourselves about what is necessary to protect resource bases, and act against policies that we know will lead to the general decline in the health of the ecosystem. Finally and perhaps this will show Norton's view best, we have an obligation to value ongoing human life and human consciousness and act in ways that will promote the ongoing success of our species. These ways will certainly include taking care of the biosphere in which we live, not simply for the short term but for the long term success of our species we will need to radically change the way we live and the way we interact with nature.

Contemporary Environmental Concerns

Now that you understand the many ways philosophers attempt to include the environment in our moral decisions, we turn to a number of contemporary concerns involving the environment raised in both the scientific and philosophical communities. What follows is a brief summary of the environmental issues that are most relevant to us today. You may find that you are familiar with most or even all of these issues. This section consists of four parts, each covering a broad environmental topic. Where possible, examples and statistics have been supplied to help you better understand why these issues are considered some of the most critical in the 21st century.

Pollution

It's a well-known fact that if humans are good at one thing, it's creating waste. From our cell phones to our hamburgers to our toxic waste, we produce massive amounts of garbage each year. It has been estimated that in the United States alone each person creates about 4.5 pounds of trash per day.[10] This of course doesn't include any industrial waste or chemical waste that is produced as a by-product of manufacturing or other commercial processes. But pollution in the form of garbage is just the beginning. As much as 90% of wastewater in developing countries flows untreated into streams, lakes, and rivers, creating biological hazards for humans and deadly habitats for aquatic animals. In addition, approximately 70% of all chemical waste from commercial production makes its way into water systems, including the ocean.[11] Quite recently, concerns about water safety were raised in Hong Kong when a dramatic decrease of the rare pink dolphin was noted. Found nowhere else in the world, this species' dramatic decline is being blamed on the ever-increasing industrial pollution being dumped into Hong Kong's waters. This particular scenario is not unique and a number of aquatic species are being classified as threatened or endangered because of degradation of their habitat.

But probably the most distressing type of pollution being created through human activity is carbon dioxide. With current levels the highest in human history, this type of pollution is becoming a problem unto itself as it sets off a range of global events that may or may not be reversible.

Global Climate Change

We've all heard that the global climate is changing and that change will without a doubt bring an overall warmer global climate. But what exactly does a few degrees warmer mean in terms of day-to-day life on this planet? In a May 2013 article in *The Guardian*,[12] the levels of carbon dioxide have reached a high of 400 ppm, higher than any other time in human history, and the news gets worse. According to an article written in 2011, recent research from the University of Washington suggests that even if we were to stop all global emissions today, the planet would continue to warm up.[13] So what exactly does a warmer planet mean? Here are some of the predicted consequences of an increased temperature of 1–3 degrees:

- **Decreased polar ice.** When the planet heats up, so do the oceans and one effect of this is loss of ice worldwide, most noticeably at the North and South Poles. As a result, a number of things will happen. First, less ice means that less sunlight is reflected out into space. This means that Earth will actually be absorbing more sunlight, leading to an even greater increase of overall temperature for the planet.
- **Decreased salinity.** The salt levels will drop in the oceans as the polar ice melts; the salinity (i.e., overall salt content) of the oceans will decrease since the polar ice releases massive

amounts of fresh water into the oceans as it melts. This will decrease the ocean's ability to effectively distribute cold and warm water from the poles to the equator and back again. This endless cycle, known as the *global ocean conveyor belt* or the *thermohaline currents*, is one of the ways the ocean helps to regulate overall global temperatures, keeping the planet climate stable. If this current is slowed or interrupted we can expect wild fluctuations in global temperatures, in addition to the loss of many oceanic species that rely on this current to bring vital nutrients to certain parts of the world at certain times. If this natural process is stopped entirely, through even higher rates of melting ice, we will be faced with nothing short of a new and quite permanent ice age.[14]

- **Melting permafrost.** The permafrost layer, or the thin layer of ice that never melts in areas such as Alaska and Siberia, is starting to melt at an alarming rate. Most disturbing is that fact that these areas, due to their geology and geography, are basically frozen peat bog and low marshy lands ripe with billions of tons of methane-rich soil and vegetation. As these areas thaw because of increases in global temperatures, this methane is released into the atmosphere as a gas. The result can be devastating for life on this planet.[15] Methane gas is a much more potent greenhouse gas than carbon dioxide and traps 20 times more heat. This would mean even faster temperature increases.
- **Droughts, hurricanes, and flooding.** Warm ocean currents are food that fuels hurricanes and with rising ocean temperatures scientists predict that we will be experiencing more and stronger hurricanes. Additionally, with temperatures rising more severe weather is in the picture, varying from location to location. Some areas such as Texas are slated to see more and longer drought conditions while the midwestern United States can expect more severe flooding and rainstorms. Heat waves are becoming a common occurrence in the western states and hurricanes like Katrina and Sandy are going to be more frequent. With severe weather there is often not only a loss of life but also food shortages and manufacturing and infrastructure breakdowns. The costs can be substantial, with Hurricane Sandy being a good example at a cost of about $100 billion.

Photo courtesy of Sherry Jansen. Modified by the author.

Species Extinction

The extinction of species is a natural process that has been happening since species first populated this planet. As a part of the process of evolution, some species will not be able to compete as well for any number of reasons and as a result their populations will decline and many species may even disappear. So we should not be alarmed at species extinction as a process. What should alarm us is the rate at which species are disappearing. It is estimated that between 150 and 200 species go extinct every 24 hours, a rate not seen since the time of the dinosaur. Species extinction is a very serious problem when it comes to maintaining healthy ecosystems. Not only does the disappearance of any one species mean less biodiversity and thus fewer opportunities for nature to fill vacant niches. The disappearance of any one species can be seen to directly impact the survival of other species within the same ecosystem. According to recent research by the University of Exeter, removal or even reduction of a species can cause other species to also disappear. This discovery was especially surprising because the individuals affected were not a direct part of the same predator–prey cycle. In fact, some animals had little or no direct relation to the reduced or extinct species. This fact underscores how little we understand about the impact of extinction. What the study's results seem to suggest is that if we think we lose only one species to extinction, we are misguided in that assertion. In fact, when we lose one species, we can almost count on losing more. So if we are aware of at least 150–200 species going extinct every 24 hours, what we may be unaware of is the 150–200 more species just added to that list due to one species' absence.[16] Species loss can result in a number of negative things. Less biodiversity means that animals and plants will become more vulnerable to disease and will have fewer opportunities to evolve, which will result in even greater species loss. With our understanding of ecosystems still in its nascent stages, we cannot fully appreciate what little it may take to disrupt ecosystems critical not only to natural process but also to human populations. We are beginning to see this in the depletion of our oceans. As we deplete certain species of fish, other species of plants and animals are taking their place. Invasive species, red algae blooms, the death of coral,

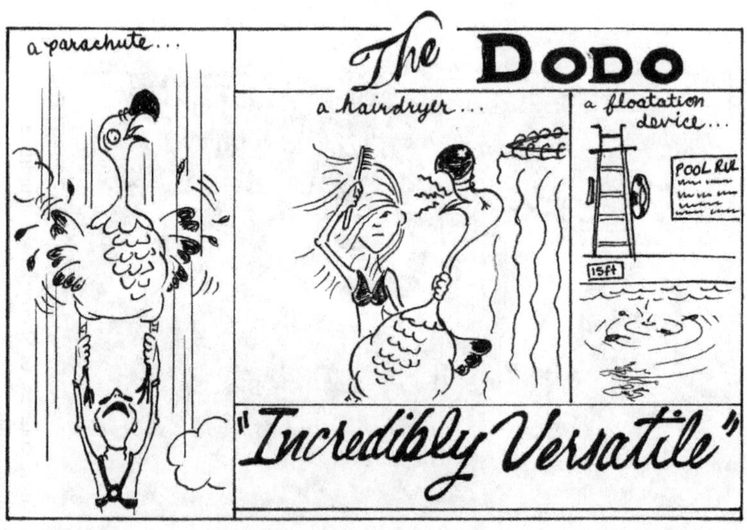

and other events are taking vital resources away from not just nature but from human populations. Additionally, species critical to the survival and reproduction of other animals and plant populations are also becoming a human problem (see the case study "Plight of the Honey Bees, Plight of the Humans" for details).

Human Population Explosion

Although the idea of discussing human beings as a population that is in need of being "regulated" is still a taboo issue, there are many studies that suggest that unchecked growth in human populations may lead to disastrous effects both for humans and for other species. Scientists at Ohio State University used models from a 2000–2004 study that predicted extinction rates would coincide with human population growth rates. The success of the 2004 model at making this prediction was recreated in a 2010 study. Both of these studies have concluded that one of the biggest threats to bird and animal species on this planet is unchecked human population growth. The more the human population increases, the higher the extinction rates.

The United States rates sixth in population growth and the study asserts that this will mean an additional 11 new endangered species will be added to the already growing list of threatened wildlife. Conversely, the study noted that the 12 countries where population growth was in decline actually also saw a modest decrease in the number of threatened species. So what does unchecked human growth mean to the diversity and complexity of life on Earth? According to Jeffery McKee, lead scientist on the study, a "loss of species, and especially so-called keystone species that are important to the environment because they function as significant predators and prey, can disrupt ecosystems. Plants and animals also help the planet adjust to climate change provide oxygen and are sources of food and medicines."[17]

But it is not just other plants and animals that are going to be negatively affected by the continued growth of the human population. Between 1999 and 2011 the human population increased by 1 billion. With this sudden increase came noticeable shortages in food, water, and essentials for millions of people. Today it is estimated that about 680 million people worldwide go hungry, with about 1 billion people not having access to clean water.[18] So what does this mean in terms of future growth? It is estimated that by 2050 the human population will have reached in excess of 9 billion people. According to author Carl Safina,[19] we are currently using the world's natural resources at a rate that is 25% faster than the world can replace them. This means that we are already living in a world that cannot currently support our consumptive needs and wants and that an increase to the population will only mean faster consumption and depletion of resources in the future, a level that the earth simply cannot sustain.

Sustaining an ever-growing human population is one thing, but like all beings we produce waste products that need to be disposed of. Currently, over 1 billion pounds of solid waste is produced in America each day. This is about 4 pounds of garbage per person and does not count industrial or commercial waste. So where does it all go? Unfortunately, much of it goes into landfills where it is eventually covered with earth and allowed to rot. Many of the household products that we send to landfills, however, take hundreds or even thousands of years to decompose, with some items such as cell phones, batteries, and computer components actually leaching harmful chemicals and heavy metals into the soil.

Notes

1. Beckerman, Wilfred, and Joanna Pasek. *Justice, Posterity and the Environment* (New York: Oxford University Press, 2001).
2. Taylor, Paul. "The Ethics of Respect for Nature." *Environmental Ethics* 3, 3 (1981): 197–218.
3. Sterba, James. "Biocentrism Defended." *Ethics, Policy and Environment* 14, 2 (2011): 167–69.
4. Ibid 168-169
5. Schmidtz, David. "Respect for Everything." *Ethics, Policy and Environment* 14, 2 (2011): 127–38.
6. Leopold, Aldo. "Aldo Leopold's Land Ethic." http://home.btconnect.com/tipiglen/landethic.html.
7. Leopold, Aldo. "North Glen." April 1, 2009.
8. Ibid.
9. Norton, Bryan G. "Environmental Ethics and Weak Anthropocentrism." http://www.uv.mx/personal/jmercon/files/2011/08/norton_env.-ethics-and-weak-anthropocentrism.pdf.
10. Curiosity.com. "How much trash does America produce." 2012.
11. UNWater.org, "Water Pollution and Environmental Degradation." 2012.
12. Carrington, Damian. "Global carbon dioxide in atmosphere passes milestone levels." *The Guardian*. 10 May 2013.
13. American Geophysical Union. "Climate commitment in an uncertain world." *ScienceDaily*, 28 January 2011. http://www.sciencedaily.com/releases/2011/01/110128095044.htm.

14. NASA. "A chilling possibility." 2004. http://science1.nasa.gov/science-news/science-at-nasa/2004/05mar_arctic/.
15. Adam, David. "Artic Permafrost Leaking Methane at Record Levels." *The Guardian.* 14 January 2010. http://www.guardian.co.uk/environment/2010/jan/14/arctic-permafrost-methane.
16. University of Exeter. "Reducing numbers of one carnivore species indirectly leads to extinction of others." *ScienceDaily.* 28 Feb. 2013. http://www.sciencedaily.com/releases/2013/02/130228124144.htm.
17. Ohio State University. "Outlook is grim for mammals and birds as human population grows." *ScienceDaily.* 19 June 2013. http://www.sciencedaily.com/release/2013/06/130619102601.htm.
18. Cohen, Joel E. "Seven Billion." *New York Times.* October 23, 2011.
19. Safina, Carl. "How many people can the world support? It Depends…" *The Blog.* May 8, 2012. http://www.huffingtonpost.com/carl-safina/population-growth_b_1499281.html.
20. CBS News.com. "Cell Phone Waste." February 11, 2009. http://www.cbsnews.com/2100-205_162-508346.html.
21. Schuetse, Christopher F. "Billions of Cell Phones Polluting the World." *International Herald Tribune.* April 29, 2013. http://rendezvous.blogs.nytimes.com/2013/04/29/billions-of-cellphones-polluting-the-world/?_r=0.
22. NRDC.org. "Bee Facts." http://www.nrdc.org/wildlife/animals/files/bees.pdf.
23. Farabough, Kane. "Pesticides Contribute to Decline in World's Bee Population." VOA News.com. June 13, 2013.
24. Holland, Jennifer S. "The Plight of the Honeybee." *National Geographic Daily News.* May 10, 2013. http://news.nationalgeographic.com/news/2013/13/130510-honeybee-bee-science-european-union-pesticides-colony-collapse-epa-science/.

Name:______________________________ Date:______________

Review Questions

1. What is environmental ethics?

2. What is one of the central questions we must answer when discussing environmental ethics?

3. What is anthropocentrism?

4. What is one problem with the anthropocentric worldview?

5. What is zoocentrism and where does it draw the line of moral considerability?

6. What is one problem a biocentrist sees with the zoocentric theories?

7. What is the difference between an egalitarian and a nonegalitarian ethical theory?

8. If I am a biocentric egalitarian, who counts and how much?

9. If I am an ecocentrist, who/what in my view has moral standing?

10. What does it mean to be an individualist/reductionist?

Name:____ Date:__________________

For Further Discussion

1. After considering the many ways we can determine moral considerability, which view do you feel is most correct and why?
2. Choose two philosophical theories and apply them to an environmental issue of your own. Do the two theories result in similar or dissimilar actions? Try to explain why this may be the case.
3. Choose an environmental issue from the section on contemporary environmental concerns and then apply the theory in this chapter that you least agree with. Did you find representing this viewpoint a challenge? Why do you feel this is so? Now apply the theory you most agree with. Are the suggested actions similar or dissimilar? Explain.

Name:_______________________________________ Date:__________________

Case Studies

The Real Cost of Upgrading Your Cell Phone

It happens to all of us. We see an ad for the latest smartphone and we just have to have it, despite the fact that our current cell phone works just fine. So we go to the mall and surrender to the temptation. Thirty minutes later we have a brand-new, shiny cell phone with all the latest features. We take it home, show a few friends, brag a bit, then 4 or 5 months later we do it all again. New is good and better is good, right? Well, it certainly is good for us and if we do the math, it isn't all that harmful to the pocketbook. But what is the real cost of upgrading your cell phone? For most of us, once we are in the mall parking lot we have all but forgotten our old phones and perhaps we don't even think much about the origins of our new phone. Perhaps we should. To date there are about 8 billion cell phone subscriptions and those numbers are expected to increase as the technologies become available to those in emerging countries. In order to keep up with the demand as it stands today, we would need more metals. Some estimate that our need for metals to manufacture cell phones is going to increase substantially,[20] by as much as three to nine times. This is more metal than is currently available on this planet. One solution to this deficit in materials would be to create more effective ways to recycle our old cell phones. However, this is proving to be difficult since many of the constituent parts are toxic and contain arsenic, copper, and lead. Many of the toxins present are deadly to humans and animals and can cause neurological problems and cancer.[21] Although many cell phone dealers participate in buyback programs, most cell phones end up in the garbage or in other municipal waste that goes directly to the landfill. With the number of cell phones increasing and the average consumer keeping a cell phone for around 18 months, cell phones and their manufacture and disposal are becoming an environmental concern.

1. Do you own a cell phone? Have you considered the environmental costs of owning this device?
2. Now that you know the environmental costs of upgrading your cell phone, would you be willing to upgrade less frequently? Use one of the theories we have discussed thus far to support your response.
3. How might an anthropocentric philosophy solve this environmental problem? What would a biocentrist do?

Plight of the Honeybees, Plight of the Humans

Humans have a mixed relationship with bees. Although we all know that bees bring great benefits to both the environment and to humans, anyone who has been stung by a bee or had to tread lightly to avoid being stung understands that bees are not one of our favorite insects. Love them or hate them, bees are a critical part of our environment and are also more critical to human survival than we once suspected. But honeybees and other species of bees are dying in alarming numbers and scientists are still trying to find out why. The numbers are disturbing: 2012–1013 data suggest that in the United States the average loss was over 45% of all hives. This is up over 78% from the previous years and beekeepers, farmers, and scientists are concerned. But why all this fuss about a bee? Bees are nature's pollinators. They provide the means for many wild and farmed crops to reproduce. About one-third of all crops grown for human consumption in the United States are reliant on these tiny insects and many crops such as alfalfa that are used to feed cows and sheep also rely on bee pollination to produce usable crops. Additionally, we would of course lose honey, a product that is directly produced by bees and made available to us not just in its raw form but as a sweetener in many of our favorite foods. The impact on food crops only tells a part of the story. Approximately 90% of all wild plants that require a pollinator to reproduce rely on bees.[22] With their decline, there will be a decrease in wild plants and this decrease will move up the food chain, resulting in fewer animal species. One of the contributors to the decline of bees has been pesticides.[23] Particular pesticides that can be purchased by consumers have been linked to bee death. Although it has been shown that the pesticides themselves are not directly harmful, these chemicals have been shown to reduce immunity responses in bees and make them more susceptible to disease. Another factor seems to be a decrease in habitat.[24] Bees need large areas to forage for a variety of different pollens. With more industry, and human housing, the opportunities for bees to seek out and find different pollens are becoming more and more difficult. Add this to the fact that most people are likely to get rid of natural hives in their yards or next to buildings and you have a situation that does not favor the recovery of bees.

1. Use Norton's view of environmental ethics. What do you feel he would recommend we do in this situation and why?
2. Consider this situation from the following perspectives: zoocentrism, biocentrism, ecocentrism, and anthropocentrism. Would any of them come to similar conclusions about what actions we should take with regard to honeybees? How would you explain this convergence? What might this tell us about environmental ethics in general?

CHAPTER FOUR

Animal Rights

Amid protests from many animal rights organizations and concerned citizens, badgers are being shot in the southwest of England in an attempt to control tuberculosis in cattle.[1] This disease, which can be transmitted from both badgers to cattle and vice versa, is deadly and vaccines that were once used regularly in cattle are becoming ineffective. Currently, the goal is set for culling 5,000 badgers but the government hopes to increase the number culled and expand the culling program to neighboring areas in the future. For this cull, no one will be monitoring whether or not decreasing the number of badgers will have any effect on the spread of the disease. Officials have stated that they are more concerned to test whether or not a badger cull can be carried out successfully, humanely, and safely. Those who are protesting the culls are saying that they are not only unnecessary but will prove to be less effective than would better vaccines and tighter control over livestock.

As this example clearly shows we have a strange and complicated relationship with animals. Some we love and keep as pets, others we eat, and still others we see as either something to enjoy as part of the wilderness experience or something that needs eradicating when their existence hampers our goals or our happiness. Part of this inconsistency may be due to the fact that throughout a good part of human history we've felt little in common with the other creatures that inhabit the earth. Another factor may be the way we've chosen to deal with, write about, and think about nonhuman animals. As we saw in the last chapter, the traditional views that have been held about our place in the world are slowing changing to reflect 21st-century advances in science, politics, and social ideas. The Cartesian model, which had been the standard well into the 1800s, viewed animals as merely complex machines, incapable of even the simplest experiences of pleasure and pain.

Now the idea that animals were mere machines did much to influence the way we looked at them morally and promoted the idea that the use of animals as everything from food to entertainment without the slightest concern for their well-being was morally acceptable. It is not unusual to see humans treating animals in a variety of ways that for some are highly morally questionable. From stories of live animals being dissected for the sake of science to news headlines involving well-known professional athletes drowning dogs in their backyard pool, it would seem that the way we should treat animals is not a moral issue that has been clearly settled. What has been settled with certainty is that the Cartesian machine model has been thoroughly dismissed as a plausible position to maintain. With the dismissal of this model, we can see that a moral theory that does not take nonhuman animals into account will be a difficult position to hold, making the way we view animals and the way we treat them a relevant moral issue to pursue.

Before we look at the moral theories surrounding animals and the issues that inform them, we first need to understand some relevant terms and then discuss the latest scientific discoveries about the capacities of many nonhuman animals. As we discuss these developments we also need to reflect on many of the long-standing myths about animals and see if the contemporary scientific discoveries can validate or overturn these ways of thinking about animals.

As you may recall from the last chapter, individuals who include animals in their moral decisions can be referred to as zoocentric in their ethical approach, that is, they look to certain features we share in common with other animals as the relevant features that make a being worthy of our moral consideration. Among these features are pleasure, pain, suffering, and sentience. In order to understand why philosophers have chosen these attributes and how they intend to focus their arguments around them, we need to understand each of these terms and how they are used by scientists and philosophers to formulate their zoocentric arguments.

Sentience and Pain

Sentience is a being's capacity to have conscious emotional states that go along with the interpretations of physical sensations such as pleasure and pain. This ability is much different from what scientists call *nociception* or the ability to sense that something is bad, harmful, or dangerous. In beings like us, nociception is the first step in a series of neurological events that eventually expresses itself as pain. In other beings, like tubeworms or clams, it may be the only step in a being's interactions with a negative event in the world. It is thought that tubeworms are simply detecting potentially dangerous or damaging stimuli through neural organs firing along a structure of what are known as *axons*. These axons then carry the information along the nerve fibers to a central processing center (tubeworms don't have brains) to instruct it to move away from the stimulus in this situation. Any stimuli that is potentially harmful to this organism can start the process, be it heat, cold, impact, or inflammation. The neural process just described in the tubeworm is very different from what we understand as actual pain. Pain requires an awareness of a relevant kind and to see the distinction we can turn to an example involving a human being. As humans, our system for detecting harms is set up just like the tubeworm at the most basic level. We both share the initial part of the process that leads the tubeworm away from harm and leads us to eventually experience what can be called *pain*. We've all experienced the unpleasantness of stubbing our toe. The experience begins with a nociceptor sensing a tremendous amount of pressure at the end of our foot. This information is immediately sent to the brain where it is processed. As the information is being transferred and processed in the brain, you yell "Ouch!" and think to yourself, "That really hurt!" Immediately you attempt to move your toe away from the initial source of the pressure. We differ from the tubeworm in that when it comes to our experience of the negative stimulus, we are consciously aware of the experience that the nervous system is transmitting to our processing center. We are not just experiencing something negative, we are aware that we are doing this. So sentience or this awareness differs from simple responses to stimuli in that a sentient being doesn't simply detect negative stimulus and then react; rather, a sentient being is aware of certain mental states that go along with the experience of negative stimulus, or put another way, pain. When we think of nonhuman animals like the tubeworm we can see distinct differences between a creature like this and a human being that would lead us perhaps to the conclusion that in terms of moral consideration there are also distinct differences, but what about a nonhuman animal that is very much like us neurologically? What about a dog, for example? Dogs, like humans, process information through a complex nervous system. They also have a brain that is very similar and functions in a similar manner to ours. When we look at nonhuman animals that are very similar to us, how are we to think about them morally? The reason why it was necessary to spend a bit of time understanding the different neurological responses to the world and how our human responses either resemble or are different from other nonhuman animals is because so many of the ethical issues that surround our treatment of animals revolves around their sentience in addition to their ability to experience pleasure, pain, and suffering. We now know that sentience is not simply experiencing a sensation but also having a conscious awareness of that sensation. So how do we define and recognize pain and suffering in nonhuman animals? Scientifically speaking, the word *pain* is defined as an adverse sense experience that alerts the body to actual or potential tissue damage. Pain is an evolutionary adaptation that tells us that some part of the body is under attack and assists us in avoiding further attack and damage by prompting us to move away from the source of the adverse experience. Pain goes well beyond a simple neurological state or nociception. Pain is both a neurological reaction plus the subjective interpretation of the discomfort (sentience).[2] So it could be said that although some beings such as the tubeworm can experience an unpleasant stimulus, they aren't necessarily in any pain as they are not subjectively conscious of this state. To date we don't have a complete list of beings that can and do experience pain, but the tubeworm seems to be a good working example of a being that doesn't experience pain, as these animals don't give us relevant cues. Probably the most compelling evidence for many nonhuman animals being able to experience pain can be found in their biological similarities with humans. We know the evolutionary processes behind the neurological developments in both human and nonhuman animals and we know that there is much in common between the structures of our brains and our nervous systems and those of nonhuman animals. We also know that in all beings that can experience it, pain is a biological advantage. The similarities between our nervous systems and those of many other animals suggests that both the neurological processes and the results of these processes are similar, that is to say that if there is a situation where we are certain that a human being would feel pain, there is no relevant reason to think that a nonhuman animal would also feel pain in a similar situation. Additionally, from an evolutionary standpoint the overall function and biological advantages of pain would also be the same in humans as they are in animals. The experience of pain seems to have evolved to provide organisms with information about tissue damage. The experience of pain motivates an organism to move away from the unpleasant stimulus as a way to avoid additional damage to itself. Following an injury an animal that is experiencing pain will recognize the damage it has incurred and will not use the injured body part in order to avoid further pain[3] and it is this refraining from limb use that is the scientific means by which we determine if an animal is capable of experiencing pain. If an animal does not avoid the use of an injured limb or body part, it is not expressing what scientists call a pain behavior, that is, it would seem that although the being recognized a negative stimulus it does not seem conscious of the fact that the body part has been injured and will still attempt to use that body part. A good example of this can be found in individuals with congenital insensitivity to pain with anhidrosis (CIPA). An individual who has this disorder is incapable of feeling pain. They are insensitive to heat and cold and will not cry if they are cut or pinched or even break an arm. Children with this illness can suffer not only external injuries that can be seen by others but can also suffer internal infections and even have organs rupture without being aware that there are any serious health threats.[4] Many do not live into adulthood and for those that do, life is a constant state of heightened awareness, often resulting in daily body checks and the administration of medicines to keep the eyes moist and the lungs working. The most frequent cause of death for persons with this illness is overheating. Interestingly enough their bodies don't know that they are getting uncomfortably warm and as a result will not know that they need to sweat to bring their own core temperatures down. In some cases in the animal kingdom we can see this kind of oblivious behavior taking place as some beings seem simply unaware that something bad has happened to them. However, most animals do express a pain behavior and thus far we have recognized it in all vertebrates and even some invertebrates such as the octopus.

Suffering

So when it comes to the experience of pain, we know that many animals have this capability. But what about capacities that are not purely physical responses but responses to emotional and psychological distress? It is certainly true that we could formulate a system that takes strictly pain into account when discussing moral consideration, but it would seem that we need to know a bit more than just the physical capabilities of other beings. Do they have inner states that can be just as, if not more, uncomfortable than pain? It would seem that we need to explore this question too in order to get a full picture of what exactly we need to take into account when attempting to determine the moral status of animals.

One of the terms we use to describe an unpleasant emotional state that is best expressed not in terms of direct physical pain (though they may be linked) but with distress is *suffering*. Emotional distress can cover anything from fear to anxiety to boredom to frustration and any being who is said to be capable of experiencing these and other emotionally distressing symptoms can be said to be suffering. Here again we need to understand the term from a scientific standpoint before we move to the question of whether or not nonhuman animals can experience it and as a result should have their suffering counted in our moral decisions. The two most common forms of distress that we hear used with regard to the moral status of animals are those of fear and anxiety. So what is fear and how does being fearful differ from being anxious?

Fear is an unpleasant emotional response to immediate danger. It motivates animals to focus their responses on the particular situation and then to prepare for identical situations in the future. Being afraid of standing too close to the edge of the Grand Canyon, for instance, will make us focus on our every step and increase our awareness of our footing and specific details such as the firmness of the ground or the stability of our footwear. It also allows us to prepare for similar events that may occur in the future, like standing on the edge of a famous building in the middle of a bustling city. Fear is another useful biological response that protects us from harm in both immediate and future situations.

Anxiety, like fear, is another unpleasant emotion that aids us in our survival in an uncertain and challenging world. Unlike fear, anxiety tends to be a less focused and more generalized emotional response to a situation. Where we tend to be afraid of something specific (heights, for instance), we tend to be anxious about situations in general (like how our fear of heights may affect our visit to the Grand Canyon overall). Anxiety leads us to feel threatened in a way that may inhibit our ability to act and we will feel a heightened state of awareness and attention to the environment in general. A good example of anxiety in humans is the feeling of being anxious right before a job interview. If you are like most people, job interviews are not pleasant activities. You are typically worried about how the interview will go in general, what impressions you will make, and what the interview will entail. Although you don't feel threatened directly, you will express nervous behaviors such as tapping your foot and you will feel much more attentive to small details such as your handshake, the position of your body, and the exact words that come out of your mouth. Other evidence that you are anxious in this situation include biological changes such as increased heart rate, sweatiness, jumpiness, inhibition of normal behaviors, and being increasingly aware of your surroundings. Think about your last job interview and then reflect on how many of these behaviors you exhibited. You will recognize most if not all of these behaviors, which would suggest to an objective observer that you were indeed anxious. Although this kind of reaction to the environment may not serve us well in our job interview, like fear it serves a very important biological function of keeping us informed about harmful and dangerous situations and allows us to avoid similar situations in the future. The increase in attention to surroundings and the increase in our pulmonary systems that accompanies both fear and anxiety all contribute to what is called our *fight-or-flight response* and helps us to react very quickly in situations that are harmful or dangerous.

Like the physical experience of pain, it is clear from observation that many nonhuman animals display physical and biological signs of both fear and anxiety. Anyone who has taken their pet to the vet can observe both of these emotional responses in action. And in a way that expresses our understanding of evolution, animals that have nervous systems similar to our own can easily be said to have the product of these systems mirror ours as well. Just as a cat is anxious and fearful when visiting the vet, a person who is admitted into the hospital is hyper-alert and focused and tends to have biological reactions that are identical to the cat's.

Animals that are used as test subjects for anxiety medicines also tend to respond to these drugs in a way that is identical to humans. In fact, it is the results of anxiety drugs on nonhuman subjects that provided the necessary evidence for pharmaceutical companies to test these drugs on human volunteers and then to successfully market them to individuals suffering from a number of distressing emotional and psychological ailments. Although the animals used in these tests tended to be mammals there is solid scientific evidence to support the statement that reptiles, birds, and amphibians also experience fear and anxiety in ways that resemble their mammalian counterparts.

From our discussion so far it should be clear why the Cartesian model had to be abandoned in favor of models that more accurately express the physical and emotional lives of nonhuman animals. Now that we have the critical scientific evidence we need to begin formulating a realistic picture of what we need to look at when formulating our moral decisions, is there anything else that may be either relevant or contentious when discussing attributes that may be relevant for our discussion of animals? There is one more that is worthy of mention. It is one that is a bit more controversial both scientifically and morally but that will affect the philosophical views of some philosophers when discussing moral considerability.

Self and Self-Awareness

The notion of self-awareness is probably the most contested issue when it comes to looking at the capabilities of animals. It is problematic because historically this ability was linked directly to reasoning ability and as we have seen it was thought that only human beings have this ability. The questions surrounding self-awareness have a great impact upon what kinds of suffering animals are really capable of experiencing as well as our thoughts about the harms that may or may not surround the killing of animals

Scientists recognize a number of ways to unpack exactly what we mean by self-awareness, but generally speaking, if a being is self-aware, that means it is not just aware of an external stimulus as in the case of pain or of a subjective emotional experience such as suffering, it is an ability to be aware of oneself as having these experiences. The idea that you are aware of a stimulus lies at the heart of what it means to be self-aware. It is quite easy to test a person for self-awareness as we simply have to ask them directed questions about their experiences to get a very descriptive account. But how do we know that an animal who clearly can't communicate vocally is self-aware?

The standard test for self-awareness involves using a mirror to determine whether or not an animal is able to recognize the reflection in the mirror as an image of themselves. An animal that can successfully pass the mirror test by recognizing themselves is said to be self-aware because they know that they are looking at themselves and not another animal. The test is conducted by placing a red dot on the animal in a place they can't see without the mirror. Then the observers wait to see if the animal reacts to its own body in a way that would suggest that they know the image in the mirror is their own. When this test was performed on dolphins they figured out that they could use the mirror to see what the spot looked like and thus they spent a great deal of time positioning themselves in front of the mirror to have a look at the odd spot on their fins and backs.[5] Both chimpanzees and elephants expressed similar reactions, not only looking at the spot but using the mirror to guide their hands and trunks to the location of the spot, giving them time to explore this strange development. Other animals have responded to the mirror test with mixed results. Dogs, for instance, don't seem to realize that the image in the mirror is not another dog and will continue to invite the stranger to play or will become increasingly aggressive at the image, as they would an intruder. Those animals that pass this test are said to have visual awareness of themselves.

There is another type of self-awareness that is critical to our understanding of animal minds and that is the self-awareness known as *temporal self-awareness*. This type of awareness is the ability to be aware of oneself as a being that exists over time, as opposed to a being that simply lives only in the present moment. The existence of this kind of self-awareness is critical to our understanding of the capacities of animals and whether or not an animal has this trait will determine the amount of suffering an animal is capable of having and will also determine the kind of moral consideration we should give them. One way to judge whether or not an animal has self-awareness over time is to determine whether or not an animal is capable of experiencing fear. Remember from our earlier discussion that fear is a directed negative emotion that requires one to feel that negative stimulus is going to happen to you either in the near or distant future. In order for a being to experience this emotion, they would need to be able to see themselves as existing into the future and not just existing in the present moment. It is a future self that stands to be harmed and it is the future self that will be aware of the suffering caused by the harm. This is just one example of how a being can be aware of themselves temporally. There are other more desirable scenarios where animals express this capability. Take the example of a dog who buries a bone in the backyard, only to dig it up many months later. In order for this scenario to have occurred the dog must have had a desire to bury the bone at one time but also to believe that at another time in the future the bone would still be located in the same place, ready to be dug up and enjoyed. We see even more evidence for the recognition of a future self in the seed-collecting activities of wild birds and chipmunks who will bury food in many different locations throughout the summer, only to return to this food source in late fall or early winter. A more sophisticated example of planning for the needs of a future self was featured in a news story about Santino, a grouchy male chimpanzee who resides in a Swedish zoo.[6] Santino was observed systematically hoarding rocks and hiding them under the hay next to the visitors center. Throughout the day, when he becomes either annoyed at the zoo patrons or bored, Santino goes to his secret stash of rocks and begins to hurl them at passersby. As zoo staff has observed he is always careful to collect and hide these rocks hours in advance, throwing them much later in the day. For scientists who study primate behavior this is a clear sign that not only is he planning ahead, but he understands that his "future self" will need this arsenal of rocks when the crowd gets to be too much.

Planning ahead in anticipation of a future is certainly one behavior that seems to point to an awareness of a self. Linking past events to future events through the emotion of fear is also suggestive of this idea. Both of these capabilities point to facts about animals and their ability to suffer, not just experience pain and a simple awareness of their surroundings. So how do these scientific discoveries affect how we view animals morally? Recall that with the Cartesian model, animals did not have any physical or emotional capacities and as a result the way we treated them was never seen as problematic. But 21st-century science has moved us well beyond this mindset and we can no longer ignore the need to consider animals as a part of our moral decision-making process. For most if not all philosophers, if a being can suffer, that suffering is reason enough to take them into account. But exactly how we view their suffering relative to human suffering and whether or not the idea of suffering is sufficient to place nonhuman animals on par with their human counterparts is something on which many philosophers don't agree. What they do agree on is that our actions can sometimes harm nonhuman animals. But what do we mean by harm?

Harm

So far we have looked at the role played by pain and suffering and how these physical and mental states can help us determine whether or not animals deserve moral consideration. Our final discussion will revolve around the idea and nature of harm and interests: what does it mean to harm an animal? What are an animal's interests and how might this help us to determine how they should be treated? So far in our discussions we have talked about negative emotions such as fear and anxiety and the negative experience of physical pain. But there is a flip side to experience and that is the experience of pleasure and benefit. As a general rule there are two ways that we can discuss the value of a pleasure or benefit. We certainly can be said to value our pleasant experiences and there are two ways in which we can do this: intrinsically and instrumentally. When we value something intrinsically, we value it for its own sake. A pleasurable experience such as being healthy can be valued in this way: we simply like it because it feels good to us. Now we can also value our health instrumentally, that is, we value it because it allows us to do other things that we find beneficial or pleasurable. For instance, if I am in good health that will allow me to go on a very long hike and enjoy other things such as nature, fresh air, and getting away from the noise and heat of the city. So in this sense, my health leads me to pursue my other interests in a way that is very pleasant. Just as good health can be seen as a benefit, so too can poor health be seen as a harm. If I am in ill health, I will not value the time I spend awake or doing things. I will be distracted by the discomfort of feeling ill and possibly suffer from physical pain, none of which I will value intrinsically. Additionally, my ill health will prevent me from doing activities I enjoy and even make activities I need to do uncomfortable. All this may even lead me to become so distracted that normal tasks will become unpleasant to the point I only want to put an end to them or perhaps even to myself. Negative mental states can be just as dangerous to my well-being and can lead to a great deal of suffering as certainly long bouts of anxiety, fear, or depression are wont to do. To inflict this type of suffering, mental or physical, can be seen as a way to harm an individual and it is this type of harm that we so often see committed by humans on animals. If you look carefully at the distinction between physical pain and emotional suffering, you'll see that they both have an inherent and instrumental value of being negative. It is safe to say from our examples that since both physical pain and suffering have an intrinsic nature, causing unwarranted pain and suffering could be seen as being intrinsically harmful to some degree. Of course, there are certain types of pain and suffering that would not be considered harms per se (e.g., taking your pet to the veterinarian to have her teeth cleaned) but most certainly would be.

Likewise, physical pain and suffering can be seen as instrumentally harmful if it prevents or frustrates a being from pursuing life goals. It is true that we as humans have goals that are likely much more sophisticated than those of other animals (going on a hike, for instance), but there is no doubt that other animals do have goals and that making them suffer will act to frustrate these goals (a deer may want to take a walk in a wooded area too, but not to escape the mental hassles of the city but perhaps to find food or shelter). So, to summarize: We as humans can cause animals harm either by causing them physical pain or by causing them to suffer. Both physical pain and suffering can be seen to have instrumental and inherent value, both negative values. Likewise, pleasure and benefit can provide instrumental and intrinsic values as well, values that are worth pursuing and values that most humans and nonhumans seek throughout their lives. When we harm an animal we can either harm them intrinsically, for example, breaking a cat's leg or causing a dog an intense amount of anxiety. We can also harm them instrumentally by creating situations where they are no longer able to enjoy aspects of their lives because the means by which they could do this have been taken from them. This could include creating environments so stressful that they cannot perform natural functions or creating physical situations that will not allow them to pursue simple pleasures such as eating and drinking or performing natural capacities such as foraging or exploring.

If we can harm animals by causing them physical pain and making them suffer, can we also harm them by killing them? If we think about all the ways that humans can be harmed, we will no doubt add death to the list. But what exactly is the harm in killing someone, especially if you kill them quickly and painlessly, and what can this harm to humans tell us about death as a harm to animals? To begin with, when we speak about death we are talking about the moment that precludes anymore experiences positive or negative. Death is not the same as dying as dying is a process that involves the living experiencing being. Generally, when we hear about someone's death, especially when the death was unexpected or tragic, we think great harm was done to the person. But if it is a harm, what exactly is the harm done? Since death is the end of all experience it would be odd to speak of it in terms of pain or suffering. Death seems entirely distinct from these two harms. We will discuss the ideas of death and killing at the end of this chapter, for now we will turn to the ways in which we view animals morally.

Image left: by Bartolomeo Passarotti (1585–1587). Robot Dog and Right Image: © Shutterstock, Inc. Modified by the author.

Moral Ways to View Animals

Throughout this chapter we have been referring to our discussion of animals and their moral status as zoocentrism. When thinking about environmental issues zoocentrism is the idea that all beings that are sentient deserve our moral consideration. This was in stark contrast both to anthropocentrism, which states that only humans deserve moral consideration, and ecocentrism, which states that species and ecosystems deserve moral consideration but not the individuals that inhabit them. It is easy to see that a chapter dedicated to questions concerning the moral status of animals is clearly a chapter filled with questions concerning a zoocentric point of view. But as you have also seen briefly, individual zoocentric philosophers unpack the idea of moral consideration, who gets it, and why in very different ways. In the remainder of this section we look at these ways in detail.

When we say that an animal deserves our moral consideration, what exactly do we mean? With this question we have clearly moved away from the Cartesian model but have yet to answer the question of our relationship to the animal. Moral consideration can take a number of forms. Probably the most familiar way to frame our relationship with animals is to use a kind of "rights" language, that is, to refer to what we owe animals as their right or entitlement to a certain kind of treatment. There are three ways that the term "right" can be applied to animals and each of these denotes a slightly different way to frame the question of what we owe them. If we are using the loosest sense of the term "right," we are simply using shorthand to say that we agree that they have some sort of moral status (i.e., they are no longer simply machines) and do deserve moral consideration. But exactly to what degree they have that status or how often this status can be overridden is far from clear. In this view it is entirely possible that the moral status they hold is much less than that of a human. Moreover, the rights they are afforded are not absolute and may be overridden for whatever "good" reason we choose to put forward. The term "good" in this case can be interpreted in many ways and could certainly include everything from medical goods to financial goods to entertainment goods. This definition of moral status is not only the least controversial of the three but is probably the most common of all the interpretations of rights we will encounter in this chapter since it still allows humans to use animals in a variety of ways, as long as justification is provided.

In a stricter sense the term "right" can be used in the equal consideration sense. If I am using the term in this sense I mean to say that if an animal has a right then it deserves equal consideration when involved in any moral issue. What is being considered equally is any interest, harm, or suffering involved in my decision.

The equal consideration model can be most closely linked to the utilitarian theories we have seen in previous chapters. As you will recall, historical utilitarians such as Bentham chose to measure pleasure and pain and contemporary utilitarians are concerned with measuring preferences satisfied. The idea that animals deserve equal consideration based on their ability to suffer has been the predominate theme for traditional and contemporary utilitarians, so it is no surprise that it is with this model that we see our scientific discoveries as aiding our ability to answer the fundamental questions about which beings are going to get our consideration as well as the distinction between equal consideration and equal treatment of beings. It has been said in this context that the content of equal consideration must be all animals, but as we have seen not all animals can

experience what is understood as pain or suffering and therefore they do not necessarily have any interests that need to be considered. So instead of offering a blanket claim about all animals, those who hold the equal consideration model can argue that what they are going to hold as equal are the pain, suffering, and interests of all those animals who are capable of such things. So our discussion could clearly center on the equal consideration of dolphins, octopi, humans, and robins, but would not include tubeworms, pill bugs, or bacteria.

Likewise, when dealing with traditional formulations of this theory we have discussed not only the ideas of sentience but also the idea of pleasure. Recall from Chapter One that contemporary philosopher Peter Singer agrees with Bentham that sentience and suffering should be the feature that determines whether or not a being has its interests considered. Recall also that Singer disagrees with attempts to measure pleasure and instead relies on the idea of preferences satisfied to determine the morally appropriate action. In the first chapter we saw the idea of pleasure versus satisfaction as applied to a number of situations. Although this example highlighted the problems created when one attempts to measure the pleasures of another person, it becomes even more evident if we attempt to measure the pleasures experienced by animals. Take, for example, an animal we are all familiar with, the chicken. Now as utilitarians working with the equal consideration model, if we had to make a moral decision involving both humans and chickens, how would we go about measuring a chicken's pleasure or happiness? It seems impossible if not laughable to try to determine what makes a chicken happy and many of us would not even know where to begin answering this question. But to ask what things a chicken might prefer seems to not only be a reasonable question, but one most of us could answer with little difficulty. It is certain that it would prefer to be healthy over being sick, full over being hungry, and live in a stress-free environment as opposed to one filled with fear and anxiety.

Likewise, Singer's principle of marginal utility works well when it comes to making decisions that negatively affect animals. Let's imagine that the circus is in town and you want to go and see the animals perform. Some of your friends are against you going because they've heard that the animals that are performing are mistreated. Furthermore, they try and argue that these animals would prefer to remain wild and have the ability to behave naturally, not dress up in silly costumes for your amusement. This leaves you with a decision where you need to weigh the consequences of your actions. Should you go to the circus? What would be the consequences of going?

As a preference utilitarian, it would seem that you could simply calculate the preferences of all those involved in your decision to go, see if the majority would have their preferences satisfied, and then do that action that satisfies the most preferences. So let's attempt to calculate the preferences that stand to be satisfied. You and many other people would prefer to be entertained as opposed to being bored, so the circus sounds like a great way to satisfy this preference. But there is more to a circus that just the audience. Often, circuses offer animal acts as a part of their entertainment lineup. The animals can range from domestic dogs to tigers and elephants. When looking to measure number of preferences satisfied, you need to take into account not only what the people would prefer but also what the animals would prefer. So it would seem that the audience full of people would prefer to be entertained and going to the circus fulfills this need. Additionally, the circus owners and performers would prefer that there is an audience that pays them so they too would get what they want by your attending the circus. But what about the nonhuman animals? As is often reported, the lives of these animals are anything but something to be preferred. They spend many uncomfortable hours on trains or in trucks moving from place to place, they are separated from their own species and not allowed to do what would come naturally to them, and often these animals are tethered, starved, beaten, and otherwise abused.[7] So despite not being able to precisely measure their suffering, it is safe to say that they very likely suffer physically, mentally, and emotionally. If we were to take their suffering into consideration we would see a slight decrease in the total amount of preferences satisfied and a slight increase in the total amount of preferences frustrated. But certainly there are more humans both attending and employed by the circus than are animals in the acts and clearly all the people involved would like to see the circus well attended. So at the outset it seems that going to the circus would still be the best thing to do as it would satisfy more preferences than it would frustrate. Sure the animals may suffer from having their preferences frustrated, but overall the calculation clearly shows that there are more preferences satisfied. So off you go to the circus.

But if you were to apply the principle of marginal utility, you would see that if the overall experience of seeing a circus would only bring us a modest amount of happiness and our attending the circus would also bring merely a modest amount of happiness to the circus performers and owners, we need to take this "modestness" into account. Additionally, we need to take the intensity of the suffering of the animals into account. Living in these harsh conditions is very stressful physically and mentally. That said it would probably bring these animals a tremendous amount of satisfaction to be afforded the opportunity to be unconfined, to live with others of their species, and to exhibit their natural behaviors. The principle of marginal utility in this case would dictate that a very large amount of satisfaction could be gained overall if these animals were not forced to entertain us under these conditions and that only a small amount of satisfaction overall would be gained by being a part of the circus experience. Therefore, the action that would increase overall satisfaction would be to not have animals perform for us as part of the circus. Therefore, I should heed the advice of my friends and find something else to cure my boredom.

In the case of the circus it seems as if we are looking at a group of beings whose vital interests are being frustrated (the animals suffering) versus a group of beings whose trivial interests are being frustrated (the humans suffering from boredom). But what happens when we are faced with a situation where both groups involved face the potential frustration of their vital interests? How do we choose between groups of humans and nonhuman animals when both have a substantial amount to lose? Here Singer relies on an examination of the kind and number of preferences a being is capable of having. He suggests that when we are facing decisions involving nonhuman animals we should look to the number of preferences one can have in addition to the kinds of preferences that are at stake. For him the more preferences one can have, the more one may stand to lose and as a result the greater the loss when these preferences are frustrated. So in cases that involve humans and nonhuman animals, the more interests one stands to have violated, the worse the violation. In "Practical Ethics" Singer writes:

> *"An action contrary to the preferences of any being is wrong, unless it is outweighed by contrary preferences.... For a preference utilitarian, the taking of the life of a person will normally be worse than taking the life of some other being since persons are highly future-oriented in their preferences."*[8]

What this means is that in a perfect world there would be no actions that frustrated the preferences of any being; however, since this is not a perfect world we can only justify frustrating preferences if more preferences are satisfied by doing so. Furthermore, when considering decisions involving persons and nonhuman animals, people tend to carry greater weight because their preferences are much more complex and tend to be future-oriented, meaning not only current but also future preferences will be frustrated. This does not mean that persons are more important or that they carry more weight simply because they are persons; we are only measuring the effects of the consequences on the preferences of those involved and attempting to satisfy as many of them as we can.

The last sense of "rights" is also the most strict and most contested version of this term. Generally linked with deontologies, we refer to this sense of right as utility-trumping. Utility-trumping rights are those that are closest to the way we view the absolute rights that pertain to humans. When we use the term "right" in this way we are saying that any being that has this kind of a right or entitlement is given a strong claim to something that cannot be overridden, even with relevant justification or with a particular "good" in mind. One example of a utility-trumping right that most Americans are familiar with is the right to freedom of speech. This right has very few exceptions and it protects an individual's freedom to say what they choose regardless of how harmful or offensive their words are perceived to be. With regard to these kinds of rights for animals, we do not see the same consensus that we do among utilitarians in the equal consideration model.

As you may recall from Chapter One, Kant creates a very distinct division between persons and nonpersons based on rationality and autonomy. Remember that rational beings are special in that they are the value-givers. This gives them an inherent worth and as such they cannot be treated as mere tools. But if it is rationality and autonomy that give us our value and our inherent worth, what becomes of those who are not rational? Kant refers to those who lack rationality as the means to an end; in other words, as tools to be used as we need and desire. According to Kant, nonrational beings are not the sort of "things" to which we have direct moral duties (since moral duties can only be upheld between rational beings) and as such we cannot wrong them morally.

For example, pretend you are out walking your dog and I stop you for a chat. All is going well and then out of the blue I kick your dog. This causes him to yelp and you to step back. Did I do anything wrong and if so, what is the nature of the wrongness? According to Kant, if I upset you by kicking your dog I did do something morally wrong, not to the dog but to you. Since your dog is not a rational being he has no value except the value we give him. That means if I choose to render him valueless, then to me he is and I can treat him in any way I please because he holds no inherent value of his own. But if you choose to value him, then he obtains instrumental value (say you value him because he makes you happy). I did nothing wrong to the dog because he is a nonrational being and as such I don't have any direct moral duties to him. I owe him nothing morally. Again, however, I do owe something to you since you are rational and if I hurt your dog, my apologies to you for injuring something that you value and I don't.

As counterintuitive as this seems, when we discuss dogs it can become even more so when we discuss those even closer to us. Imagine a tiny 2-day-old baby. As you probably know infants are not able to be rational in any sense of the word (in fact, they are probably less rational than the dogs in the previous examples). According to Kant, do these tiny beings have inherent value? Should we afford them equality? Do we owe them anything morally? Again, a Kantian would have to respond "no" to all the above questions. As much as we love them, babies are not rational or autonomous and therefore cannot be said to be value-creators. So until they reach the age when they can denote value on other things, they are not value-creators and thus have no special value of their own. Likewise, they cannot be afforded equality and similar to a dog, cannot be owed anything morally. A note of caution would be in order here because this seems to imply that Kant believes we should have no concern for those that are not rational. This is not altogether true. Although Kant firmly believes that these beings are owed no direct moral consideration, this does not mean that he feels we should be able to treat them in any way we choose. Remember I do have moral obligations to dog owners and proud parents of babies and so I would be discouraged from not fulfilling my moral obligations to them. Additionally, even if these beings were to have no one to value them (the stray dogs), this would not mean I should express cruelty toward them. For Kant, being cruel and causing wanton suffering is always something to be frowned upon, not because of what you do directly to the nonrational being but because this creates in you a propensity for cruelty that may very well transfer over to your treatment of rational beings. Kant felt that if a person was cruel to nonrational entities he was creating a situation where being cruel to rational entities would also be perfectly acceptable. So regardless of the direct duties and inherent value that may be lacked by these creatures, this lack is never an excuse to be outrightly cruel to any sentient being.

Unlike the equal consideration model, if we were to say that animals have utility-trumping rights and one of those rights included a right to be protected from bodily harm, then all animal experimentation that is invasive and causes harm would have to end, regardless of the medical benefits to humans or even to other animals. To get a better sense of this, you may recall Kant's categorical imperatives. Both the first and second categorical imperatives are utility-trumping in that regardless of good outcomes one is not allowed to break a universal moral law and one is not allowed to treat humans as tools. These imperatives have influenced philosophers who are interested in securing the same kinds of rights for animals as those enjoyed by humans. Animal rights theorist Tom Regan is one philosopher who asserts the second Kantian categorical imperative to not treat humans as tools applies equally to animals.

Regan offers us interpretations of Kant that focus not on one's ability to reason but on sentience itself as the relevant moral feature by which we determine who receives utility-trumping rights. In Regan's case he refers to sentient beings as those who are "subjects of a life" and counts all mammals and most vertebrates as beings who have this attribute. Asserting what we have called a *utility-trumping view* of rights, Regan argues that animals, like humans, have rights that are fundamental and should be respected regardless of what benefits social or otherwise could be gained by violating them. Using the second categorical imperative as his guide, Regan asserts that neither animals nor persons should ever be used as tools. In his book *The Case for Animal Rights,* he expresses this absolute assertion by calling for the abolition of all farming, hunting, experimentation, and entertainment that involves animals. This strong view is supported by the scientific discoveries that animals not only suffer but are capable of having "beliefs and desires; perception, memory, and a sense of the future, including their own future; an emotional life together with feelings of pleasure and pain-preference and welfare-interests…".[9] For Regan, all of these attributes constitute the particular attributes that make a being worthy of not only equal consideration but of strong rights that need to be recognized and protected. It is from these abilities that our inherent value is derived and since many nonhuman animals have these abilities, they are also inherently valuable. As we understand the term "inherent value," all beings that hold this attribute hold it equally. This would mean that a dog (who is clearly a "subject of a life") has the same inherent value that I do as a human. So, I cannot in keeping with Regan treat this animal as if it merely has instrumental value. I cannot treat it like a tool.

However, not all Kantians agree with Regan's interpretation of Kant and some, like Roger Scruton, support a much more inegalitarian or an unequal approach to the question of rights for animals.

It is this inegalitarian approach that we turn to now. As you will see, despite the different ways philosophers have thus far defined a right, one thing they have held in common is that regardless of how rights are defined all human and nonhuman animals should have their interests weighted equally when we make our moral decisions. Nonegalitarians such as Roger Scruton and

Mary Midgley will reject this approach and instead argue that there are several reasons why the interests of humans should carry more weight than those of other animals. Scruton will argue that it is our moral agency that makes us count for more than other animals. Midgley will argue it is the importance of our social bonds that are the distinction that should carry more weight when we are looking at moral issues involving humans and animals. We look at the argument presented by these two philosophers and then consider whether or not they are compelling enough to override the assertions made by egalitarians like Singer and Regan.

In his book *Animal Rights and Wrongs*,[10] Scruton argues for the distinction between nonrational animals and rational persons. He argues that animals are not members of our moral community and as a result they have neither rights to be treated in a certain way, nor duties to treat others in a certain way. This type of argument is known as the *appeal to moral agency*, which states that in order for a being to have full moral status and to be given equal moral consideration, a being must be a moral agent, that is, the being must be both rational and autonomous. For philosophers such as Scruton that hold this view, only beings that can judge actions as either right or wrong and who are capable of acting on these judgments are worthy of full moral consideration. Beings that are not rational or autonomous could certainly deserve moral consideration but they do not deserve as much moral consideration as rational beings do. That said, any being in Scruton's view that is not rational is not intrinsically valuable and as such, its value is determined by persons.

Take, for example, the difference in our relationships between a deer in the wild and a pet dog. For value-makers, the value of these creatures rests solely upon the value we choose to give them. We generally think of our pet dogs as members of our families and as a result we feel special obligations toward them. Unlike our pets, we value wild animals quite differently. A wild deer may be valued for its beauty, but it could certainly also be valued for its meat. We do not value a deer in the same way we value our pets and since how we view them determines their value, we seem to assert that our dogs have a special claim over us since we are their caregivers and our relationship is much different from our relationship to a wild animal. In both cases, however, these creatures don't have value in themselves and since that is true we have no direct Kantian duties to avoid treating them as means to ends. Nor do we need to include them in our formulations of universal moral laws. "Don't murder" does not apply to the animal kingdom.

This demarcation along rational lines certainly begs the question of what we should "do" with those humans who are what Scruton refers to as "premoral" (infants who will grow up to be rational persons) and "postmoral" or "nonmoral" (those adult humans who will never reach full personhood). According to Scruton, premoral humans should be treated as potential persons and as such should be afforded all the value of full persons, though this does not mean that they are afforded (for practical reasons) the full rights of persons. Postmoral and nonmoral persons present more of a challenge for Scruton. Since they cannot be considered potential persons there may be other sentimental reasons for not killing them, but there is certainly no moral mandate that states we can't. In his words:

> *Infanticide is an inexcusable crime; but the killing of a human vegetable, however much we shirk from it, may often strike us as understandable, even excusable. Although the law may treat this act as murder, we ourselves, and especially those upon whom the burden falls to protect and nurture this unfortunate creature, will seldom see it in such a light.*[11]

Although this may sound shocking, it is certainly reflective of a person who takes the idea of personhood quite seriously. It should be noted that just because Scruton recognizes personhood as the line that divides those of intrinsic worth from those of instrumental worth, this does not give one a license to be cruel or callous toward any being, regardless of value.

Akin to Kant, he sees that even though nonmoral persons are not a part of our moral community, our treatment of them reflects what we are as humans and it is an affront to our personhood if we intentionally harm them and also an affront to what Scruton refers to as our virtue and piety. Also akin to Kant, Scruton feels that although nonhuman animals are not intrinsically valuable, they still should not be mistreated and, furthermore, we do have some responsibility to care for them, provided they are domesticated and dependent upon us.

As admirably rational as Scruton's views may be, for many people the idea that it is morally acceptable to kill another human being is not something they feel comfortable endorsing. So what does this say about making moral agency something so special that only those who possess it are considered worthy of certain protections? As with so many moral theories, what initially sounds like a good justification for inequality turns out to be much more problematic than many people are willing to accept.

Philosopher Mary Midgley recognized the inherent problem with making moral agency the relevant characteristic that afforded people more moral consideration than nonhuman animals and attempts to show us that although the basic idea of our "specialness" holds true, it is not moral agency but the strength of our social bonds that makes humans unique. Midgley argues that the bonds created between humans are much more important than the bonds created between nonhuman animals. It is the bonds between human beings that ground our stronger obligations to them than those that other animals experience between one another and more importantly than those we experience with them. She reasons that as humans our strongest bonds are with other humans. The strongest bonds we possess are those between close family and friends. Although weaker, we have bonds to other humans that live in our neighborhoods and our wider communities, with the weakest of our bonds being to total strangers. Despite our weakening bonds we are still bound to human strangers as members of what she refers to as the human community, that is, we view our fellow humans as a part of the human family, despite the fact that we may not know them personally. If we examine our bonds with animals we can see quite clearly that outside of our exceptional bonds with our pets (usually cats and dogs), we have few if any social bonds with animals. It is the strength of the social bonds themselves that result in our much stronger moral obligations to our fellow humans and thus when we are taking beings into consideration, it is our fellow human beings who will receive special consideration because they are members of the human community.

This inegalitarian argument seems to fare a bit better than the argument the appeal to moral agency, but as with all inegalitarian arguments there are serious questions posted by egalitarian philosophers that bring to light difficulties with this position. It certainly seems correct to say that the moral obligation I owe to my child is greater than the obligation I owe to my neighbor's child. But since my moral bonds toward my neighbor's child are much weaker, does that mean I am free to kidnap, torture, or kill my neighbor's child? It would seem that when I deal with other human beings the strength of my social bonds does not denote a difference in my obligations. I am obligated to keep my neighbor's child safe and free from harm if it is in my power to do so. So if in this case there are clearly weakening social bonds but clearly not weakening moral obligations, why doesn't this work the same way with nonhuman animals? After all, if it is simply a matter of the strength of our social bonds, it would seem that my obligations would change but clearly in the case of children they don't. Although this seems to suggest a weakness, it is not the most questionable consequence of Midgley's view. Many egalitarian philosophers have pointed out that if Midgley is correct and it is the strength of my social bonds that determine my moral obligations, it would not be out of the question to say that a group of individuals could exist who felt very strongly obligated to their own race, ethnicity, religion, or gender (this is their group) but felt much less obligated to other races, ethnicities, religions, or genders. This kind of hierarchical way of thinking about moral obligations can lead directly to racism or sexism, in that moral consideration or special consideration is afforded to members of one's own gender or race just as it is afforded to one's species in Midgley's argument.

So do animals deserve equal consideration? This is a question that philosophers have yet to resolve. For those who hold that egalitarianism is correct, it stands to reason that the burden of proof will lie with the inegalitarian camp. In essence, if there is to be a marked distinction between how humans and animals are considered morally, it will be up to those who hold there is a relevant distinction to justify it. So far, the theories that have been presented have not been convincing enough for one to hold them beyond question.

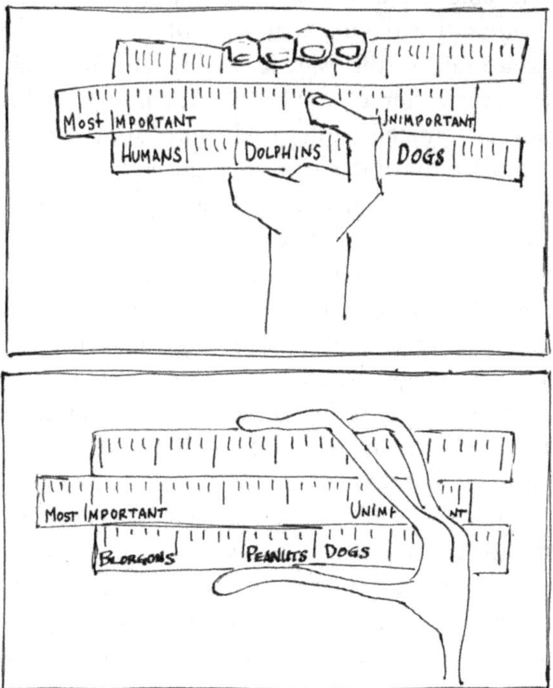

Thus far we have discussed the moral status of animals with regard to their sentience. We have looked at both the egalitarian and inegalitarian ways to view the interests of both humans and nonhuman animals and we have explored a number of ways to view the term "rights" as it pertains to nonhuman animals. There is one more significant moral issue we need to discuss with regard to animals and that is the notion of death and the idea of killing an animal. We have probably all faced the prospect of having to kill an animal. Whether it is a spider in our bathtub, a rat in our attic, or having a sickly pet euthanized, the question that we now need to address is not one of interests but one of harm done when we act in a way that extinguishes an animal's ability to have interests.

Moral Considerations Concerning Death

As with looking at issues concerning animals' interests, there are also a number of philosophical theories that attempt to explain how we should look at the death of an animal. Philosophers generally consider death a harm, at least from a human standpoint. But can death also be considered a harm when thinking about nonhuman animals? It is to this final and morally relevant question we now turn.

Typically there are three distinct views about the harms to humans that are caused by their death: (1) death is a harm because it thwarts a being's central desire to live, (2) death thwarts all central desires that one was capable of having, and (3) death is an instrumental harm in that it ends all future opportunities.

In the first view, a person under normal circumstances will value his or her life not only instrumentally but more importantly inherently. They will value it instrumentally in the sense that by being alive they are able to pursue goals and projects, but its real value is the simple fact that living is valuable in itself. It is the inherent value of a person's life that is taken away with death. If we are looking at death in this way, it would seem then that only those beings who can value their lives inherently suffer a harm when their lives are taken from them. It is clear that many people are capable of understanding and appreciating the inherent value of their own lives. But what are the implications of this view to animals? It would seem that at least as far as we currently know, very few animals understand or can express the inherent value they place on their own lives. In fact, it would be difficult to demonstrate that any animal can express a wish to stay alive let alone their understanding of the inherent value of life itself. These concepts are very abstract and it seems that only adult human beings are capable of expressing such desires. That being the case, if we are going to look at the harm of death as a harm to the inherent value of our lives, it would seem that those beings who are incapable of expressing or understanding this idea are not harmed if they are killed. So in the first instance, killing a person would be causing a harm because they are being deprived of the inherent value of life itself. If, however, we were to kill a cat or even a dog painlessly, in this first sense we would not be causing a harm because neither a cat nor a dog understands or appreciates the inherent value of life and thus nothing of value is being taken from them. As with other actions that require abstract thinking in order to be considered morally wrong, this first view asserts that there is nothing morally wrong with killing one who does not understand the inherent value of life and therefore cannot express a desire to remain alive for life's sake. If we were to apply this example to a newborn infant or to a person who is severely mentally challenged, we can see that the implications of this view are probably something most people would not feel comfortable withholding.

Other philosophers recognizing this problem maintain that it is not the abstract desire to remain alive that is thwarted when a person is killed but, rather, death ends all of our central desires, whatever they may be. If we assert the second reason why death is a harm, we can see that by killing someone we are taking away the possibility of having any of their future desires realized. So according to this view it is not simply the desire to live being thwarted that causes a person harm but it is the fact that all the desires a person has would be destroyed if they were to be killed. If I had desired to go to Paris next spring, write a novel, learn to swim, or fall in love, all of these desires would be stripped from me if someone were to end my life (or if I were to die through natural causes). It is the ability to desire that is so valuable to me and when this ability to desire is taken from me I have lost something of value and as a result have been harmed. This certainly takes away a bit of the abstract nature of the first model in that I don't have to understand the value of life itself in order to desire things for my future. However, with this model we have yet to sufficiently respond to the question why we can't kill infants or the mentally challenged. These individuals can no more desire things for the future than can non-human animals. In many instances it is unclear if many of these individuals can conceptualize a future at all. Certainly we could argue that newborns and the severely mentally challenged seem to express simple desires for the future such as eating and staying warm, but couldn't we also argue that animals too seem to express these simple desires? Here we are faced with one of two choices: We either need to assert that since both humans and nonhuman animals can express similar simple desires, death in both cases is a harm, or we need to look at the idea of desires as a sort of sliding scale wherein the more complex desires you are capable of having, the more valuable these desires are and the more harm is done to you if you are killed. In the first case, you would need to grant animals the same status as humans when it comes to death because it seems that death harms both humans and animals in similar ways or, in the sliding scale model, you would have to accept the fact that the lives of adult humans are more valuable than are the lives of both nonhuman animals and infants or mentally challenged humans. In the sliding scale death would certainly be a harm to an adult human, but it is unclear if it is a harm to an infant. If it is unclear, we may conclude that killing an infant is not as morally wrong as killing an adult human.

The final way of looking at the harm that death may cause is by appealing to what is called the *instrumental harm model.* As the name suggests, death is a harm because it ends all opportunities that a future would bring. Although this model resembles the desires model just discussed, it is different in that it doesn't focus on the desires (or the awareness of these desires) so much as it focuses simply on opportunities that are afforded a person or being that is alive to experience them. In this model, a being does not need to be consciously aware of future possibilities in order for these opportunities to unfold. A being need only be aware or sentient in order for these opportunities to present themselves and if it turns out that the opportunities and experiences that are pleasurable far more often than they are painful, it can be said that taking them away is harmful.

Now that we have introduced all three alternative ways to view death as a harm, let's imagine a situation where we are faced with the decision of whether or not to kill an animal and then, applying the three models, see how each would impact our decision.

You have just moved into a new home and find you have a colony of bats living in your attic. As they are destructive and can spread disease, leaving them in the attic is not an option.

You can either call an exterminator to have them poisoned or you could call a bat removal company who will humanely remove and relocate the bats. If you were to have the bats humanely removed you would certainly be causing them the stress and fear of being captured, confined, and then relocated. Bats are social creatures and you may be causing additional suffering if you are not able to capture all of them, separating them from their colony mates. Alternatively, the exterminator has assured you that the poison used on the bats is painless and they will not suffer, just gently die in their sleep. How does looking at the situation through the different models affect our actions?

According to our first model, the bats would need to be aware of and appreciate the inherent value of their own lives. Although we don't know for certain, it is pretty safe to say that bats don't express a wish to live for the sake of living nor do they express an understanding of the value of life itself. In this case, then, considering the fact that relocation would cause some stress, fear, and suffering, it would seem best to have the exterminator poison them. Although we do know that suffering is a harm it is clear in this model that death is not, so if we were to rely on the first model killing the bats would seem to be the most moral thing to do.

If we were to use the second model it certainly can be said that bats have desires even if these desires may be simple in their nature. On this model, we would need to consider that their desires, whatever they may be, are being taken away from them if they are killed and as a result we would need to carefully assess the stress and suffering they would experience relative to the desires for the future they would stand to lose. If it turns out that a lifetime of relatively pain-free experiences along with many of their desires being met outweighs the brief suffering that may occur as they are captured and moved, then we are obligated to have them treated humanely and not killed.

In the instrumental model it becomes quite clear that killing the bats is indeed causing them greater harm than would humanely relocating them. By having them exterminated we are essentially destroying any future opportunities that could be had by these creatures. These opportunities will certainly involve both pleasure and pain, but if the pleasure outweighs the pain then their future opportunities are of value. Having them humanely removed will cause them some duress but if they are relocated with care there is no reason to think that pleasurable opportunities await them.

The way that we view death and the reasons we give for it being a harm to humans will greatly influence whether or not we see it as a harm to animals. Of the three models it would seem that the only the instrumental model is capable of including all human beings in our decisions about killing and the harm that it can do; this seems preferable to many philosophers, who would rather include nonhuman animals in our considerations about the harms of death than to exclude the most vulnerable humans among us.

So, through looking at both the scientific research into the capabilities of nonhuman animals and exploring the ways in which we can give moral consideration to animals, you may have noticed some very interesting parallels between what we know, how we attempt to process what we know into our moral thinking, and the three ethical theories we keep returning to throughout this text. As we continue to explore moral issues it will become clearer as to where the lines between our moral theories are drawn and what contributes to these lines.

Contemporary Animals Rights Concerns

Factory Farming

As described by its name, factory farming predominates in most industrialized countries where many animals are raised as quickly and in as little space as possible in order to maximize profits. As many people now know, with an emphasis on profitability there is little if no concern given to the well-being of the animals on these "farms." Most will spend their short lives in cages that are too small to stand up properly or turn around. Many will be exposed to noxious levels of ammonia from their own urine and feces and all will face an uncomfortable and crowded ride to a slaughterhouse where many of them will end their conscious lives being dropped in boiling water or being stripped of their skin. For individuals involved in the factory farming process, it is a matter of producing a product and the animals are treated as ends with no moral status at all.

In addition to living in squalor and confinement, many of these animals are mutilated without anesthetic, having their beaks, tails, or genitals removed. As with all animals kept under duress, they are fed a constant supply of antibiotics and other unnatural food supplements to prevent them from dying prematurely. This does not mean they are in good health, as many of them suffer from infections, broken bones, or other ailments derived from their confinement.

Added to the physical pain these animals endure lasting emotional and psychological suffering as well. Deprived of the ability to exhibit their natural dispositions, many develop neurotic or compulsive behaviors such as mutilating their cage mates, headshaking, or teeth-gnashing. The suffering of these animals individually is staggering but their numbers are even more astonishing. It is estimated that approximately 9.7 billion animals are systematically "processed" yearly in this country. With numbers and practices like these, it is clear to see why factory farming is thought to cause more harm to animals than does any other institution or practice. With no legislation in the United States to protect farm animals, this is truly one area where maximization of profits at any cost has truly flourished.

Animal Experimentation

Of all the ethical issues involving animals, probably the most widely known and protested is that of animal experimentation. When discussions regarding animal experimentation arise, images of monkeys with electrodes implanted in their brains or rats running through mazes surface, but experimentation that uses animals is varied and diverse. Animals are used in order to give us original scientific knowledge, to test new products either medical or commercial, and for educational purposes that can include dissections and surgical procedures. Similar to the life experiences of animals on factory farms, animals involved in all types of testing are often confined, uncomfortable, and suffering from both physical and mental duress. Unlike a factory farm animal, however, there are many laws and regulations that help to minimize the pain and distress of research animals. Certainly these regulations do not make life any more pleasant for animals involved in invasive or toxic testing and interestingly animal welfare laws in the United States do not protect two of the most used species in research: rats and mice. Given that, it stands to reason that most animals currently being used in all facets of research are seen as having no moral status. Currently there are no exact numbers on how many animals are killed each year and estimates range from 40 to 100 million. One of the biggest controversies that surround animal experimentation is its overall usefulness to humans. Although many experiments using animals have yielded great medical breakthroughs (like the use of dogs to perfect insulin), most either do not accomplish what they set out to prove or have little or no practical application to human welfare. One of the most controversial areas where this has proved to be the case is in cosmetic and other commercial testing. One particular test that has received widespread criticism is the LD50 tests that basically require the force-feeding of a particular product (e.g., mascara or air freshener) to animals until half the animals die. Although the food and drug administration no longer required this test post 1983, many commercial and cosmetics companies still use this test for their products.

Animals as Entertainment

Humans have been collecting animals for display for thousands of years, and the idea of the zoo has been around since at least ancient Egypt and possibly longer. Zoos have performed many functions over the years; not only have they been strictly for entertainment but they have also been used for educational and scientific purposes. Most recently, zoos have claimed to be tasked with preservation of endangered species and breeding programs for species threatened with extinction. It seems that zoos are not only harmless, interesting pastimes for animal-loving people, but also a critical part of helping endangered species. There are those who feel quite strongly that this sort of entertainment is not harmless, but in fact it is quite harmful for the animals and should be abolished. One of the examples that is often cited is how animals arrive at zoos to begin with. Animals that are captured from the wild to be placed in zoos often die or become quite ill in transit. Not only will they face potential abuse and infection, but they often have a difficult time making the transition to a captive environment. It is not unheard of for perfectly healthy animals to die of heart attacks or strokes due to the stress of captivity. Not only that, some animals that are captured and taken to zoos no doubt belonged to social groups in the wild. With their group slaughtered, poisoned, or also taken captive and then split up, social animals suffer the additional burden of being taken out of their social group, another stress factor that cannot be mitigated. Zoos also differ in quality, with many zoos offering animals too little space with too little stimulus. Although many zoos are moving away from the barren cage and toward naturalistic habitats, the quality of the enclosures vary greatly and depend on the funding available. By and large, zoos that are created strictly for entertainment purposes are designed to give visitors maximum accessibility to the animals while at the same time keeping it safe. These zoos are designed around human needs and will often forego places where animals can hide from the prying eyes of humans. Even zoos that tout themselves as being breeding centers and habitats for endangered species are often seen as much better morally than those whose purpose is for entertainment only. But it is a well-known fact that many animals involved in breeding programs simply don't procreate, possibly due to the stress of captivity. It is also well known that of the thousands of species that are endangered, zoos only make serious efforts to protect a very small number of them. Usually cuddly mammals such as the Chinese panda, the paltry efforts made by zoos to protect species seems like a need to appeal to our desires at best.

Notes

1. BBC News. "Badger Cull: The Environment Secretary reports pleasure at progress." September 2, 2013. http://www.bbc.co.uk/news/uk-england-23929964
2. The Free Dictionary by Farlex. "Definition of Pain."2009 http://medical-dictionary.thefreedictionary.com/pain.
3. Degrazia, David. *Animal Rights: A Very Short Introduction* (New York: Oxford University Press, 2002), chap 3.
4. Oppenheim, Kenith. "Life full of danger for little girl who can't feel pain." CNN. February 3, 2006. http://www.cnn.com/2006/HEALTH/conditions/02/03/btsc.oppenheim/.
5. Morell, Virginia, *Animal Wise: The Thoughts and Emotions of Our Fellow Creatures* (New York: Crown Publishing, 2013), 174–78.
6. Wrenn, Eddie. "What a chimp! Bored Santino hides rocks under hay in order to attack zoo visitors . . . And his planning shows he has a sense of "self." *The Daily Mail.* May 11, 2012.
7. International Institute for Animal Law. "Prohibiting the Exploitation of Animals for Entertainment by Circuses."2001 http://www.animallaw.com/circus/cfm.
8. Singer, Peter. *Practical Ethics* (New York: Cambridge University Press, 2011), 134.
9. Tom Regan, "The Case for Animal Rights," *The Animal Ethics Reader, eds.* Susan J. Armstrong and Richard G. Botzler (New York: Routledge, 2003), 20.
10. Scruton, Roger. *Animal Rights and Wrongs* (New York: Continuum Publishing, 2006), 51–56.
11. Ibid., 79–83.
12. Morell, Virginia, *Animal Wise: The Thoughts and Emotions of Our Fellow Creatures* (New York: Crown Publishing, 2013), 126–35.
13. Ibid., 37–58.
14. Kluger, Jeffery. "Inside the Minds of Animals." *Time* (August 16· 2010): 36–43.
15. Morell, Virginia, *Animal Wise: The Thoughts and Emotions of Our Fellow Creatures* (New York: Crown Publishing, 2013), 254–55.

Name:____________________________________ Date:________________

Review Questions

1. What is nociception and how does it differ from sentience?

2. What is the scientific definition of pain?

3. Why is pain biologically important?

4. What is fear?

5. What is self-awareness?

6. How is equal consideration different from equal treatment?

7. What are the three ways to discuss the term "right"?

8. How does Tom Regan use Kant to assert that animals have rights?

9. What is suffering and why is it relevant to know what types of beings can suffer?

10. What is factory farming and why is it morally objectionable?

Name:______________________________ Date:______________

For Further Discussion

1. Consider your own views on either factory farming or animal experimentation and then compare them with one of the theories discussed in this chapter. Do your views reflect an anthropomorphic view or are they more utilitarian?
2. When thinking about how to treat nonhuman animals, how important do you feel the scientific facts should be in our decision-making process?
3. Go online and research one animal that is of interest to you. In your research have you found anything to indicate that this animal is capable of suffering? What evidence (if any) did you find that this animal is self-aware? Does this change the way you think about how they are treated? Explain.

Name:______________________________ Date:______________

Case Studies

Truth and Consequences

Many of us hold ideas about the nature of nonhuman animals. But have you stopped to wonder if any of these popular ideas are actually true? Many times we have "knowledge" that is neither confirmed nor examined but taken for granted. So what do you actually know about animals and does this knowledge stand up to recent scientific evidence? If we are going to understand how to treat animals, as we have seen from this chapter we need to know what they are like and what interests they are capable of possessing. Here is a list of some common "facts" about nonhuman animals and recent scientific evidence that disproves it:

A. **Only humans have emotions.** Is laughter really the best medicine? It is if you're a rat! Neuroscientist Jaak Panksepp tickles rats for a living. Once thought to be a strictly human activity, laughter has been discovered in a number of animals but most recently in lab rats. For his research Panksepp literally tickles young rats, encouraging them to play and then mapping these happy emotions in their brain activity. To date, not only has play and happiness been mapped but also fear, rage, panic, and grief. It would seem that these emotions occupy specific centers or systems in the brain and rat and human brains are surprisingly similar. So why haven't we ever heard rat laughter before? Well, two reasons: one, we probably weren't expecting rats to laugh so we never thought to look and, two, rats laugh at a frequency that humans simply can't hear. Certainly they chirp or squeak but this is not what is considered laughter. A sonogram can pick up these frequencies and they resemble something like a human giggle. So why is laughter in other animals so significant? According to Panksepp, laughter is about joy and it, as well as other emotions, is not just uniquely human; there are many animals that are capable of a whole host of wide-ranging emotional experiences.[12]

B. **Only humans can teach and learn; animals just work on instinct.** It has long been asserted that nonhuman animals don't make conscious, intentional decisions but act according to preprogrammed instincts. But this notion is being challenged at the most fundamental levels in the most unlikely beings: ants. As strange as it sounds, science has now shown us that what we once thought to be preprogrammed "behaviors" are far from it. Professor Nigel Franks of the University of Bristol has studied ants for over 10 years and has discovered that when performing critical duties such as looking for a new home, ants will teach other ants how to find a new home by leading them along and waiting ever patiently for the new pupil to learn the lay of the land and make it safely to and from the new nest. The teacher in this pair waits for certain signals from her student that let her know the geography lesson has been learned and it is time to move forward. Now the practice of teaching is defined by one being (the teacher) modifying her behavior often at great cost to herself in order to impart certain knowledge onto the pupil. What is so surprising about this experiment is that it raised questions about our understanding of learning versus instinct. Of all the animals to assert a learning behavior and not an instinctual behavior, one would think we could be solid in our observations of insects, but as these experiments have proved, we need to modify our view regarding animal behavior and think in terms of animal consciousness and thought.[13]

C. **Only humans can learn complex languages.** In a 2010 *Time* magazine article, Jeffery Kluger writes about his morning coffee with Kanzi. This meeting took place at The Great Ape Trust in Des Moines, Iowa, where Kanzi, a 29-year-old bonobo chimpanzee, has spent his entire life. Described as a "fellow of few words,"[14] Kanzi communicates his thoughts and desires through laminated picture cards. A formal count shows that he can use about 384 human words but he probably knows dozens more. Not only can Kanzi communicate using these picture symbols, Kanzi can create his own vocabulary when presented with unfamiliar objects and situations, express emotions, and reference the past and the future. Indeed, according to the author of the article, the idea for coffee was not his but Kanzi's. Kanzi is not alone in his ability to learn and use a language as complex as human language. In fact, he is only one of many great apes that have been taught human language and use it quite fluently. Although Kanzi and other apes do not have the vocal physiology to speak, they can use cards, laminate sheets, or even computer programs to express themselves through human language. But it is not only the great apes that seem to have mastered complex language. In 2001, a dog named Rico appeared on German television. Rico has the ability to understand human language. He knows the names of at least 200 items and would fetch them by name when prompted by his owner. Scientists who later studied Rico's behavior discovered he could learn language and remember words as quickly as a toddler. These findings were not just anecdotal, but were published in the peer-reviewed journal *Science.*[15]

1. How important is having the correct knowledge about what animals are like in answering moral questions about the treatment of animals?
2. Were you aware of the facts presented above or did you still hold onto the myths? Did this fact change your view about which animals deserve moral consideration? Explain.
3. Try to explain the moral view of an inegalitarian in light of the recent scientific facts surrounding what animals are like. What challenges does an inegalitarian face in light of these facts?

So Who Counts as a Person?: Whales and Dolphins, That's Who!

Personhood, or the ability to be rational and autonomous, has traditionally been thought to be linked to only one species on the planet: humans. But over the past several years many groups from around the world are starting to rethink personhood and who should be considered a person.

In early 2012, the American Association for the Advancement of Science held a meeting to discuss whether or not cetaceans (whales and dolphins) should have rights. Speakers at the meeting suggested that these animals should not only be afforded the status of persons but also deserve all legal rights and protections that are currently afforded to humans. The scientists based their arguments on scientific evidence that suggests these creatures not only have a high degree of intelligence but are also self-aware. Furthermore, their brains are surprisingly similar to ours, with all the nerve cells required for abstract reasoning and problem solving. Additionally, they are one of several species now being acknowledged to have complex cultures similar in complexity to human cultures. In an interview in *The Economist*, Kari Koski of the Whale Museum in the San Juan Islands in Washington State recounts how a pod of killer whales who make their home near Vancouver, Canada, were recently afforded legal protection because they have been defined by their culture, not their species. They were placed on the endangered species list not because there is a shortage of killer whales, but simply because their culture is found nowhere else in the world. The idea of rights for nonhuman animals may still be controversial, but whales are not the first animals to be considered. Our closest living relatives the great apes have also been considered for full legal protections under the notion of personhood and in 2007 one country, the Balearic Islands, an autonomous province of Spain, has granted legal personhood rights to all great apes. However, they were not the first to recognize the unique status of our closest relations. In 1999, New Zealand passed legislation granting the five great apes basic human rights which means they can no longer be used in research, testing, or teaching. The United States is also reconsidering the rights of apes and as of 2012, all invasive research involving great apes is no longer funded by the National Institutes of Health.

1. Can another species be considered a person? Why or why not? Support your response.
2. Would philosophers such as Regan or Singer require the designation of person to ensure that animals were given moral consideration? Explain.
3. If we did grant personhood to dolphins and whales, what changes would we as individuals have to make in order to make sure these rights were protected? Would you be willing to do this? Explain.

CHAPTER FIVE

Bioethics

Images © Shutterstock, Inc. Modified by the author.

If we had to name one thing in the 21st century that most people couldn't live without it would be modern medical advances and technologies. From breakthroughs in antibiotic therapy to brain surgery, medicine is one of the most useful and fastest progressing areas in our modern world. Recently, a team of international scientists successfully mapped the genomes of the tiger, lion, and snow leopard in an effort to protect these endangered species from extinction. Genetic mapping may seem like old news to us in the 21st century, but to date very few animals have had their genetic makeup mapped and prior to these recent efforts the domestic housecat was the only member of the feline species whose genome had been fully sequenced. Scientists plan to use this new genetic information to make more informed choices about breeding, promote species diversity, and in a worst-case scenario have the appropriate genetic material on hand to assist in reintroduction of species if these felines become extinct. There is no question that our understanding of biology and its applications are growing every day and with rapid progress can come moral dilemmas. Over the last few decades a new branch of applied ethics has emerged to deal with these cutting-edge issues. Known as *bioethics*, it encompasses the ethical and social issues generated by biotechnology. Biotechnology is the application of science and technology to living organisms. It can incorporate moral issues involving humans, animals, plants, insects, or bacteria. Any living organism that can be affectively manipulated by technology falls under the category of biotechnology and bioethics is geared toward understanding our moral obligations in this realm. In this chapter it will be our job as philosophers to look at what these scientists are doing and what potential moral issues may arise when scientists manipulate living organisms.

The study of bioethics requires at least a fundamental knowledge of the processes, procedures, and scientific vocabulary used by the medical community in order for us to understand what questions are raised in conjunction with them. So before we examine the fundamental moral problems that may arise in this area of applied ethics, we first need to look at the latest medical advances in the most prominent fields of biotechnology. What follows then is a brief look at the processes and biology behind gene therapy, cloning, and bioengineering.

Gene Therapy and Genetic Enhancement

The cell is one of the fundamental building blocks of life. Nearly all life on Earth is comprised of a multitude of cells, each programmed to perform specific and sophisticated tasks. At the heart of this programming is DNA, or deoxyribonucleic acid. DNA provides a detailed plan for constructing and operating an entire complex organism. The molecular structure of DNA consists of what is known as a *double helix*, a structure that resembles a twisted ladder. Each rung of this ladder consists of a pair of chemical bases, four bases in all, sewn together in a number of variations. DNA "instructs" cells by varying the sequence of these base pairs along the length of the double helix. One way to think about this process is to think of the base pairs of DNA as computer code or a simple sequence of 0s and 1s. Each time DNA instructs a cell to do something, the sequences are laid out like a computer code. If the DNA wants to change the instructions, it simply has to create a different code with the same 0s and 1s. For every instruction you give to a computer there is a unique strand of code and this is the same for DNA. Each unique sequence signifies a unique set of instructions for the cells to interpret.

What we refer to as *genes* are the specific sections of the DNA sequence that are acting as the basic conveyors of inherited properties. So when we say that someone "has it in her genes," what we mean is that this person carries a specific sequence of DNA in her cells. Of the two, your genetic structures are larger and less numerous, with an average human having about 3 billion base pairs of DNA, but only close to about 25,000 genes or DNA sections. It's within the structure of these genes that science is doing the lion's share of work in the fields of gene therapy and gene modification.

Gene therapy is an experimental technique used to directly change genes in order to prevent or treat a disease. There are many diseases and conditions in humans that are caused by genetic errors and in instances where genes are defective or absent gene therapy can play a role in repairing or inserting genes, thus improving the quality of life for many people. Currently our biotechnology has progressed to the point where we have now mapped the entire human genome (a *genome* is simply an organism's complete set of DNA) and have found ways to detect genetic defects or disorders in individuals. We are even able to, in some instances, detect genetic disorders before they have manifest themselves. It's important to note that even though we are able to diagnose current and potential disorders in human beings, our ability to fix these genetic defects has yet to be tested. To date, this form of gene therapy has yet to be performed safely on humans and has only been performed on plants and animals with mixed success.

What scientists are hoping to do in the very near future is to take a copy of a normal gene and introduce it into the cells in such a way that those cells who may be carrying a defective instance of the gene will no longer "listen" to the defective gene but will begin to replicate the new, normal gene that has been introduced. A gene can't simply be inserted into a cell and left there to do its work since the insertion of foreign genes could cause cells to malfunction. To help scientists insert good genes without destroying the cell completely, they need to find a mechanism that will penetrate a cell almost unnoticed and then change the genetic structure from within. Currently, many scientists are exploring the use of viruses to aid them in penetrating cell walls and inserting genetic material without harming the cell. This is something that a virus can do naturally and science hopes to someday rely on specially altered viruses to harmlessly insert themselves into a cell nucleus, "encouraging" the cell to start the production process for a genetically healthy cell that will replicate and eventually, through the process of cell turnover and production, will become the dominate cell within the body.

For our purposes we discuss two general groups of cells: somatic cells or body cells and germline cells or reproductive cells. When we are discussing gene therapies we are usually discussing therapies that deal with somatic cells, because these are the cells that make up the bulk of your body tissues and are most likely affected by genetic defects. As with most medical therapies, only the patient who receives the genetic therapy will be affected by genetic changes involving somatic cells; the benefits can't be passed onto future generations.

Germline cells, however, are sperm and egg cells and gene therapies designed to effectively alter these genes will have an impact not only on the patient but also on his or her offspring. For example, if the genes are altered in either the sperm or the egg, the alterations will be inherited by both the immediate offspring and also by all the offspring in that genetic line. Again, therapies that involve genetic manipulation of this kind have never been performed on humans and again have met mixed results when performed on animals and plants. If and when it may occur in humans, germline therapy would most likely involve manipulating the genes of a child in the very early stages of development, before cells have had time to mature and genetic structures have established themselves. To distinguish it from somatic therapies, germline therapies are generally thought of as "enhancement" therapies because many people foresee a time when we will have the ability to actually change bloodline characteristics as a means to create "better" people.

Of course this description oversimplifies the distinction between somatic and germline therapies as well as the distinction between a positive (enhancing) or a negative (therapeutic) therapy as there is much gray area between the two. As many scientists know, it's possible to introduce genetic material into somatic cells only to find that this material has made its way to the germline cells, so to draw this distinction based on cell type serves only as a means to discuss the moral issues raised by these processes. Additionally, there are ongoing discussions about what kinds of genetic alterations are therapeutic and which should be considered enhancements. It is debates such as these that intrigue philosophers because they open up a wealth of possible moral issues.

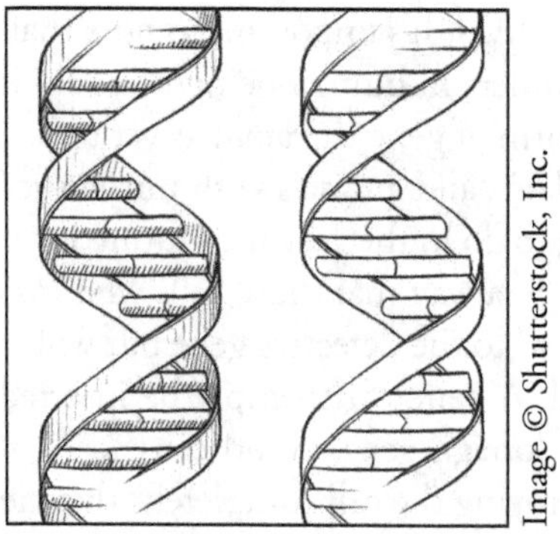

Image © Shutterstock, Inc.

Take, for example, the genetic attribute known as intelligence. Many individuals would argue that genetically increasing a person's intelligence is clearly something that is an "enhancement" and not simply a fix for a genetic defect. But what if the increase in intelligence was from 80 IQ points to 100 IQ points (100 IQ is considered by most to be "normal")? Would this increase still be seen as an enhancement or is it actually therapeutic, a way to bring a person to normalcy? Much of the controversy that surrounds the distinction between negative and positive gene therapy rests on the distinction between health and disease and abnormality and normality and these terms can be very vague. What we think of as "normal" in any given situation is not so much a concrete number; rather, it is a range or a percentage. For example, someone with an intelligence quotient of 100 would be considered just as normal as a person with an intelligence quotient of 90 or even 105. We are ultimately the ones who determine these ranges and we need to understand that an IQ of 106 is essentially not markedly different from an IQ of 104. In fact, you probably wouldn't even consider someone who scored an 89 on an IQ test abnormal despite the fact that the scoring speaks otherwise. Moreover, some people with what would be considered "disabilities" don't see themselves as disabled. To them, they are simply "other-abled" and don't lack anything at all. This is especially true of some in the deaf community. Many deaf individuals have argued that the genetic factors that cause deafness are not defects but variations that should not be weeded out of the gene pool. For them, being deaf is not an abnormality, it's just another way of being human.

Already it should be starting to become clear that there are many moral issues surrounding the gray area between enhancement and therapy. Later in this chapter we look more closely at the implications of these issues and what philosophers suggest as a best course of action when dealing with genetic therapies. Keep in mind that although our examples and our emphasis thus far has been on the genetic enhancements and therapies for humans, there are many additional issues surrounding the use of this technology on both plants and animals.

Genetic Modifications and Cloning

Genetic enhancements involving plants and animals are more well known and a bit less controversial than their human-based counterparts. We are all familiar with the acronym GMO, or *genetically modified organism*. This term is used to describe any organism that has undergone the process of genetic modification. Currently there are a number of bacteria and viruses that have undergone genetic modification in order to serve us in our medical needs. Viruses have been radically altered in the hope that someday they can act as vehicles for DNA and certain types of bacteria have been modified to produce human insulin. However, did you know that a large portion of our staple foods have been genetically engineered? In the United States alone it is estimated that approximately 80–95% of all soybeans, sugar beets, cotton, and feed corn have been genetically altered. Why is it that we genetically modify so many of our food crops? Many people believe that the only way to keep up with demand and continue to feed an ever-growing population is to modify food organisms, making them mature faster, produce more, and resist pests and diseases more effectively. It's also thought that in some instances genetic modifications will enhance the nutritional value of many crops, allowing those in the poorer areas of the world to receive nutritional benefits they would not normally receive. One instance of this is the addition of daffodil genes into the rice genome. The resulting rice, which is yellow in color, was actually able to provide vitamin A, an essential vitamin, to children in areas such as Bangladesh and other places where they may not be able to acquire this nutrient from their traditional food. Further genetic experiments have taken place in many African countries where the Bio Cassava Plus program hopes to create more nutrient-dense forms of the cassava plant. Although a staple, cassava, like white rice, lacks many of the fundamental vitamins and nutrients necessary for health. By creating a plant that can provide more nutrients, many African nations can curb malnutrition and improve the quality of the lives of their citizens.[1]

It is certainly fairly common to encounter genetically modified plants in the supermarkets and on our tables, but what about genetically modified animals? Unlike genetically modified plants that don't need the approval of the Food and Drug Administration (FDA) to be sold to consumers, genetically modified animals do need to go through a strict testing and approval process before they reach supermarkets and are purchased for consumption. As of 2012, there are no genetically modified animals that are approved for use as food. However, a genetically modified salmon, which has been altered to reach maturity at twice its natural weight, is currently being considered by the FDA for sale to consumers.

Probably the most radical and controversial form of genetic manipulation is not therapies or enhancements but genetic cloning. When scientists clone a being they produce a genetically identical copy of an existing biological entity. There are three types of cloning currently performed by scientists. The first type is fairly uncontroversial but the last two have proved to be hotbeds of moral controversy. Possibly the most uncontroversial type of cloning is known as *DNA cloning*. This type of cloning is fairly widespread in the scientific community and involves copying particular genes for later research and study. One of the reasons why it is probably so uncontroversial is that the entities that are cloned are not complete biological beings, or beings that we can identify as individuals. As you may recall from Chapter Three, most of our moral theories are focused on individuals and their well-being. Since DNA strands are not individuals, most philosophers and most people don't regard them as entities worthy of our moral consideration. As a result, they tend to fall "under the radar" in terms of moral concern.

The second type of cloning is known as *therapeutic cloning* and involves duplicating human embryos for use in research aimed at treating particular diseases. This type of cloning has been linked very closely to the stem cell debate because it involves harvesting stem cells from cloned embryos. An embryo is the name given to a being that is in a very specific stage of development, defined as occurring between the very early stages of fetal development and about the 14th day after conception. For a human being as for all other mammals, there is a marked difference between an embryo and a fetus. Human gestation begins in a 24-hour period known as *fertilization* and is completed when the genetic information from the sperm and the egg have fused together. The product of this fusion is a zygote, which is a single-celled organism. After about 5 days, the zygote becomes a ball of about 100 cells called a *blastocyst*. This ball of cells constitutes the material from which most of the embryo will be produced with some of the material forming the placenta and the rest forming the umbilical cord. About 2 days after formation the blastocyst will implant itself in the womb. Only about 25% of all blastocysts will successfully implant, sending signals to the female's body to continue the process of embryonic development. It's not until about 14 days after fertilization that the cells in the blastocyst start to differentiate, that is, start creating the beginnings of a nervous system, organs, and other vital features. It will be another 7 weeks of development before anything resembling organs occurs and this is when an embryo becomes a fetus in medical terminology. So when we speak of embryonic research, we are talking about the stages of development up to about 7 weeks. As you may deduce from the information presented here, the reason scientists use embryos in genetic research is because the cells in an embryo have not yet been "assigned" a function; that is, they have not differentiated sufficiently enough to become a specific organ or body part. This is the stage whereby the embryo is basically a mass of cells from which all other cells "stem" or are developed. A stem cell is unique in that it hasn't become a specialized cell. They have the unique ability to generate almost any kind of specialized cell in the body: skin cells, heart cells, liver cells, and so on. The hope is that since they are programmable at this stage, they can eventually be harvested and then artificially programmed to replace defective cells in already living beings. Stem cell research holds the promise of curing cancer, heart disease, and neurological disorders such as Parkinson's.

The first example of embryonic stem cells grown in a culture occurred in 1998 at the University of Wisconsin. Even at these early stages the potential for these cells to change lives was already well understood. Growing "spare" organs, creating cures for disease, and increasing lifespans had already been linked to the use of stem cells even before it was possible to grow them artificially. But these goods were quickly overshadowed by controversy as it was discovered that in order to harvest these cells human embryos had to be destroyed. This began the debate about the value of an embryo as a human, a person, or an individual which is still being determined.

Although the use of stem cells and cloned human embryos is very controversial, it is not nearly as controversial as the idea of cloning an individual human being. Reproductive cloning not only evokes the strongest reactions in most people but it is also the type of cloning that fascinates us and terrifies us at the same time. There are many misconceptions about what a clone is and what attributes a clone will possess. Most of these misconceptions stem from Hollywood films that portray clones as exact duplicates or as mindless copies of another person. Other misconceptions about clones arise from the fact that cloning is seen as something unnatural and only possible through advances in modern science. But both of these notions are simply untrue.

Reproductive cloning at its most basic involves the duplication of a fully developed human or animal. The method used to clone a fully developed animal is called *somatic cell nuclear transfer* (SCNT). The process is as follows: The nucleus of an egg cell is removed and then it is replaced with the nucleus of a somatic cell extracted from an adult living animal. Either electricity or chemicals are used to activate the growth of the new cell to the embryo stage. At this point the embryo is implanted into the uterus of an adult animal and several months later the adult female gives birth to the cloned animal in the normal way.

Although this process still sounds like science fiction, it is not the only way that clones can and are produced. In fact, nature creates clones all the time. Identical twins are true clones in that they possess almost identical DNA. As we know, twins, triplets, and even quadruplets are born all the time and in many cases there is no science to the process, just simple biology. As far as clones being exact duplicates or mindless copies of another being, the reality couldn't be further from the truth. Although clones share identical DNA with another living being, they have their own minds and own life experiences. A clone that grows up in a lab, for instance, will have a very different life experience than an animal that grew up on a farm. It would be no different in the case of a human being. If we were to clone a person, say your grandmother, she may resemble Grandma in every way but since your grandmother grew up many decades before Internet, the microwave oven, or even television, her clone would be experiencing a very different world than your original grandmother. These environmental changes would certainly affect how the clone viewed the world and as a result she would not be exactly like your grandmother with regard to worldview, personality, or life experience. Moreover, researchers have discovered that clones need not even physically resemble their adult counterpart. For example, scientists who have worked with cloned cats have found it impossible to create an exact duplicate of a calico cat through cloning. It seems that through random genetic mutation the calico pattern will always be unique. So even if you were to clone your beloved calico kitty, you still wouldn't get an exact copy, in color, pattern, or personality. With that in mind, it might be best to save your $50,000 and adopt a new calico kitten from the local shelter.

As if the cloning of adult humans wasn't strange enough, science has introduced one final manifestation of the cloning process known as *chimera cloning* or *chimera production*. This process takes its name from a mythical beast that was said to possess a lion's head, a goat's body, and the tail of a snake. Chimeras, like the mythological beasts, are actually a combination of the DNA from at least two other beings. To create a chimera the egg cells of one being has the nucleus removed and then the missing nucleus is replaced with the nucleus of another animal. So if we were to create a human chimera we could take the cell of a mouse, remove the nucleus, and then replace it with a human nucleus. As the egg develops, the resulting embryo would be 99% human and 1% rodent. Again, this sounds like science gone wrong but the truth is that chimeras are created quite frequently in laboratories and the reason for chimera production may not be as sinister as you might think. Genetic hybrids of this kind are created mainly because human egg cells are in such short supply. So the use of hybrids is a good way to ensure the continuation of research in the areas of gene therapy and DNA cloning without having to rely on human donors.

Despite our tendency to let our imaginations run wild with thoughts of half-human/half-rodent beasts roaming the earth, chimera production serves practical purposes and is regulated very strictly. So at least for now, we need not worry about animal chimeras, although it's not altogether certain that we can entirely discount the possibility.

Fundamental Moral Principles

Now that we have a basic understanding of the science behind the numerous biotechnologies that are present today, we can turn our attention to the ethical issues that some of these processes, procedures, and products may create. In order to do this, it will be helpful to our discussion if we look at some additional ethical principles to guide our thinking. Here we examine four ethical principles and one assessment tool in detail. As you may recall from Chapter One, an ethical principle is a fundamental standard of conduct from which other standards and judgments draw support. Principles are the ideas that we propose to guide our actions. The three principles that we are going to work with here are principles that are presupposed in all the ethical theories, so you will use them whether you are a utilitarian, a virtue ethicist, or a deontologist. Moreover, some of these principles may seem familiar or self-evident because they happen to form the backbone of much moral thought in general.

At the center of any discussion in bioethics is the principle of respect for autonomy. You have now seen the term "autonomy" in many places throughout this book and understand that autonomy is simply defined as the ability to govern oneself and to act on the rational choices one has made. An autonomous person is both free from external constraints and has critical mental capabilities that allow him or her to understand the consequences of his or her decisions.

A respect for autonomy in the field of bioethics comes down to allowing one to remain free of controlling influences, that is, to make and act upon the rational choices that one feels are best in the given situation. We see this principle called upon most frequently when a patient has to make critical life decisions that reflect his or her beliefs and values. For example, if an autonomous person states that he doesn't want a certain lifesaving procedure, those in the medical community must show him respect for this decision by not forcing him into a procedure he doesn't want. A standard example of respect for autonomy is when a Jehovah's Witness refuses a blood transfusion. Even if the procedure is necessary to save a patient's life, if a person has refused treatment based on religious grounds, that refusal must be respected and no treatment should be administered. Another medical example can be seen in the decision of a patient to stop chemotherapy or radiation therapy when they feel that the treatment is no longer helping. Even if the doctors and nurses insist that there would be benefits to continued treatment, the patient's wishes and thus her autonomy to make her decision must be respected.

But respect for autonomy need not be relegated to cases of life or death. Issues involving autonomy can also include simple situations such as exchanges between doctor a and a patient, a nurse, a researcher, and a volunteer or any other situation where one person is relying on another person's professionalism and expertise to help make critical decisions about one's own well-being. Listening to a patient's concerns and not treating volunteers in a patronizing fashion are examples of the principle of respect for autonomy in non-life-threatening situations.

The second principle we need to understand is the principle of beneficence. This term has many meanings but for our purposes we can say that beneficence means actively promoting goodness, kindness, or charity. In bioethics this term is eluded to in the famous Hippocratic Oath, "Above all, do no harm." So whenever we are interacting with people, we have a moral duty to prevent injury and harm whenever possible and to promote the interests of the person by removing any possible harms. The phrase "whenever possible" is often used in discussing the principle of beneficence as there are some cases where people cannot remove a possible harm without great risk to themselves or the harm that is caused can't be mitigated in any way by the people involved. The principle requires that we do our best to promote the good but it doesn't require people to put themselves at great risk in order to promote the good of others or to mitigate a harm being done to them. Again, we can turn to medicine to see this principle well illustrated. Both doctors and nurses have a responsibility to promote the good of their patients. Whether it's to cure a disease or to fix an injury, these professions are obligated to promote the good and do no intentional harm. In the event that a patient's treatment is bringing about more benefits than harms, it is the doctor's responsibility to make sure the patient continues to get treatment. But in cases where treatment is no longer doing any good or is doing the patient more harm than good (recall the cancer patient example), then it is the doctor's responsibility to discuss this with the patient and then use the principle of respect for autonomy, allowing the patient to decide whether or not to continue with treatment. So the principle of beneficence in medicine can either be a proactive principle meaning that doctors and nurses actively seek to cure a patient or it may be a passive principle in cases where healthcare professionals refrain from treating the patient any further or in cases where the treatment would cause more suffering than benefit.

The last principle that we need to discuss is one that most of us are probably familiar with at least in name and that is the principle of justice. Although this term is used frequently outside of philosophy, like the term "argument" it is used by philosophers in a very specific way. We are familiar with it in the general sense, which is that justice occurs when a person gets what's owed to them. What is owed to a person will of course depend on the situation. Situations such as exchanging the appropriate amount of money for a promised good, receiving the grade that you earned, or, after breaking the law, being given a punishment equal to the crime. The first two examples are instances of what can be referred to as distributive justice and is the focus of our use of this principle in bioethics. As you may have noticed distributive justice deals with questions surrounding the distribution of goods and services within a society. What constitutes a fair price in a transaction and what an individual has earned in a class all point to the idea that there is a good that needs to be given to members of society. Exactly how these goods are distributed and what constitutes the best or most fair distribution is going to be one of the key concerns in bioethics. The reason why the distribution of goods is one of the central concerns in bioethics is that the services and goods created by innovations in medicine and the biological sciences are goods and services that affect the health and well-being of individuals. These are not just trivial items but are items that can determine critical outcomes in our lives.

We've already discussed the idea of equal consideration in the last two chapters, but it's important to note here that the idea of equality is the fundamental idea that underlies notions of justice. If we are to receive a payment, a grade, or a punishment, the idea is that all people in similar or equal circumstances will receive the same payment, grade, or punishment. It would hardly seem just to demand more work from one student than another in order for both of them to receive the same grade. From this idea of equality the well-worn phrase "equal treatment for equals" has been derived. But what exactly does this phrase mean and how does it apply to the idea of justice or getting what is owed to you? Like so many other essential ideas in philosophy, who we consider equal is really a matter of which trait, characteristic, or factor we choose to focus on as the most relevant. So, in order to say that two people are equals, we need to understand and state very clearly the traits, characteristics, or factors we are considering to be most relevant.

We can imagine two people, both in need of a job. Let's imagine further that there is only one job opening at a particular corporation and both of these individuals have applied for the position. The first individual meets all the job criteria in addition to having 10 years of experience in the field. The second individual meets about 50% of the job criteria and has no experience in the field. According the principle of justice who should get the job? Most would say the first candidate because he goes above and beyond the qualifications and it's the job qualifications in this situation that are the relevant determining factors. So in this circumstance we have two candidates, but these candidates turn out to be unequal when it comes to qualifications and experience. According to the principle of justice, which states "equal treatment for equals," these two are clearly unequal and as a result it is not unjust to treat them unequally, that is, to offer one the job and not the other. Now take another example. This time we have two students, both of whom have excelled in their applied ethics course. They've done equal amounts of work and their work has been equally exceptional. At the end of the quarter, however, one of the students receives an "A" in the course and the other a "C–". If we are looking at this using the principle of justice, has justice been served? Clearly not, because these students are equal in relevant ways and they were treated unequally. Now in both of these situations when we look to the relevant characteristics of the participants we see that the characteristic we are looking at is what these individuals have earned. In the job opportunity example, the employer is looking at the experience the person has in addition to the qualifications earned through formal schooling or on-the-job training. In the second instance we also have a case where the individuals, through hard work and dedication, have earned very high marks. Both of these examples serve as instances of justice based on merit, one of many different ways that goods and services can be distributed among equals.

Aside from merit, there are a number of other ways to distribute goods and services in a just fashion. Those most important to our understanding of the ethical issues surrounding the distribution of biotechnology as a good are:

1. A person is owed something according to the positive contributions they make to their society. Thus a philanthropist is owed more goods and services than a criminal simply because philanthropists make positive contributions to society and criminals do not.
2. A person is owed something according to the effort they expend. In this case, if a person works hard, then they deserve more than a person who doesn't work as hard or doesn't work at all.
3. A person is owed something based on their needs. In this case, those who are able to make their own way are given much less than those who can't make it on their own. This doesn't mean that access to goods and services are unavailable to those who are not in a situation of need; it just means that some individuals will get extra help.
4. All people are provided with an equal share of all the goods and services in a society.

When thinking about biotechnologies and medical advances it's important to keep these views in mind as biotechnologies are considered vital goods and services and are not unlimited in their nature. Who should receive gene therapy, genetically modified foods, and the latest stem cell treatments all comes down to how one views what constitutes a just distribution of limited but valuable goods.

One final ethical principle that warrants discussion is called the *principle of double effect* (sometimes called the *doctrine of double effect*). This principle is usually associated with situations where serious harm is the likely side effect of our attempts to promote a good end or mitigate a great harm. Again we can call on the example of a cancer patient to illustrate this principle at work. In treating many aggressive cancers, patients are often exposed to large doses of harmful radiation. This radiation given as a medication is actually very harmful to all the cells in the patient's body, not just the cancerous ones. When a person undergoes radiation therapy, in a sense they are slowly being poisoned. Although this fact is well known, the end result that doctors are hoping to achieve is the remission of the cancer that is growing inside the patient. So the good end that the doctors are trying to achieve is killing the cancer; the unfortunate side effect of their efforts is the poisoning of the person's entire body. The doctor doesn't want to nor is she trying to intentionally harm the patient; in fact, she does all she can not to harm the patient. Rather, the harm is a "side effect" of the treatment that is supposed to support the good outcome.

Using the principles of respect for autonomy, beneficence, and double effect, we can now begin to frame our discussion of the ethical issues that may arise from advances in biotechnology. With regard to justice we have also seen how the idea of equal treatment for equals is understood and some of the ways goods and services can justly be distributed within a society. One final aspect of just distribution has to do not with goods and services but with harms. In addition to looking at ways that the goods and services of biotechnology are distributed, we also need to consider the actual and potential harms that the use of biotechnology may create.

Risk

We tend to speak of potential harms in biotechnology in terms of the risks associated with them. At its most simple risk is simply being exposed to harm or exposing others to it. All ethical theories will at least allude to the idea of risk and each has particular concerns regarding what can and should be the focus of our risk assessment. Utilitarians must weigh the risks if they are to determine the course of action that creates the most satisfaction. Deontologists must weigh the risks in determining whether or not we are needlessly endangering the lives of people or exchanging a respect for autonomy for a good outcome. And finally, a virtue ethicist would need to weigh the risks of any given action to determine whether or not the action would be one that a rational person would accept given all the information.

If we judge the known risks of any particular biotechnology to be too high or if the risks associated with a biotechnology are unknown but potentially irreversible and dangerous, an ethical person would want to reconsider moving forward with that particular technology since placing themselves or others in direct harm violates the principles of autonomy, beneficence, and justice.

It's fairly safe to say that every day we take risks. Whether it's driving to work or eating in a restaurant, potential harms are all around us. We weigh these risks all the time and are well aware that every time we get into our cars, we risk being involved in a fatal accident and every time we eat at a restaurant, we risk contracting a foodborne illness. So if we are aware of these risks, why do we continue doing these activities? Well, if you take a measured approach and weigh the risks you will find that it is less likely that you will end up in a serious accident as opposed to making it home safely from the grocery store. Likewise, it's more likely that you will eat an enjoyable meal without incident than it is that you will contract a serious illness. We don't normally use a formal system to determine these everyday risks, we generally just do a quick pro/con reflection and then move forward with our decision. In everyday situations this quick assessment is quite efficient, but what about risks that have much higher consequences or risks where the chances of the outcome are unknown? This type of risk scenario is more common when looking at biotechnologies than it is in our everyday lives and as a result it may be helpful to understand a more formal way of looking at the risk factors involved in this area.

Traditionally, risk assessments for more high-risk situations have been guided by the idea that we should be free to create products or act in a particular way unless there is evidence that our product or our actions create unacceptable risks. That is, we are free to do what we like as long as there is no evidence that a great harm will follow. On this model of risk assessment, it is perfectly acceptable to proceed with technologies or processes if there is no evidence to suggest that moving forward would cause any substantial harm.

A more recent and more widely accepted model of risk assessment is what is called *precautionary risk assessment*. This model differs from the traditional model in that one must provide evidence to show there is no unacceptable risk associated with our product or actions. That is, we are not free to create until we have shown with a substantial amount of certainty that moving forward will not cause harm.[2] The distinction between these two models is subtle and rests on a distinction about where the burden of proof for harm lies. An example of the two models may help to make this distinction more clear.

Let's take a very controversial example, one where the risks are not well known. Let's assume there is a corporation that would like to clone human beings. They have the technology and the investors to start marketing this technology to consumers. Should this corporation be allowed to do this? If we are looking at the risks through the traditional model, those who want to clone the humans would have to present their formal materials, and those who are concerned need to present their own formal materials. If those who oppose human cloning cannot present evidence that this process is sufficiently harmful, then the corporation should be free to create clones for consumers.

Using the precautionary model, the corporation would be responsible for showing us that there are no risks associated with cloning. Other parties need not be involved as the burden of proof lies with the corporation; they must show it is not harmful in order for them to be free to sell their product to consumers.

Both of these models offer us interesting challenges with their use. The precautionary model seems to suggest that the corporation needs to show us that there are no risks involved in the cloning process. In other words, they are left with trying to prove a negative, there are no substantial risks and never will be any substantial risks. This certainly does raise the question as to whether or not this kind of evidence is even possible. After all, how do you prove that something is not there and never will be? How do you create a sufficient number of tests to rule out future risks? It would seem this model asks the corporation to do the impossible, and that would not be a very reasonable expectation. On the other hand, the traditional model places the burden of proof on those who oppose cloning to begin with and are at odds with the process. This is problematic because it moves the assessment of risk to those outside the practice of cloning altogether.

Contemporary Bioethics Concerns

There are an immense number of factors we need to take into account when looking at biotechnology and some of the ethical issues it creates. We need to be able to not only apply the ethical principles and do a risk assessment, but we also need to understand when these ethical principles stand to be violated and which risk assessment model seems most appropriate to the task at hand. We now return to the medical advances discussed in the first part of this chapter and then look at some of the issues that may be raised through the use of these biotechnologies.

Looking at the principles of respect for autonomy, beneficence, and justice, gene therapy does not seem to create any moral quandaries. If a person is aware that the cell therapy is being performed and that person freely accepts the treatment, there is no violation of autonomy in administering it. If the therapy alleviates pain and suffering at little cost to the patient, then the therapy can be seen as adhering to the principle of beneficence. Since most gene therapy would consist in getting a shot or a series of shots, it would seem that the benefits would far outweigh the burdens. If this therapy is made available to all those with the genetic disorder, it would seem that distributive justice would also be well served. Finally, in terms of risks, at this point the actual risks to an individual are not well known. It has, however, been shown that manipulation of genetic structures on plants and animals have been done successfully with no known harms incurred.

If the process was well tested and the risks that could be incurred would be those equal to what we now see in plants and animals, it would seem that this kind of therapy would be acceptable on this front as well. So as far as gene therapy is concerned there is very little controversy in the way it could be administrated, and distributed, or the risks incurred.

With other types of genetic manipulation we have discussed, answers to these questions are not as clear-cut. Genetic enhancement of germline cells and genetic cloning are much more problematic.

Recall that germline therapies are those genetic therapies that involve genetic alterations that can be passed on to the next generation. Genetic cloning also involves creating genetic material that is passed directly to offspring; in fact, it is the creation of the offspring themselves. One of the most obvious moral concerns at this point in time when discussing these therapies is their safety. No germline therapies of any kind have been safely performed on humans. Science is working toward this possibility but cautiously as there are currently so many unknowns that it is difficult to even assess the risks of these procedures. But there are many human activities where the risk factors can't all be accounted for but the benefits are obvious. Genetic enhancement or germline therapies could be seen as similar to the risk incurred by people who perform, tasks such as driving on the ice roads of Canada or launching a space shuttle. Perhaps germline therapies should be looked at in a similar way. This response to the use of germline therapy is very much in line with a utilitarian framework in that our goal in making these enhancements available will be to create the most benefits with the least amount of harm. If our decisions to allow genetic enhancements move along utilitarian lines it would indeed be nothing more than weighing out a potential benefit with a potential burden and then "calculating" which one would outweigh the other.

If we were to calculate this out to, say, one generation of individuals who had received genetic enhancements, weighing out these benefits and burdens may be a challenge to grapple with but certainly we could make a fair prediction. But remember the reason why germline therapies are so controversial is that any adjustments made in this generation would subsequently be passed onto the next generation and all future generations. In both a risk assessment and utilitarian framework any attempts to weigh the benefits and burdens over many generations into the future is likely to fail as we simply cannot with any real certainty know what effects our current genetic manipulations will have on people 5, 10, or 20 generations in the future.

A good example of this would be to genetically enhance people with increased intelligence. This sounds like a great idea, after all wouldn't it be better for everyone if people were more intelligent? This would certainly be true, but what if our current enhancement of intelligence had unintended and serious consequences for future generations? What if, for instance, we were to attempt to enhance intelligence but in doing so we inadvertently reduced empathy? As generation after generation lost their ability to empathize there is no doubt that the results to society overall would be disastrous. If future people are incapable of empathizing, they would have little concern for others and thus our increase in intelligence may be directly connected to more violent, selfish, and apathetic behaviors that hadn't existed before the enhancement. This scenario represents not only the benefits and burdens that must be weighed when considering genetic enhancements but also the risks involved. Using either model, if we knew that enhancing humans today would lead to a more violent society in the future, the benefits would clearly not be worth the risks.

Even if we were to calculate the risks as being acceptable, there is the question of which character traits we should value most and who should choose the enhanced traits we give to successive generations. Whenever we think of creating better humans, we can't help but think of the eugenics programs that were instituted in the past. The term "eugenic" simply refers to the science of modifying human populations to increase desirable traits. Possibly the most infamous eugenics programs were those instituted in the 1940s by the Nazi party. Their pursuit of a master race has been cited by those who are against genetically enhancing humans as a potential outcome of our manipulating DNA to improve the human species. Government-sponsored eugenics programs in the past have focused on low IQ, particular physical characteristics, or certain ethnic backgrounds as traits that should be selected against. Those who are wary of genetic enhancement see modern DNA manipulation as simply another eugenics program similar to those in the past. But those who are in favor of genetic enhancement don't see the problem as one of gene selection but rather of autonomy. They will argue that in the past, it was the government that decided which traits were valuable, taking the decision away from the parents of the children and the citizens of the countries. For those who support genetic enhancement, the fears of many could be allayed by making the parents of the children responsible for choosing which traits are desirable and thus which the child should have enhanced. This would not only ensure that the autonomy of those who are rearing the child is respected but also could prevent scenarios such as the enhanced intelligence/lack of empathy problem since not all parents will value intelligence over other traits. This certainly could resolve autonomy and risk issues, but does it resolve the entire controversy surrounding genetic enhancement? According to bioethicist Jonathan Glover,[3] leaving these choices up to the parents brings about controversy of another kind. The first involves gender selection and the second involves parents making genetic choices that will put a child at a severe disadvantage. As you may be aware in many countries male children are preferred over female children. Currently there are no therapies that ensure that parents will conceive a male child but with germline therapies this would be entirely possible. If germline therapy choices were left up to the parents we could experience a worldwide shortage of female children. Eventually as a species we could reach a crisis point where sustaining populations will not be possible. We could be putting future generations at a serious disadvantage by creating a situation where there are not enough females to maintain populations.

But choosing a child's gender would only be one choice among many that a parent could make when creating a genetically enhanced person. Some parents either through ignorance or misinformation may request enhancements that are actually disadvantages, not advantages. Jonathan Glover gives us an imaginary example of a very religious couple who requests that their children are given an inability to read or write so their faith can never be tested. In the parents' mind of course this would seem like an advantage, as having one's faith tested can be uncomfortable and runs the risk of destroying faith. But modifying children so they cannot read or write puts them at severe social, political, and economic disadvantages that far outweigh the benefits the parents think they are giving them. A more realistic and currently ongoing discussion has to do with genetic deafness. According to many deaf parents, being deaf is not a defect, a challenge, or a disability. Some parents see deafness as being not abnormal but "other normal" and have protested genetic work that would allow for genetic deafness to be eradicated. They argue that eradicating genetic deafness is similar to the eugenics programs of the Nazis because those who have their hearing judge being deaf as a disability. They argue further that any research that aims to eradicate this other normalness is discriminatory and ought to be stopped. So given this situation it is certainly plausible that some deaf parents would want to make sure that their children are born deaf as well. Again, this raises issues about what is considered a disadvantage or an advantage and how these critical decisions made by parents can affect the future of their children in potentially negative ways.

A middle ground to determining who should decide which characteristics should be enhanced is offered by philosopher Robert Nozick.[4] His solution is to offer parents the ability to choose their child's character traits under very general constraints set up by governmental agencies. This solution lies midway between parents being solely responsible for gene selection and governments being solely responsible. He calls his solution the "Genetic Supermarket" model. He feels that in this model the government could compile gender data that was readily accessible to future parents. This information would allow potential parents to know which gender is in short supply at any given time. If the parents want a girl they would simply wait until the numbers suggested that girls were in short supply; if they wanted a boy they would wait until there was a shortage of boys. This, according to Nozick, would still empower parents to make their own choices about their children while at the same time maintain gender balance, ensuring the survival of our species. Nozick also recommends governmental protections for children that would cover certain genetic decisions. If minimal protections were put into place similar to those currently in place to protect children, the scenario of the very religious parents would be prevented. It is not altogether clear, however, that it would solve the scenario involving the deaf parents.

If we can, through Nozick's suggestions, solve some potential problems that arise from germline therapies, there are still issues of autonomy and justice that have yet to be addressed. We have discussed in brief how the autonomy of the parents should be respected through allowing parents to make critical decisions about their children, even if there are some constraints to their choices. But what about the autonomy of the child? The question of what happens to a person's autonomy when they are created in a certain way is another issue that surfaces when considering designing human beings. Some fear that if we create "designer babies" those children will lose their autonomy in addition to losing some of their personhood. In cases where parents decide the traits of their children it would seem that in some ways they are predisposing them to act a certain way or to have certain capabilities. By creating people to be more intelligent, faster, or more morally inclined you are in a way determining the way they will act. Since the idea of autonomy is that a person is free to make their own choices and decisions, you can see how predisposing a person to act in a certain way is not being respectful of their autonomy. Additionally, if you were to argue that you are giving your child certain traits so they can be assured a happier, productive future, aren't you in fact treating the person as a means to an end? After all, if happiness and productivity is the goal and this goal can be achieved through taking away a person's autonomy, it would seem that you are in violation of not only the principle of autonomy but also of Kant's second categorical imperative.

We could certainly imagine a situation where if we could create the perfect child we would be tempted to do so. You might, for instance, not only could you want to select a boy but you may also want your child to have dark eyes and light-colored hair, have an average build but be a bit taller than other boys. Of course you would also want your child to have above-average intelligence and perhaps have a talent for leadership. But why stop there? You've always wanted to have musical abilities, why not endow your son with the talents you've always wanted? If I could create a list of attributes that would comprise a "perfect" child, why wouldn't I? Why leave to chance what I can construct? Of course at this point in time the ability to create these designer babies is still in the far-flung future, but this sort of genetic engineering has already proved successful on a number of other species. We currently use genetically enhanced microorganisms to produce human insulin, human growth hormones, and other medical substances and it is no secret that both animals and plants have been successfully "modified" to produce more milk, fruits, and grains. The use of such processes raises its own series of moral questions that are discussed in the next section but suffice it is to say that creating designer people is not something that can't be done and in the near future may become as common as our genetic practices with plants and animals.

Thus far we have looked at situations that reflect questions about the risks involved in genetic enhancements and also questions regarding respect for autonomy. There is one other issue that arises from discussions of the genetic enhancement of humans and that is the issue involving just distribution of these enhancements. As we discussed earlier there are a number of ways to justly distribute goods and services within a society. Distribution based on merit, need, and contribution are just a few of the ways that were outlined earlier in this chapter. Assuming we can get past both risk factors and autonomy issues we are still left with questions about the just distribution of genetic enhancements. If future generations are going to be genetically enhanced, who should have access to these enhancements and on what grounds should they have them? Looking at the current state of biomedical advances many philosophers are concerned that the processes involved in genetically enhancing our children will prove to be expensive and difficult for the average person to obtain. This concern in addition to the current maldistribution of biotechnologies worldwide leaves philosophers wondering who will reap the benefits of genetic enhancement and who will suffer the ill effects. It is quite plausible to imagine that only a handful of very wealthy parents in the United States would be able to afford to have their children genetically enhanced. Given that most parents would be inclined to choose advantageous traits such as enhanced intelligence, motivation, competition, strength, and good looks, they are ensuring that their children are created with advantages that natural selection cannot consistently provide. Clearly their children will reap the rewards of these enhancements and as a result will get into the best schools, get the most job opportunities, and become more successful overall than their average peers. But the advantages would not stop there as these children will not only have been made for success but each successive generation in their line has also been altered for success. With each generation the children of parents who were genetically enhanced will become even more intelligent, motivated, and good-looking. So what happens to the children whose parents couldn't afford to have these genetic enhancements? Clearly they will not only be at a disadvantage to begin with but each successive generation who cannot afford these enhancements will be put at a disadvantage. The gap between the advantaged and the disadvantaged will grow larger with each generation as the wealthier and genetically enhanced will always be in a position to outdo their average peers. It would seem that if genetic enhancement therapies were distributed based on who could afford them, even if this distribution model lasted one or two generations it would disadvantage a large portion of the population for generations or possibly forever. So it would seem that in order to distribute genetic enhancement therapies justly there would have to be systems in place that would either make these therapies available to all at a reasonable price or would limit the ways that these therapies could be used by the very rich. Working with the current methods we have at our disposal, it would seem that the only just way to distribute access to genetic therapies is also the most difficult to employ. If we were to look at the benefits and harms that could be incurred through this practice only equal distribution of the medical technology seems to be most compatible with what would be equal treatment for equals. If we were to assert any other type of distribution, it simply would not make sense. For example, we could not distribute genetic enhancements based on need, since enhancements are not something one needs, but rather something one wants. Additionally, if we were to distribute these enhancements based on merit, it is unclear what one would have to do in order to merit use of this technology.

So, genetic enhancements or germline therapies certainly carry great promise, but the ethical issues that are still unresolved leave many thinking that these therapies are simply ethically unsound and that genetic enhancement is best left to modifications of plants and animals. Animals and plants whose DNA has been altered are known as *GMOs*, or *genetically modified organisms*. Genetic modification of plants and animals has been occurring for hundreds or even thousands of years. From selective breeding of dogs to get certain genetically desirable traits to creating strains of peas and corn that are resistant to mold, GMOs are a part of our human history. But it has only been recently that organisms that are genetically modified are modified purposefully at the cellular level.

Probably one of the most prominent areas of modification is in the food industry. Many of the foods we consume have been modified in some way and it has only been recently that consumers are starting to question the wisdom of eating food that is created in a lab. Though much of the controversy surrounding genetically modified food has to do with consumers wanting to know what foods have been modified, there have been a number of additional controversies surrounding the creation and consumption of modified foods. Questions concerning the risks to human health, the loss of autonomy over food choices and food crops, and the destruction of the environment are three of the most frequently voiced ethical concerns when it comes to the genetic modification of our food.

Attempting to determine the risks involved in creating and consuming genetically modified food products is difficult. The corporations who create and market these foods can be said to apply the precautionary model of risk in that they have stated that there are no known risks associated with consuming genetically modified foods. Recall that under the precautionary model, the corporation is free to sell their product until there is evidence that genetically modified foods pose a risk. Interestingly enough, the FDA leaves all testing of modified foods up to the corporations and does not require that tests for safety be conducted by external government agencies. Many corporations test their products on a voluntary basis, and have yet to cite conclusive evidence that the modified products are harmful. This is a concrete illustration of the one problem with the precautionary model, that in order for a modified food to be banned it must first be shown to be harmful. This means that there is the potential for harmful foods to be consumed by humans before they are banned as opposed to testing the food before it reaches our tables since future risks cannot always be shown to not exist. So would the traditional model be more in line with assessing the risks of modified foods? For many it seems to offer a better way to look at this situation since the corporation would be free to create and sell these foods only if there is no evidence of unacceptable risk. This clearly places the burden of proof on an external resource and some argue that this burden should lie with the FDA.

In the case of genetically modified foods, if it is the risk that is our concern it would seem that since not all foods have been genetically altered we as autonomous individuals can mitigate any risks by simply not buying and consuming modified foods. But this is not as simple as it sounds. To date the federal government has been reluctant to require companies to inform consumers about the use of genetically modified organisms in their foods. Without proper labeling, it is impossible for a consumer to know whether or not the items they are consuming have been genetically modified. The reasons for this are many, but some have argued that a failure to supply consumers with the information they need to make choices that could affect their health is a violation of the principle of autonomy. In order for a person to make real choices and follow through with these choices, the person needs to be informed. As an autonomous person, you should be free to make choices that affect your health and no one should prevent you from making said choices. By refusing to label their products, corporations have in essence created a situation whereby your ability to make choices has been prevented. If you don't want to take the potential risks involved in consuming genetically modified foods you need to be aware of which foods contain modified organisms and which don't. If you are unable to make this distinction because a producer had decided not to inform you, in a sense you are being denied a respect for autonomy as your ability to make relevant choices is being prevented by those who do not want you to know about what you are eating. So it seems that by not labeling foods, the government and the corporations are not respecting our autonomy.[5]

Reduced [redacted]

[redacted] De-Lish

Nutrition Facts

Serving Size 4 bites	Servings Per Container 8
Amount Per Serving	
Calories 400	Calories from Fat 320
	% Daily Value
Total Fat 32g	**10%**
Saturated Fat 28mg	**8%**
Trans Fat 4g	**2%**
Cholesterol 80g	**55%**
Sodium 600g	
Total Carbohydrate 0g	**0%**
Dietary [redacted] less than 1g	
Sugars 60mg	
Protein 22g	
Vitamin A 0%	Vitamin C 0%
Calcium 0%	Iron 1%

Ingredients: Enriched [redacted], niacin, reduced [redacted] thiamin, rye, [redacted]nitrate,[redacted]acid, soybean), sugar, palm oil, flavors, nut [redacted], dextrose, mextrose, plextrose, more [redacted] high [redacted] syrup, highest [redacted], lowest [redacted] syrup, beef fat,[redacted] tail, eye of [redacted] monoca lcium phosphate, Astatine, ununhexium, sodium bicarbonate, salt, xantham, modified cornstarch, autolyzed [redacted] hydrolyzed [redacted], paralyzed maltode xtrin, spice, partially [redacted] oil, [redacted] skin, [redacted] pieces, [redacted] lips and bh's, ampersands

In cases involving the labeling of genetically modified foods it is easy to see the influence corporations can have when it comes to our ability to make rational choices. This is made even clearer when one considers the almost singular influence these corporations are beginning to have over the farmers who grow many of our vital food crops. Food is a vital commodity that none of us can live without. As a basic need, the fair distribution of food is critical for survival and the distribution of the means for growing food is equally critical. It wasn't too long ago that the farm that produced the food you ate was local, small, and run by generations of farmers. However, in the 21st century this is no longer the case. Although approximately 19% of all land in the United States is used for farming,[6] only about 1% of the population claim to be farmers and only about 2% actually live on farms.[7] Farming, like so many other aspects of our modern lives, is becoming incorporated and multinational. What this means is that as more farms are incorporated, our food supply becomes more strictly regulated by fewer and fewer individuals. Again, we look at the idea of risk versus benefit and see that there are certainly many benefits to centralizing food production and distribution. Centralization allows for more efficient transportation and thus a better-quality product. It also allows us to coordinate food distribution from faraway places, leading to items such as tropically grown bananas being available for purchase even in the dead of winter. But this kind of centralization means that there must be entities large enough to coordinate these operations and some worry about the influence large corporations are having on how smaller farmers operate, where they buy their seeds, and how they sell their products on the market.

Take, for example, the Monsanto Corporation. Monsanto is a giant in the genetic industry and also in the farming industry. Owning over 90% of the soybean seeds and over 85% of the corn seeds, this corporation is notorious for suing farmers who attempt to use seeds produced by the plants they have already paid for to reseed their soil. What this means is that instead of adhering to the age-old practice of saving some seeds from a current crop to seed next year's crop, farmers are forced to purchase new seeds each year. Farmers who are caught "reseeding" are sued and can lose great amounts of money and even their farms to the Monsanto Corporation. Reseeding is one way for smaller family farms to save money that is reinvested into their farms. Having to buy seed each year can be expensive and many family farms have gone out of business because they are not able to reseed.

Of course, Monsanto Corporation has created many seed varieties that are genetically altered to resist pests and weeds and these genetic modifications are considered property. When a farmer uses genetically altered seeds from Monsanto, the seeds remain the property of the corporation and are not owned by the farmers who use them.[8] Monsanto argues that since the seeds belong to the corporation, any attempt to reseed amounts to stealing property from the corporation. Again, a respect for the autonomy of the farmers is in question as there are very few other seed companies to buy from and buying seeds that are not modified to resist pests and weeds may ultimately lead to crop failure. The influence of Monsanto over crop production not only hurts smaller farmers financially but it creates what is potentially a monopoly on many of the basic food crops in America and abroad. Monopolies are destructive for capitalist economies as they do not promote fair market competition and they are also unfair to consumers as there they create a situation where prices and distribution can be controlled by one entity, removing the potential for consumers to make choices regarding where and how their food is produced.

Despite the fact that many of our food crops have been genetically altered, both pests and weeds are returning as animals and plants are themselves evolving to resist the modifications that have been created in the lab. When examining issues involving genetically engineered organisms creating resistant weeds and insects, we need to understand that the creation of modified organisms doesn't stop nature from evolving to meet the challenges posed by them. One of the newest concerns surrounding GMOs is the resurgence of pests and weeds that were thought to have been eradicated. Known as *super bugs* or *super weeds*, these are organisms that have developed resistance to many of the herbicides, pesticides, and genetic alterations to our food.

In early 2013 a report was released stating that the corn that Monsanto Corporation had genetically altered to resist rootworms was no longer effective. Over the last several years, farmers have noticed an increase in rootworm damage to their corn crops. As a result, many of them have had to return to the heavy use of pesticides to kill what has been identified as a new strain of rootworm, which is resistant to the genetically modified corn. In the past 2 years, sales of insecticides and herbicides have increased by 50–100% and some fear a return to the days when farmers sprayed so much poison on their crops that the soil itself became poisonous. According to crop consultant Dan Steiner in the past many of the farm workers and consultants who worked directly with the soil would experience nausea and even vomit after handling soil samples without gloves.[9] Of course, additional pesticide and herbicide use is not good for the environment any more than it is for the people who are poisoned when they come in contact with the soil on their farms. Overuse of chemicals has been connected to birth defects, polluted streams and rivers, and even with a reduction in bee populations worldwide. The problem that farmers are currently facing in the Midwest is not an isolated one. As rootworms become more and more resistant, we can count on this genetic mutation spreading to other areas of the United States and even to other parts of the world. The creation of super bugs and super weeds could have a direct and devastating effect on future food production. The more pesticide- and herbicide-resistant organisms we inadvertently create through our genetic modifications the more likely we are to have worldwide food shortages or worse crops that are vulnerable to a number of super bugs and super weeds that we can't modify food crops against. Weighing the risks, we should ask ourselves: "Are we willing to continue using a product that has a very high chance of making basic food items scarce in the future?"

Although we are faced with many moral issues when thinking about our food and our future genetic makeup these concerns are thought to be mild compared to the perceived potential consequences of genetic cloning. For many years this technology was thought to be the stuff of science fiction, then in 1997, the world was stunned with the news that Scottish researchers had successfully cloned the very first mammal, a sheep they named Dolly. Overnight Dolly became a celebrity and the once far-fetched concerns surrounding genetic cloning has become a reality. Since that time, many more mammals have been successfully cloned including horses, cows, dogs, cats, and rabbits. But our short description of the cloning process and the extent to which it has been successful hides some of the difficulties with the process. The case of Dolly may help to illustrate some of the more problematic moral issues involved with reproductive cloning.

Dolly's attempt to blend in with the flock proved unsuccessful

First and foremost, the cloning process is an extremely inefficient way to create life. Most cloned embryos will die and very few clones will ever make it to adulthood. In the case of Dolly, it took about 275 unsuccessful embryo implants to produce one sheep that was able to live to adulthood. Although Dolly was lucky enough to make it as far as she did, she was plagued with health problems such as arthritis and immunity defects. She eventually died of lung disease at the age of 6, which is about half as long as the lifespan of a normal sheep. In addition to immunity problems and arthritis, clones tend to be more susceptible to abnormalities in organs and organ function along with premature aging.

Following the success with Dolly, the question of cloning humans loomed large in the media. If scientists could successfully clone an animal, what would prevent them from cloning a human? The initial public outcry against cloning far exceeded the scope of what science was capable of doing, but at the time it seemed inevitable that human cloning was just around the corner. To date no human beings have ever been cloned and many countries have enacted legislation that prohibits human cloning and research involving human embryos for cloning purposes. Although some aspects of cloning are uncontroversial, the successful cloning of Dolly raised serious moral issues about whether or not we should use this technology and for what purpose.

As discussed earlier in this chapter there are a number of types of cloning. There is the cloning of tissues and organs, the cloning of nonhuman animals and plants and the cloning of human beings.

Cloning tissues and organs is thought by most to be therapeutic and it is this type of cloning that is generally thought of as fairly uncontroversial. Most individuals welcome the ability to clone tissues (e.g., bone marrow) or organs (e.g., the liver) as a technology that could save many lives. In this type of cloning, organs and tissues are grown using a patient's DNA. This exact duplication decreases the chance of the new tissue being rejected and could be used to ensure that all those who need an organ would have a perfect match available for their use at any time. This process could eventually replace organ donor lists and allow for organs to be replaced as needed and not when they become available.

Although it is the therapeutic aspects of cloning organs and tissues that received the bulk of media attention, there are other nontherapeutic uses for cloned tissues that have recently been explored. Experiments using cloned animal tissue have yielded some interesting results that some say may actually help us solve hunger, save the environment and even prevent animal cruelty. In 2008, the animal rights group PETA offered $1 million to anyone who could create "test tube meat," that is, meat that was produced in a lab and did not come from a live animal. In early 2013 scientists in both the University of Missouri and the University of Maastricht in the Netherlands have been working with chicken and cow stem cells, in the hopes of creating the world's first cloned meat product. In late 2013, the University of Maastricht served up the world's first lab burger made from the cloned tissue of a cow. Although the process is currently prohibitively expensive, these researchers hope to perfect the technique and even create lab meat cloned from chickens and pigs. Again, when we think of this type of cloning, most will see few negative moral issues surrounding it; in fact, this may be another area where cloning helps us to solve some of our most pressing moral problems with regard to the environment, animals, and global food distribution.

The cloning of an entire biological organism however has been met with mixed reactions from both the general public and philosophers. Concerns not only for the animals themselves but concerns over decreased biodiversity and the potential hazards associated with cloned animals being accidently introduced into the environment have raised questions as to whether or not this practice should be allowed. It is well known that cloned animals rarely live normal lives. Most have shortened lifespans and the short lives they do live involve diseases and defects that affect their quality of life. Indeed, many individuals are skeptical as to why one would want to clone an animal where there are noninvasive and natural ways to produce them. Another concern is that of risks to the environment and to biodiversity in general. Although animals that are cloned rarely leave the labs where they were created, there is always the risk of animals escaping or being let loose intentionally or by accident. If set free there is no way to know how these animals may affect the environment or native animal populations. If they did survive in the wild, they could potentially reproduce offspring that carry genetic mutations we are as of yet unaware of. It is much more likely, however, that since these animals are usually bred to reach maturity and grow faster than their natural counterparts, they could invade environments and based on their genetic dispositions could outcompete the indigenous wildlife. Moral issues involving nonhuman animal cloning generally fall into two categories: risk assessment and the potential to cause suffering to sentient beings. Since we have successfully cloned many animals we are aware that they tend have shorter lives and suffer from many physical ailments. As we know these facts, we would need to make an assessment of the quality of life afforded to these animals. Clearly the question of whether or not we should clone nonhuman animals will rest on how much suffering would result, the strength of our use of "rights" with regard to animals, and other factors discussed in our last chapter. The risks involved are also fairly well known and would need to be assessed using either the traditional model of risk assessment or the precautionary model of risk to determine whether or not this practice should continue. On a more practical note, many question our motivations for cloning nonhuman animals when success is so marginal and the benefits not entirely clear. Although not a moral issue in itself, the question of why or if we should do something just because we can is a thought-provoking one.

Clearly the most controversial issue surrounding cloning is the cloning of human beings. Issues involving nonhuman animal cloning are compounded and other issues are raised when scientists start discussing human cloning. As with therapeutic cloning, there is not simply one straightforward response to the question of what human cloning is and what exactly it entails. What follows are some of the types of human cloning that are or could be possible in the future with a brief summary of some of the moral issues that accompany them.

The first type of human cloning we will discuss is the cloning of human embryos for stem cell research. We then turn to the cloning of actual human beings as members of society. Recall that stem cells are those cells that have not differentiated into specific cells that perform specific tasks in the body. Since the cells start the differentiation process at about the 14th day after conception, stem cell researchers tend to work with cells up to this time and then any surviving cells are destroyed. Important ethical questions concerning this research revolve around the fact that cloned human embryos either die or are killed after only 14 days. This is objectionable because potential humans are created with the understanding and intent that they will not be allowed to develop into human beings.

Some hold the view that a human being's life begins at conception. If this is true, the resulting embryo is considered a human being and should be afforded all the rights of a human being, including the right not to be killed unjustly.[10] But here we need to think carefully about what we mean by "human being" and consider whether or not this term can reasonably be applied to an embryo. As we have learned in previous chapters, it is thought that all human beings deserve moral consideration. It is when we attempt to determine what makes human beings "special" that we find a variety of justifications. Traditional theories justify this by simply referring to our humanness or our sequence of DNA. Others look to reason or our ability to value as the relevant factors for moral consideration. Reflecting on what we have read thus far about the justifications that humans deserve special treatment, can any of them be reasonably applied to an embryo? Being human may mean many things, but when we assert the specialness of any human regardless of the attribute we choose as our focal point, we are always referring to an individual being that has a myriad of attributes and potentialities. Does this same basic description apply to an embryo? Certainly no one would argue that a human embryo has the appropriate sequence of DNA to be identified as human. But does it have the individuality and the potentiality that a fetus, an infant, or an adult human being possesses? We know that an embryo prior to the 14th day is merely identified as a clump of undifferentiated cells. These cells haven't developed into anything that is recognizable as an individual human being. In fact, at this stage cells are still capable of twinning, that is, they are capable of becoming not only one but possibly two or more individuals.

With this in mind it would be difficult to define an embryo as an individual human being with individual traits and potentialities since it could still become more than one human being. It is in this way that embryos are quite different from what we normally think of as a human being and it's this difference that makes the idea of equal moral consideration for humans and embryos an interesting and possibly impassible logical problem. If we were to look for close comparisons between an embryo and another organism, probably the best candidate would be other cells in the human body. Embryonic cells prior to the 14th day of conception are simply a group of cells waiting for further chemical instructions about how to proceed. The cells in my body, such as liver or skin cells, are also simply a group of cells that are also awaiting certain chemical instructions on when and how to process toxins or when and how to produce more melanin. We see this same grouping of cells awaiting instruction in cancer cells. So embryonic stem cells, liver cells, and cancer cells are all simply bundles or clumps of cells awaiting chemical instructions. Considering how close these three examples are in kind, if we are going to give one clump of cells moral consideration equal to an individual human being, how do we justify not granting moral consideration to the other two types of clumped cells? These examples certainly have more in common than do an individual human and a 3-day-old embryo and if we are to remove our bias and grant certain consideration to those beings that have the most similarities, then it is the most rational and logical course of action to treat the clumps of cells equally as opposed to treating one type of cell clump as morally relevant but the other two as irrelevant. So if we choose to give the embryos used in stem cell research the same moral status as human beings, we must also assert that liver cells and cancer cells also hold the same moral status. The result of this would mean that we shouldn't be allowed to do things that may kill liver cells (e.g., drinking alcohol) or attempt to kill cancer cells through chemotherapy or radiation. For most people the thought of liver cells or cancer cells being given the same moral consideration as a full-fledged human being seems highly problematic. Which in turn may suggest that granting an embryo the same moral consideration as a human would also prove problematic.

At this point in time, the ability to clone a full human being is not within our capacities. However, with future advances in biotechnology it should not be seen as entirely out of the question. Many of the moral issues that surround the cloning of human beings stem from our experience with cloning nonhuman animals. Questions of efficiency, environmental risks, and suffering have already been raised but take on new dimensions when applied to human beings. Additional elements such as issues involving our autonomy and the principle of beneficence are added concerns when we consider the potential negative consequences of creating human clones.

There is no relevant reason to suppose that cloning humans would be any more efficient a process than cloning other nonhuman animals. That would mean for each successful human clone, there would have to be a substantial number of failures that preceded it. Even if we could make this process more efficient it is unlikely that it will ever be as successful as natural human procreation. If it takes over 200 tries to successfully bring one cloned being into adulthood, this may speak of an underlying problem with the process itself. It has been well documented that nonhuman animal clones suffer from a number of maladies and this raises questions about the cloning process as being a viable means for creating healthy individuals at all. There is much speculation about why the cloning process is so unsuccessful and some argue that this lack of success is nature's way of telling us that this process should be abandoned.

As has already been mentioned, animal clones rarely enjoy healthy, happy, and long lives. This fact raises questions concerning beneficence and the potential suffering of cloned humans. Recall that the principle of beneficence urges us to do what is good and avoid doing what is harmful. If we knowingly bring humans into the world that will die young and suffer from malformed organs, compromised immune systems, premature aging, or any number of illnesses, aren't we violating the principle of beneficence? To bring individuals into being knowing that it is likely they will not live full and pain-free lives is actually creating a situation where you are doing a harm to those you create. You could certainly argue that this is a risk factor that should be taken into account, but given the statistics we have on current cloning techniques and cloned animals it seems quite likely that cloned humans are created with built-in disadvantages that will cause them to live a compromised life.

The issues we have just discussed only cover issues of cloning humans as the process exits today. But what if the process is modified and refined in the future? It is altogether plausible that the success rates could increase and the health problems decrease. If we could achieve these goals in the far-flung future, would we have successfully resolved all the moral issues surrounding human cloning? Even if we were to improve the process, many are concerned that it would still violate the principle of respect for autonomy. There are two related autonomy issues that arise when we consider cloning human beings. The first concerns a person's right to be a unique individual and the second concerns the right of a person to have an open future.

One of the things that makes humans feel valuable and important is directly linked to the fact that each of us is a unique individual. But what if you woke up one day and found out there was another person in the world that was exactly like you, down to the DNA? Some worry that by cloning human beings we are detracting from both the uniqueness of the person who is cloned and also the uniqueness of the clone. After all, it is quite likely that the two people will share a substantial number of character traits and physical attributes. This may lead the clone to feel that she is not an individual, but merely a copy of a previous person. But is this entirely true? Would a clone be much like the donor person in enough relevant respects that she could no longer have an identity of her own? If this was the case, it certainly does seem like this is a violation of her autonomy. After all, if a clone was identical to the donor in every way, it would seem that many of her actions would be predetermined based on the donor's actions, her likes and dislikes determined by the donor's DNA, and her moral character based strictly on the donor's moral character. In essence it would seem that the clone would not possess the autonomy that we normally attribute to persons. If we were to intentionally create such a people it would seem that we did violate their autonomy by preprogramming them to live and act a particular way—a way that they did not choose but was picked for them. But is cloning really capable of violating a person's autonomy in this way? Although we can't say for certain, we do know that the process does not create an exact duplicate identical in every way. Remember that cloning occurs naturally in cases of twins and triplets and we know from looking at sets of twins that they are not identical in either their looks or their mannerisms. In fact, there are always differences despite their genetic origins. The same has held true for cloned animals. Although they may carry the exact same DNA, natural variability is still at work and animals will have both different personalities and at times look very different from their donor parents. Finally, we mustn't forget about the role played by our environment. Although much of what we do depends on our attributes, there are environmental factors at work as well. Even if a clone looked like me and had similar mannerisms, they would still be growing up under vastly different circumstances. These circumstances would certainly contribute to the choices presented to this individual and thus the choices they would make. So the notion that creating a clone would be a direct violation of a person's autonomy because they had lost their right to be unique or that they had lost their right to ignorance may not be powerful enough arguments against the practice.

The second concern about cloning human beings also rests on the issue of autonomy, but this is an issue not of uniqueness but a related idea, that of a person's right to an open future. The open future argument has also been referred to as the right to ignorance argument because it rests on the idea that we humans are not only ignorant of our futures but we have a right to this ignorance.[11] This argument goes essentially like this: A person's genes may determine to some extent what life choices are open to that person. Since there is no one with my exact same genetic makeup I don't as of yet see the potential course my life could/would take. But if I could observe a person with the exact same genetic makeup as my own, I would be able to observe at least one way that my life could go. This could predispose me to the view that certain possibilities are closed to me and this knowledge could seriously curtail my sense of being able to choose options for my own life. So if one was a clone, one could get a general picture of what one's life will be like. If one's donor was a filing clerk who hated school when she was younger, one could certainly assert that having identical DNA puts you in a position to also dislike school and also end up working at a job as a clerk. What follows from the argument from ignorance is that essentially as a clone even if life choices are not determined at the genetic level it certainly stands to reason that they could be perceived to be determined at the psychological level. As in the first situation if life choices feel predetermined there is concern that they will unfold as predetermined and one will feel as if their autonomy is seriously curtailed. By curtailing another person's autonomy we have again shown a sincere disrespect for them as persons and again we have violated a very important ethical principle.

It seems that much of what we discuss ethically concerning genetics and cloning revolves around the unknown. Since these technologies are still in their infancy, it is difficult to assess them in a concrete manner. Science is helping us to bridge the gap between ignorance and knowledge and this will inevitably lead to our ability to better formulate ethical solutions to the problems presented by the new technologies. But what we can know is that there are general guidelines that each theory we have looked at in this course will follow in order to make the most moral decisions regarding gene therapies, enhancements, and cloning technologies. Our guide throughout this chapter has been the four moral principles set out at the beginning: respect for autonomy, beneficence, justice, and double effect.

Notes

1. Talbot, Marianne. *Bioethics, An Introduction* (New York: Cambridge University Press, 2012), 332.
2. Wellcome Trust. "Tibbs the cat and the precautionary principle."2013 http://www.wellcome.ac.uk/Education-resources/Education-and-learning/Big-Picture/All-issues/Nanoscience/Articles/WTD015852.htm.
3. Kuhse, Helga, and Peter Singer. *Bioethics: An Anthology* (Victoria, Australia: Blackwell, 2006), chap. 18.
4. Ibid., 194–95.
5. Wikipedia. "Bovine Somatotrophin." May 2013. http://en.wikipedia.org/wiki/Bovine_somatotropin.
6. Lubowski, Ruben, and Bucholtz et al. "2002 USDA Economic Research Service Report." 2002. http://www.ers.usda.gov/publications/eib-economic-information-bulletin/eib14.aspx#.Un63bvmsiSo
7. US EPA Ag 101 Demographics.2013. http://www.epa.gov/agriculture/ag101/demographics.html.

8. Monsanto. "Why does Monsanto sue farmers who save seeds?" 2013 http://www.monsanto.com/newsviews/Pages/why-does-monsanto-sue-farmers-who-save-seeds.aspx.
9. Charles, Dan. "As Biotech seeds falter, insecticide use surges in corn belt." *NPR.* July 9, 2013. http://www.npr.org/blogs/thesalt/2013/07/09/198051447/as-biotech-seed-falters-insecticide-use-surges-in-corn-belt.
10. Judith Jarvis Thomson, "A Defense of Abortion," *Philosophy & Public Affairs* 1, 1 (1971): 47–66.
11. Kuhse, Helga, and Peter Singer. *Bioethics: an Anthology* (Victoria, Australia: Blackwell, 2006), 162–76.
12. Business Insider. "Facts about McDonalds that will blow your mind."2011 http://www.businessinsider.com/facts-about-mcdonalds-blow-your-mind-2011-11?op=1
13. For more on this topic or to view the entire article, see "Hamburger Junction," *The Economist* (February 25, 2012): 94.
14. "Bioengineering humans to tackle climate change, says philosophers." *The Guardian.* March 14, 2012. http://www.theguardian.com/environment/blog/2012/mar/14/human-engineering-climate-change-philosophy.

Name:____________________________________ Date:________________

Review Questions

1. What is bioethics?

2. What is beneficence?

3. In what two ways can we assess risk and why is this distinction important?

4. What is genetic enhancement?

5. What is a clone?

6. What does the term "eugenic" mean and why is it a concern for bioethicists?

7. What are two moral issues that arise when discussing germline therapies?

8. How does the controversy over labeling GMO foods reflect a potential problem with respect for autonomy?

9. What are the two main ethical issues surrounding the cloning of human beings?

10. In what two relevant ways is an embryo not like a human being?

Name:____ Date:____________________

For Further Discussion

1. Would it really be so wrong to genetically enhance people to make them more moral? Choose one of the three moral theories and respond to this question from the point of view of a deontologist, a utilitarian, or a virtue ethicist.
2. If you were given the opportunity to "enhance" one of the characteristics of your offspring, which one would you choose and why? What if you and only a handful of other people were given this opportunity? Would you still do it? If so, would your action be just? Explain.
3. Go online and research AquAdvantage® Salmon. What interesting connections can you make between this product and the moral issues that have been discussed in this chapter?

Name:_______________________________ Date:_______________

Case Studies

Would You Like Fries with Your "Lab Burger"?

As we all are aware, hamburgers are big business. With McDonald's selling over 75 burgers a second,[12] it is one of the most consumed fast foods in the world. But this delicious food comes with a price. Raising cattle is a resource-intensive process, with about 30% of the world's ice-free land dedicated to either raising the plants for cattle to eat or the grassland needed for cattle to graze. As the human population grows and more individuals in countries worldwide experience increased economic prosperity, it seems to be a fact that the demand for meat will only increase in the years to come. But with so many resources already dedicated to the production of beef, will there be enough to support the growing demand? Researchers such as Dr. Mark Post at Eindhoven University in the Netherlands thinks that there will be plenty of room, and then some. Dr. Post and his team have recently been able to grow what he hopes will serve as a prototype for beef in their lab. Using stem cells from cattle muscle, Dr. Post created a sheet of cattle muscle about 1.18 inches long, .59 inches wide, and .059 inches deep. Although this amount of cattle muscle is quite small (it would take about 3,000 more of these to make a hamburger), this could be the future of meat production. Although this technology is still in its infancy, Dr. Post and his team have already devised ways for this tiny muscle to exercise and build up strength and for that extra fat to make the meat juicy, they have used the same process to produce fatty cells, which are grown separately, to be combined at the end right before the cooking process. Although this sounds just like science fiction, the benefits are quite real. The more lab meat that can be produced, the fewer cattle will exist to take up resources and pollute the environment. If this process is perfected, even countries that could not raise beef would be able to enjoy a hamburger now and again. As for vegetarians, no animals will be harmed in this type of meat production. A simply muscle biopsy is all that would be required to get the process started. So perhaps in the near future even they might be one of the billions and billions served each day.[13]

1. How is the use of stem cells to create food different from using genetically modified organisms to create food? Is this distinction important? Explain.
2. Which risk model seems most appropriate to use on this issue and why?
3. If you apply the traditional risk model, would we be more inclined to put this type of food on the market than we would if we applied the precautionary model? Explain.
4. Would you buy a hamburger made from bovine stem cells? If so, why? If not, why not?

Fix the People, Not the Climate: Bioengineering for Climate Change

In early 2012 an article ran in *The Atlantic* magazine that set the virtual world ablaze with criticism and abuse. S. Matthew Liao, a New York University Professor of Philosophy and Bioethics, had coauthored a paper suggesting that one solution to climate change that needs to be considered is that of bioengineering humans. Bioenhancements could potentially aid us in coping with the inevitable climate and resource changes that are in our future. Although the paper did not in any way endorse such a plan, it did suggest that this was a potential solution that had, up to that time, been largely ignored. Among the bioenhancements discussed by the paper were "making humans smaller via gene imprinting . . .; lowering birth rates through "cognitive enhancement"; genetically engineering eyesight to work better in the dark to help reduce the need for lighting; and the pharmacological enhancement of altruism and empathy."[14] Although he received a vast amount of criticism, Liao's paper was set to be published in the journal *Ethics, Policy and Environment* later that year and, amidst criticism, he is unapologetic about the article. He asserts that many individuals simply assumed that he was proposing bioengineering as an actual solution, something the paper does not claim. He also asserts that people who read the article and assumed it was written in support of eugenics are simply misguided.

Underlying his paper is the idea that we need to view ourselves as something more than simply biological entities. The fact that we need to change in order to mitigate the terrible effect of climate change is a given, what is not a given is how those changes will occur or what they will entail. For Liao's coauthor, Anders Sandberg, it is not just science fiction but a scientific fact that if humanity is to survive we need to move beyond what we are now and become what he calls "post human."

1. What ethical issues arise when we discuss bioengineering future humans to deal with the effect of climate change?
2. When people heard about this article they were enraged. Do you feel their reactions were warranted? Explain.
3. If genetic enhancements were proved to be quite safe and if they were made available to everyone, would there be anything wrong with making people able to see better in the dark? Explain.

CHAPTER SIX

Ethics and Technology

In 2002 Super Bowl fans were treated to an unpleasant surprise when they opened their newspapers that Monday morning. Without their knowledge or consent the government had employed facial recognition technology to scan the faces of all those attending the game. This scanning technology was linked to a database containing the images of known criminals and suspected terrorists. The hope was that this event would attract not only innocent football fans but perhaps some unsavory individuals who could easily be confronted and arrested following the game. Most fans were outraged and deeply troubled by the implications of these random scans. They complained that they had done nothing wrong and this practice constituted an invasion of their privacy since they were not informed they were under surveillance and that their images were being scanned.

The technologies that are available to us today are certainly wonders, allowing us to talk to someone halfway around the world, find our way in a new city, or even get a recipe for stir fry at the click of a button. When we think about technology it is clear that with every new technology new questions and issues about its use or misuse are in need of being answered. One of the most fundamental issues that seems to arise is that of personal privacy: what it means, who is entitled to it, and why. Was facial scanning at the Super Bowl a violation of privacy? Does privacy extend to the public realm or is it confined to our homes? What does it mean to say that our right to privacy has been violated? Why does a violation of our privacy matter in the first place? In this chapter we look not only at the concept of privacy but also look at some new technologies that have philosophers concerned about a loss of our privacy and what this may mean to us in the future.

Personal Privacy

The idea of personal privacy or a right to privacy is a foundational part of our thinking as Americans. It is this idea of privacy that helps us formulate our other rights and laws that constitute what people would say are our fundamental freedoms. But what exactly was meant by privacy and what constituted a violation of it has been a topic of discussion since the early 1800s. With the invention of the camera, the idea of a right to your image and a right to your privacy moved this discussion from the legal realm to the public realm. Before the photograph newspaper articles relied on pen and ink illustrations to make their stories more interesting and appealing to the general public. Unlike rendering an event through illustration, photographs were visual images of an actual event that could be recorded and distributed to a large number of people. The images contained not only events but the people associated with those events and it was the fact that your image in connection with an event could be distributed to strangers that troubled many people. This distribution led to the question of whether or not a person's image could appear in print without their express permission and to some of the first discussions about technology and personal privacy.

Of course, the camera was just the beginning of the wave of new technologies that were to come: video cameras, tape recorders, cell phones, and other devices that are able to capture personal information have continued to be a catalyst for discussions about personal privacy. We've come a long way since the camera and the technologies we use now are not only more sophisticated but can gather more data and disburse it more quickly to more people than those living in the 1800s could have ever dreamed. This is what makes the technologies of today so much more problematic than the invention of the camera, the telephone, or even the television. Unlike the camera or the telephone of the past, technologies today can provide us with more personal information at a faster rate. Information that would have taken many people weeks and months to compile can now be obtained by one person in a matter of minutes. Moreover, the information we can store and retrieve is not like a photograph taken with a film camera. The digital information available to us can be stored almost indefinitely and never needs to be destroyed due to lack of physical storage space.

An easy way to see an example of the ease with which personal data can be retrieved and how much data can actually be available to anyone with an Internet connection is to do an Internet search on yourself. It comes as a surprise to many people who perform this search that not only is public information such as the social networks you belong are easily accessible, but so is information about where you work, how much money you make, your current and past addresses, your phone number, where you attended school, what you look like, and even who you are related to. Fifty years ago it would take a person many months to get this diverse information about someone; now it takes less than 10 minutes. As you search it may be interesting to note how old the information is that you uncover. Information that you may have posted many years or even a decade ago may still be available and accessible to those who search long enough. The Internet stores your past as well as your present and both are available to just about anyone.

The availability and amount of personal information that can be obtained by anyone is unlike anything we have experienced in history. It would seem that with so many ways to access information about individuals, the very idea of privacy is in question. So in the contemporary world what constitutes privacy and why might it still be relevant?

If you ask a variety of people what constitutes privacy you will probably get very different answers. For many in the 21st century the idea of privacy will probably be described as a quaint notion used by people in former generations. For others concerns about privacy seem to be linked to generational attitudes or even cultural attitudes that have been fostered in their youth. Take, for example, the different attitudes toward privacy between the generation known as the *millennials* (those born between 1980 and 2000) and the baby boomers (those born between 1946 and 1964). The millennial generation grew up with the Internet, social networking, and cell phones. This generation tends to view privacy and privacy concerns as non-issues since they spend so much of their time with technologies that not only allow for but also encourage the free sharing of personal information. The baby boom generation, however, grew up in a period of time where distrust of authority and governmental agencies was a part of the wider cultural experience. Lacking social media and other fast-paced ways of gathering and getting information, this generation sees privacy as a fundamental right and is hesitant to make public their most personal information.

In addition to generational differences with respect to the importance of privacy, this idea seems to be something that is valued by more democratic societies. Many cultures who don't have a history of strong democratic ideals tend not to be as concerned about privacy and are more willing to give up privacy rights if doing so would, for example, contribute to national security (as in the case of the Super Bowl). So it would seem that the idea of privacy isn't a universal value or principle. Does this mean that the value of privacy is simply subjective in nature or could we perhaps make a case for it based on either its inherent or instrumental value? In earlier chapters, we discussed the ideas of inherent and instrumental value with regard to the environment and animals, but these terms may also apply to ideas such as privacy. Recall that something has inherent value if we value a thing for itself. On the other hand, we value something instrumentally because it gives us further opportunities to obtain other things we value or it allows us to do other things we value. In the case of inherent value it would seem unlikely that privacy would be something that we could value simply in itself. Privacy seems to be connected to the way we would like to control the actions of others with regard to our personal information and to have direct control over our personal information. That said, it would seem that there may not be inherent value in privacy; however, there is certainly a case for our privacy having instrumental value. For instance, what might maintaining our privacy allow us to have and do as individuals? For one thing, having some of our information and activities remain private allows us the freedom to act as we would like to with the understanding that no one will ever know about these actions. We would be able to purchase items of interest, read the books we like, and join organizations we believe in. When the freedom to live as we please without the prying eyes of others is protected, it seems to promote independent actions and thoughts as we know that what we do will not be scrutinized publically. Although some may argue that they still think independently and act without inhibition even if they know they are being watched, thought experiments have shown that this is not necessarily true. The very idea that your behavior might be monitored has been asserted to be a very powerful way to modify human behavior, for good or ill. In fact, philosopher Jeremy Bentham, whom you were introduced to in Chapter One, created the blueprint for a prison structure he called the "Panopticon." This building was designed as a circle with all rooms facing in upon a guard house set directly in the middle. From their cells the prisoners could never see the guards so they never knew if they were being observed or not. He asserted that since the prisoners never knew whether or not they were being watched they would more than likely conform since the fear of possibly being watched would be enough to modify their behaviors.

From the idea of an actual prison to the idea of the Panopticon as a metaphor, contemporary social critics have argued that the all-pervasive existence of monitoring technology has the same effect on our behaviors as Bentham's actual prison. From surveillance cameras on street corners to monitoring technology on the Internet, the simple thought of being watched may alter a person's behavior dramatically. If you are uncertain that this holds true, another thought experiment may help to illustrate that your behavior does change when you know (or assume) that someone is watching. The next time you are at a stop light that is monitored by a camera reflect on your inclination to speed through a yellow light at that intersection as opposed to an intersection that is not being monitored. Are you more inclined to risk running a yellow light at an intersection that is not monitored by a camera? Did the knowledge that there was a camera affect the way you behaved? What if you weren't sure if the camera was real or a decoy? Chances are you act differently at intersections that you assume are being monitored than at those you are sure are not. Simply the thought of potentially getting caught running a yellow light is enough to make you extra cautious and pay more attention to your driving habits, a classic example of the Panopticon metaphor at work. Reflecting on how we act if we know our behaviors may be monitored as opposed to knowing they are not may be sufficient evidence to assert that although privacy may have no value in itself, it may still have an amount of instrumental value sufficient enough to make a case for its preservation.

We have looked at privacy as something that may have a value above and beyond simple subjective preference, but we have yet to come to an understanding of what the term actually means. This is in part because there are many ways to define privacy, and no set definition seems to be adequate to explain all the ways we view what is private as opposed to what is public. One thing we do know about privacy is that it is a term that is in a constant state of evolution. This evolutionary process is certainly fed by advances in our technologies but is also fed by how we view ourselves. In general there are three distinct ways that the term "privacy" can be used: the historical sense or the idea of freedom from intrusion, the legal sense or freedom from interference, and most recently, control over the flow of our personal information. These three ways of viewing privacy are known as *accessibility privacy*, *decisional privacy*, and *informational privacy*, respectively.

Although most Americans take for granted that they possess something called a *right to privacy*, there are no mentions of this right in the Declaration of Independence, the Bill of Rights, or the Constitution of the United States. Many legal experts recognized this fact early on and attempted to interpret particular amendments as alluding to this right, although it was not stated distinctly. This historical sense of privacy or "accessibility privacy" is a direct result of these interpretations and can be defined as a right to having one's physical being left alone or being free from having one's physical space intruded upon.[1] Interpretations of the Fourth Amendment, which prohibits unwarranted search and seizure, is a good example of accessibility privacy in that one is protected from the government intruding on your personal space without just cause. Although accessibility privacy is linked most closely to our governmental documents, it is decisional privacy that is probably the most well known and is frequently used in the 21st century. This type of privacy is generally recognized from legal cases where certain decisions regarding our life choices or our bodies are at issue. Decisional privacy entails your ability to make free decisions about how you live your life. These decisions should be free from the intrusion of others. Possibly the most famous and controversial court case that involved the idea of decisional privacy is *Roe v. Wade* in which it was determined that neither the government nor private individuals could intrude upon the decisions women make about their bodies up to and including the right to terminate a pregnancy. Other legal battles involving critical medical procedures have also been determined along decisional privacy lines. We have seen examples of this type of right when discussing certain medical procedures in Chapter Five. Recall the example of a person who for religious reasons refused a blood transfusion. In our last chapter the ability to make your own decisions and to have others respect them was linked to the principle of respect for autonomy. Likewise, this ability is also linked to decisional privacy in that autonomous adults have a right to dictate what happens to their own bodies. Decisional privacy is acknowledged as a fundamental principle that allows for respect for autonomy and self-determination.

The third definition of privacy is a fairly recent development in the evolution of the term and it will come as no surprise that its development coincides almost directly with the invention of new technologies. By definition, informational privacy is control over one's personal information as opposed to one's physical person or one's decisions. Control over one's personal information covers what kind of information can be accessed, how much information can be accessed, and how this information can be used. We can relate this definition of privacy to the Internet search you were encouraged to do earlier in this chapter. When you searched for yourself were you surprised at the type of information available to you? Did you find information about yourself you didn't know was accessible to others? How much control do you have over your information? Can you delete it, block it, or hide it? What if you didn't want some of the information you found to be public? Do you have a choice? Although the majority of this chapter focuses on the idea of informational privacy and how recent technologies are challenging the idea that there can be such a thing, the definition of informational privacy will be modestly revised and then clarified by philosophers in an attempt to arrive at a more coherent definition of privacy as it is discussed in the 21st century. Philosophy professors such as James Moor and communications professors such as Helen Nissenbaum work to create a working definition of privacy that can cover not only the technological aspects but all aspects of our private lives.

To delineate the complex nature of privacy, philosopher James Moor incorporates all three views of privacy we have just discussed, adding a very specific element to the definition that he refers to as *situation*. Moor writes: "An individual [has] privacy in a situation with regard to others if and only if in that situation the individual [is] protected from intrusion, interference and information access by others."[2] This definition is unique not only in the way it utilizes all three definitions of privacy but in the way that Moor specifies how privacy or a lack of it does not occur in isolation. We judge privacy or a lack of it as it occurs during an activity, within a space as part of a relationship, or with regard to storage and access. It is through an examination of the various activities we are engaged in that allows us to determine when our privacy has been violated or when it has simply been lost. Situations where our privacy stands to be lost are called *naturally private situations* and situations where our privacy is violated are called *normatively private situations*.[3] A naturally private situation is one in which an individual's privacy is protected by natural or physical means, for example, a walk in the park or working alone late at the office. Although different in some respects these two situations are similar in that they both offer a physical way for a person to be alone. In these situations, if someone else were to happen to be in the same place, say you come across someone else on the trail or your coworker stops by to pick up some files, it is not considered a violation of your privacy because in these situations although you would like to be alone, you simply cannot expect that you have a right to be left alone or that you have a right to privacy in such spaces. On the other hand, a normatively private situation is one that is set apart and aside by society as a situation where you can expect that others will not invade your space. These spaces are those that are and deserve to be protected either through laws or through social prohibitions. The office space you work in is characterized very differently from the office space you have created in your home. Your home office is a place where both legally and as a part of our social rules is off limits to people except by invitation. This would be the same as a patio or a barbecue in your backyard. To have another person intrude upon your quiet nature walk in the forest is one type of situation. To have a stranger sunning herself on your patio and using your barbecue without permission are two different situations entirely. Likewise, it is an entirely different kind of action when a coworker barges in on you at the office as opposed to barging in on you, uninvited, into your home office or living room. For Moor the difference is not in the intrusion itself, but in the type of situation upon which the person intrudes. An intrusion into spaces that are designated as normatively private is a clear violation of privacy, but intrusion into public spaces is simply loss of privacy and thus we cannot say that our privacy has been violated.

Even with the addition of this critical element, some are not satisfied that this definition of privacy is adequate to help us solve moral issues surrounding information technology specifically. In an attempt to make Moor's initial definition of privacy less vague and more meaningful with regard to technological concerns, Helen Nissenbaum argues that instead of referring simply to "situations," we should look at our daily activities in terms of what she refers to as "spheres of life."[4] A sphere of life is that space in which the process, procedures, and activities we engage in are distinct from other spaces in our lives. Everyone is involved in a variety of distinct spheres throughout their day. These spheres can include our work sphere, our education sphere, our political sphere, and our leisure-time sphere. With regard to our privacy, the processes that are used within each sphere must be appropriate to the given context of the sphere and must also comply with the particular norms or rules that govern the flow of our personal information within the context of any given sphere. The kind of information that is presented in any particular sphere can be given out either appropriately or inappropriately based on norms or rules that can help us make this determination. Along with the rules that regulate the kind of information that is appropriately given out within each sphere, there are also rules of distribution that determine when our personal information should be restricted or when the flow of personal information should be limited either within a particular sphere or across the many spheres that exist in our lives. When both the appropriateness and the distribution rules are followed, our privacy is not violated, but when either of these rules is broken, a violation of privacy has occurred.

An academic example of how Nissenbaum's spheres of life model works with regard to personal privacy should make her ideas more clear. Let's imagine that your professor has you fill out a survey card on the first day of class. You are asked for some personal information, namely your age, telephone number, mailing address, and email address. It also asks if you have any allergies or medical problems and, if so, what medications you are taking. She plans to file this information in her office and she will be the only person who can access it. She assures you that she will only access this information in the event of a class cancellation or medical emergency. In this context, is divulging your personal information including your medical history appropriate? Is the way this information is distributed, to whom, and for what reason appropriate? In this case it would seem that both the information requested and its distribution are reasonable within this context. The professor seems to be following rules of conduct regarding your personal information in a way that conforms to legal and social norms so in this instance a violation of privacy has not occurred.

Now let's imagine that midway through the course the professor meets up with a friend from out of town who happens to be in the pharmaceutical industry. Her friend explains that they have a new asthma drug and they are getting ready to start testing it on human volunteers. She needs at least six volunteers that suffer from moderate to severe asthma and who are currently on medication. You know from your survey that there are at least 10 people attending your class that cited asthma as one of their medical conditions. Additionally, you know there are six of them who are currently on medication. In this situation you could provide not only the names but the addresses, phone numbers, and email addresses of these students to your friend who could then target them with advertising about volunteering as test subjects. Consider this situation and then ask yourself whether or not your professor would be violating their privacy. According to the Nissenbaum model, if the professor provides personal information to her friend, then indeed the students' rights have been violated. Although in the first instance it was perfectly appropriate for the professor to gather personal information within the context of the classroom situation, it was to be used for emergency purposes only and was to be distributed to her and her alone. If the professor were to give this information to her friend in the pharmaceutical industry, it would be a violation of the privacy norms established for the educational sphere in that students revealed this information to be used for a specific purpose and to be revealed only to specific persons. It is also a violation of the norms of distribution as the students did not give their permission for this information to be distributed to persons outside of the academic setting. Although violations of personal privacy rarely occur in academic settings, they are quite frequent in the digital world. Many people who have had experiences where their private information has been given or sold to corporations or advertisers understand how the students in our scenario would feel if they found out their professor had given away private information without their permission. In fact, many people would see a direct parallel between information selling and gathering and our professor and her friend. In thinking about what privacy means in our spheres of life one cannot help but acknowledge that one of the most prominent spheres we interact within is the virtual one. To examine this sphere in more detail we turn to some of the most current virtual practices, how they work, who uses them, and how they may threaten our privacy. These are the practices of data gathering, data exchange, and data mining.

If you've ever filled out a survey card that asks for personal information or participated in local census polls, you've participated in a data-collecting exercise. Data collection is an ancient exercise, with biblical texts referring to census and other data being recorded on a regular basis. Today data is collected by corporations, educational institutions, governments, and special interest groups. Data collection is big business in the 21st century and more and more of your personal data is being made available to individuals and organizations without your knowledge every day. As we saw when we searched for ourselves on the Internet, many things about your life can be found at the click of a button, but much of what can be known about you does not exist on the Internet itself. In addition to the tangible information that can easily be seen, a lot of intangible information exists about you that you may not even be aware of. Internet sites can monitor your transactions, cookies and can record them, even your cell phone can make your physical location known by those who have the appropriate technology. This intangible information, how it is gathered, and who has access to it raises some critical privacy issues that requires a basic understanding of the technologies and how they work to see how these critical issues unfold and their implications to personal privacy.

Contemporary Privacy Concerns

One of the most common methods that websites use to monitor your Internet information is what are called *Internet cookies*. Cookies are files that particular websites send to your computer to retrieve information about you. Their function is to enable website owners to collect information about Web users' browsing preferences. When you visit a site that uses cookies, it will send out a program that is stored on your computer which records all of your browsing activity on that particular site. If you visit the website again, the cookie will remember your browsing preferences and direct you to information of interest, suggest products for you, or simply track which items are most popular. For philosophers who discuss personal privacy there are some troubling aspects in the use of cookies to track user information. The first and probably of most concern is the fact that cookie programs are devices that are actually installed on your computer, often without your knowledge, and used by website owners and operators to extract personal information from you. The fact that the program is actually loaded onto your computer is atypical of most monitoring devices that are generally kept with the monitor and not the person being monitored. This combined with the fact that websites don't always inform visitors that their programs are being installed seems to be not only a violation of your physical property but also of your privacy.

Another way technologies can monitor both objects and sometimes individuals comes in the form of a microchip tag. Referred to as *radio frequency identification (RFID) tags*, these tiny tags can be embedded into clothing, packaging, and even living organisms, such as our pets. RFID tags work as little electronic circuits that store data complete with an antenna that broadcasts the stored data through radio waves. The data on an RFID tag can be accessed using what is known as a *RFID reader*, which is a handheld device that converts radio waves into digital data. Initially this technology was created in order to keep track of items that were bought and sold. The benefit of embedding this type of tag into an object is that the object could then be monitored through every step of the production process. If a tag was embedded at the factory it could be tracked to overseas outlets and then to specific retail stores. The retail store could then use the tag information for inventory control as well as protection from theft. RFID tags can also be injected into our pets as a way to ensure that they are identified and returned to us if they can ever lost or stolen. Law enforcement in many states have advocated these tags for schoolchildren as a way to monitor or identify them if they are abducted. But RFID technology has been incorporated into much more than inventory tracking systems and identification tags for lost pets. This technology has been installed in car keys, passports, and even placed in clothing to monitor items after they have been purchased by customers. So what do RFID tags mean to our privacy? In instances where these tags have been integrated into clothing, passports, or car keys, there are concerns that the tags could be used to pinpoint a person's location or even monitor who is wearing a particular product. Tags placed in car keys could easily provide access to not only a person's location but also about how much time a user spends on the road, what routes they frequent, and even whether or not they speed on a consistent basis. In clothing these tags could be programmed to record information about clothing size, where the item was purchased, or even how the clothing is worn or stored. Again, we are faced with a situation where the person driving the car or wearing the clothing may have no idea that a tag has been installed and that personal information is being collected. RFID tags, like the installation of Internet cookies, generally go unannounced and unnoticed by the public and again, concerns about consent and also about distribution are present with this technology too.

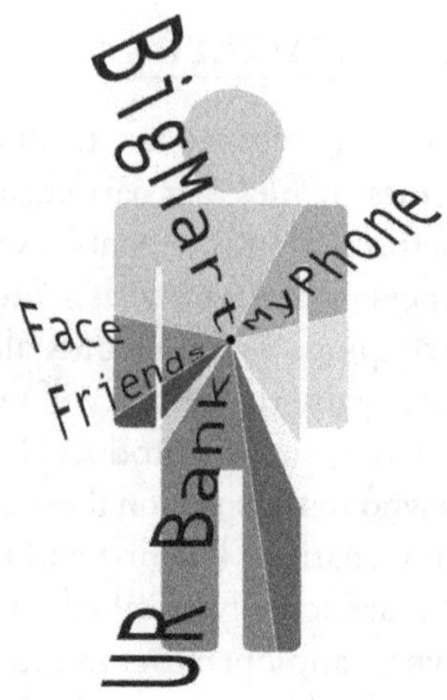

Up to this point we have looked at data gathering that seems to be connected with commercial transactions and businesses attempting to monitor our browsing and purchasing activities. But corporations and companies are not the only entities that are trying to gather information about you. It is no secret that governments also use technologies to gather information or monitor our activities. As you recall the facial recognition technology used at the Super Bowl was used by governmental agencies in an attempt to locate suspected terrorists. Certainly there are advantages to this use of technology as it may keep the American public safe by locating suspected terrorists, especially terrorists who are attending events where many people stand to be injured or killed. But as with the Super Bowl example, with every advantage this technology brings questions are raised about the privacy of innocent citizens who have no intention of wrongdoing. Government agencies have a number of technologies available that allow them to monitor and intercept phone and email messages and even gather information on our website search requests and cell phone calls. While much of this activity by governmental agencies is justified and protects us from both foreign and domestic threats, some forms of data collection do not seem to be directly related to terrorism or terrorist-related activities. Take, for example, the telephone monitoring scandal of 2013. Early that year, a whistleblower by the name of Edward Snowden came forward with information that suggested that the National Security Agency (NSA) had been collecting data on all cell phone use by American citizens. According to several reports that were made public, the NSA was compiling data that included the phone numbers of incoming and outgoing calls, the location of the person making the calls and also the amount of time persons were spending on each call. Of course there is still speculation about whether or not this was the full extent of the kind of information the NSA was gathering and some sources believe that other types of information were also being gathered without anyone's knowledge. It is unclear why the NSA needs this much specific information on its own citizens and even though it seems that the data gathering they are doing is legal, it does again raise an issue about whether or not this kind of information gathering is moral in terms of personal privacy.[5]

If we were to take a moment to assess each of these situations using Nissenbaum's idea of appropriate and inappropriate information gathering and distribution, we will note that although vastly different in some respects they are similar in many important ways.

Looking at Internet cookies we can see that immediately there are two problems: the information being given and the information being distributed. When you visit a website, you generally assume that any information about your purchases and the pages you visit is information that only you are privy to. But you are also aware that like a physical store the owner may also know what areas of the store you visit and may observe what items are of interest to you. If a website owner is informed about the places you visit on her website and she keeps that information contained on the website, then it would seem that this is not a violation of privacy as one would expect a retailer to know what you purchased or what items were of interest to you. However, the fact that cookies are placed on your computer without your knowledge may in fact be a violation. Remember that, like the example of the student and the professor, you need to be informed that information is being gathered and you also need to be afforded the opportunity to opt out if you don't want to share personal information. So merchants monitoring our purchases may not violate our privacy, but not being informed that this is being done just may violate our privacy rights. Additionally, if the Web owner or operator decides to sell our information to another party and does so without our consent, similar to the professor giving our personal information to her friend without our permission, a violation of distributional norms has occurred and if this happens our privacy has again been violated. Similarly, it would seem that the use of RFID tags poses no problem in the event we know that the tag is there and we are aware of what information is being transmitted and who has access to it. Micro-chipping pets or even small children is not entirely problematic insofar as those involved who can give consent understand what is being done and are aware of the information that can be accessed. When it comes to RFID tags in keys or clothing again whether or not this would be a violation of either information giving, gathering, or distribution would be contingent upon whether or not the person who owns the keys or buys the clothing is aware of this technology, understands who has access to it, and grants permission to use the information that may be accessed. By now you may be noticing a pattern in our thinking about the giving and distribution of information and that is knowledge and consent. This is going to also be the case with the NSA and its data-collecting activities. Here again we can see that our privacy was clearly violated in that a government entity was gathering information that we were not aware we were divulging. Within the context of a private citizen making an ordinary phone call, it seems that this level of monitoring is inappropriate (an appropriate context may be one in which there is reasonable suspicion of illegal activity). Likewise, the distribution of our personal information is not controlled by us and cannot be controlled. We have no idea who can access this information and what this information is used for. According to Nissenbaum's theory, this would be an inappropriate distribution.

It seems that one of the biggest concerns that we face when trying to frame issues of informational privacy is that often we are not informed that data is even being gathered. Without knowing this it is very difficult to control the distribution of this information. The difficulty increases as many businesses and corporations have been created for the sole purpose not only of collecting but also of merging the electronic records of individuals.

Simple data collection has limited uses for corporations and advertisers but collections of data or the merging of a person's personal data can prove to be quite useful. Information merging is a process by which companies or other entities will share your information with other companies or organizations. For example, when you apply for a car loan the dealership will run a credit check to see what sort of financing for which you are eligible. When you apply for a job, certain background checks can legitimately be performed before you are hired and if you buy insurance for your home other personal information will be requested before the insurance is granted. In each situation, we have freely given relevant personal information to those persons involved in our transactions. But what if these businesses turned around and shared the information they had gathered on you with the other businesses? What if the insurance company now had your credit score and your car dealership had your background check? What if all this information was in turn combined with information about your political affiliations, the websites you visited, and whether or not you frequently speed on the freeway? The practice of taking unrelated bits of information about a person and then sharing them with other businesses or storing them in a central location is known as *data merging*. Indeed, *third-party merging*, that is, merging of your data by an outside company or corporation, goes on quite frequently and the results of this merging can be sold to other companies, businesses, corporations, or governments to help them get a more complete picture of who you are as a person.

Computer matching is a process that works in a similar way. Computer matching is used to merge computerized records and then cross-checking this information in two or more unrelated databases to produce matching records or hits. Fans at the Super Bowl in 2002 were unwilling participants in the process of computer matching. After the computer took a photo of a fan it was entered into a database and run against a known criminal database and a suspected terrorist database. If the computer was able to come up with any "hits," those who were monitoring the program would know that this was a person of interest and could apprehend them either during or after the game. Computer matching with visual images is one of the most sophisticated forms of computer matching. It usually involves taking large databases of input information being run through specific algorithms that can lead to certain kinds of information being traced back to a single person via a Social Security card, driver's license, passport, or other individual specific item of information. Once relevant data has been filtered it can then be stored in a number of places or can be placed in a central database for later use. Routine checks of the data can be performed to include more personal information about you as it becomes available, creating an even more detailed description of you. Again this information can be used to apprehend criminals, catch people who regularly cheat on their taxes, or even locate terrorists, but it again encourages us to think about whether this practice is violating our privacy either through our inability to monitor and determine the amount and type of personal information that is available or whether or not this matching is a violation of the norms of distribution of our information, since we did not give companies and business entities permission to use our information to cross-reference other information about us. Two additional considerations need to be added to the idea of data collection they are the longevity of the data and also the risk that legitimate databases may be hacked. As you may recall, one of the reasons why modern technology is of such a concern surrounding issues of privacy is because the information is not only eternal but data can be collected indefinitely. The databases set up by the NSA to gather our cell phone information are vast enough to collect more information than most of us can comprehend and this information is eternal, that is it can be stored for an indefinite amount of time and will exist no doubt longer than we will. That means the information has the potential to exist through many presidential elections, global upheavals, and any other events that may be in our future. So who will have access to this data 10, 20, or even 50 years from now? What will they do with it (if anything)? The issues of distribution in this case are ones not just of present time and space, but also of future time and space. If we are not in control of our information today, it is quite certain we will have even less control as the years progress.

A final and legitimate concern for those of us who understand computers and electronic information is that it is never completely safe. Even information that we freely give to banks and businesses can be hacked and stolen. Computer hacking is becoming more sophisticated, with criminals hacking everything from the Sony PlayStation to the U.S. government, and stealing everything from credit card numbers to nuclear weapons codes. There is no reason to think that our personal information could not be hacked. Not only does this bring to light issues of privacy but if you recall in our last chapter in discussions about the nature and measurement of risk you will see that any time we make electronic information available there is always the risk that those who don't have permission to use it will.

The practice of data mining is very different from data gathering in that it is a form of analysis that involves the indirect gathering of personal data that is then analyzed for implicit patterns. These patterns often generate new and often nonobvious information that is then classified, categorized, and linked to individuals. The categories and classifications created through this process might involve individuals in groups or classifications that they themselves are unaware exist. One of the most interesting and controversial parts about data mining is that the information generated about individuals is not explicit information, it is not information that appears or exists in any database; rather, it is implicit information that means that the information obtained through data mining does not exist in the form of an electronic record but is the result of the process of merging explicit information. Since no concrete data is actually obtained, any information collected through this process is considered public and is not confidential. Additionally the information obtained through the mining process is not exchanged between databases but usually resides in a single database within a large data warehouse.

Unlike data collection, data mining seems to bypass many of the concerns about information giving and information distribution that were criteria for a violation of privacy in that it would seem that no confidential information was being obtained and no information was being distributed across databases. So how might this type of implicit data gathering affect us and how might it raise concerns about personal privacy? To help us understand what concerns may be raised, it might be useful to look at a concrete example of how data mining is done and some of the consequences that may arise from this process.

Let's say that you are a customer applying for a bank loan. You are asked a series of questions about how much money you make, how much you have in savings, how long you have been at your current job or residence, and how much outstanding debt you have. All of these questions are perfectly appropriate to the situation or the business sphere of your life. This of course means that you are willing to fill out the forms that request this information and you are also willing to give these forms to the bank in the hopes they will grant you the loan. But what if your information was mined? By mining the information received by the bank certain information patterns may emerge that suggest that individuals within your age group, who earn the amount of money you do per year, who have the same amount of outstanding debt that you have, and who have been at a job as long as you have are also very likely to quit their current job and move to a larger city. In addition to being in the category of likely to quit your job and move to a larger city, the mining program also reveals that persons in your line of work, with similar work experience and similar amounts of money saved, are also more likely to default on your loans within the first 2 years. Now the idea of leaving your current job and moving somewhere else are not part of any of your future plans. In fact, you love your job and were hoping to stay where you are and start a family. But the data-mining program has revealed that contrary to what you assume you will do, you are likely to do otherwise. This implicit information runs contrary to the explicit information and shows you to be a high-risk investment. If the bank chooses to use mined information to help them determine your eligibility, you may be denied the loan since statistically you do fall into a high-risk investment group.

It may seem far-fetched but data profiling of this kind has actually occurred in instances where credit card companies have cancelled consumer credit cards or reduced the card limits based on information obtained through data mining. Consumers who lived in a certain town, had certain shopping habits, and whose homes were held by a particular title company had their cards cancelled without warning even though they had good credit scores and had always paid their bills on time. In this case, the credit card company based their decision on risk factors that were obtained from the data-mining process and not from actual explicit consumer data. But data mining is not confined to transactions that take place in the physical world. Many websites buy and sell consumer transaction information, which allow other businesses to create a detailed

hypothetical profile of many consumers. Even sites that don't sell you a product can be involved in buying and selling your information to companies who can then either market directly to you or in turn can monitor your online use to generate general patterns that can again be bought, sold, and then mined. One of the most famous examples of data mining on the Internet involved the social networking site Facebook. In 2007, the site announced that it would be trying a new marketing tool that would allow users to share their online activities with their friends. To make this information available, external websites would send purchasing and browsing information back to Facebook, which would then be uploaded into an individual's news feed page. This practice became controversial when it was revealed that it allowed Facebook to disclose what external website users were visiting and what purchases were being made and then displaying this information to the users' "friends." Many people were surprised to see their purchases and website activity displayed without their permission but more people were surprised to know that this information was not just shared among "friends"; rather, this information was being shared with businesses in order to market products to consumers. Again, this is a form of data mining in that one site compiles and displays your online habits in order to provide marketers with vital information about potential interests, browsing preferences, and purchasing habits. These user profiles can be used to generate profits by looking for patterns implicit in your purchases and then marketing products directly to you, without your knowing you are being targeted.

Moral questions surrounding the practice of data mining are more complex than simple data gathering or data monitoring since we are not dealing with any personal information directly nor are we faced with a situation where our personal information is being distributed to others in the same way that data gathering seemed to do. So how do we frame privacy issues and data mining? One way we can look at this issue is to think about the difference between information being used as explicit data versus information being used as implicit data. In the case of the bank loan, the credit card, and Facebook newsfeed, it would seem that individuals did offer all of this information freely, but in all three cases individuals offered the explicit information to be used explicitly, that is, they offered concrete data to be used to determine whether they qualify for a loan, pay bills on time, or shop at a certain website. In none of these situations did they give companies permission to use their information implicitly. They had no idea companies would use it to generate general patterns or create categories or classifications above and beyond the explicit data itself. In this sense, data mining violates the distribution principle in that individuals did authorize the use of their personal information in the explicit sense but they did not authorize its use in the implicit sense.

Thus far we have looked at new technologies and some of the emerging questions they raise about personal privacy. It is obvious that with new technologies new questions will arise that philosophers, lawmakers, and citizens attempt to respond to, often attempting to figure out the moral and legal implications as we go along. In addition to privacy issues, very likely the second most discussed philosophical idea to raise moral questions is that of virtual and intellectual property. Like issues surrounding privacy, issues surrounding intellectual property have been the topic of conversations for hundreds of years, with the concept of property in general being much older. But the idea of virtual property is something quite new and how virtual intellectual property is protected, disbursed, and managed is the next topic for discussion.

As with our discussion of privacy, it would be good to start with an understanding of what property is, how it is a person comes to obtain her or his property, and the distinct concepts and issues surrounding intellectual property in particular. Then we can move to a discussion about the idea of virtual property and why it can be so morally problematic. Let's start our discussion with a very famous (perhaps infamous) website whose "property" will help us understand these concepts more clearly.

Property and Ownership

In the late 1990s Shawn Fanning created Napster, the first website that allowed Internet users to upload and share music. The MP3 format allowed anyone with a computer to upload or download music for free. Hundreds, thousands, and eventually millions of files were available for download and millions of users took advantage of the technology. It wasn't long before Napster was being sued by artists and record companies for the illegal distribution of copyrighted music and its free use days were over almost as soon as they began. Napster reemerged as a pay-per-song site but the idea of the free flow of information, music, movies, and everything else had taken off and for every pay-per-song site there are at least two or three free sites that still allowed file sharing. It was the advent of this technology that fueled discussions about intellectual and virtual property and the efficacy of the legal protection of both.

One of the arguments proposed by Fanning and others who supported sites like Napster is that the digital information that was being exchanged originated on a CD and that CD was legitimately purchased. That said, the CD was technically the property of the purchaser and as such can legally be shared, copied, or even destroyed by that person. This description of what counts as property and what one is allowed to do with that property is a description that in general terms most of us would agree with. The CD is a physical object and one certainly has a right to do what one chooses with physical property. But people in the legal and philosophical community tend to think of the idea of property less in terms of a physical object and more in terms of relationships to an object. Take the CD example. In this case there seem to be three elements involved in owning the CD as property. First there is the owner, me; there is the object, the CD; and there is my relationship to other individuals with respect to the object (the CD). In this sense the owner controls what happens to the CD relative to others around them. The owner controls who gets to listen to the CD, who gets to borrow it, or who gets it when they die. So, the idea of property is a bit more complicated an idea than just the possession of a simple object; it is how that object is controlled, by whom, and for what reasons.

Now this is a very good illustration of a physical object, and the philosophical theories that have been proposed to determine not only what property is but who is entitled to the property and why can be traced back hundreds of years. Three very influential philosophers have helped to shape our views of property: John Locke, Jeremy Bentham, and G. W. F. Hegel. At the time of their writings, there was no such thing as virtual property but intellectual and physical property existed so it is on the latter that we focus our attention.

Possibly the most influential of the three views is that of John Locke. In many of his works, Locke argues that what nature provides should be made available to all persons in common.

A person's claim to property comes in when a person through her or his own labor "mixes" the natural world with their own toil and sweat. So a forest full of trees belongs to all in common, but if I go in and chop down a tree and then turn that tree into firewood, that firewood belongs to me since I took a natural object and "mixed" it with my labor. Similarly, if I earn the money, drive to the store, stand in line, and purchase a CD it is through the labor of earning the money and preforming all the tasks to acquire the CD that makes this object mine and no one else's. For Locke, property is intimately tied to labor and if one works for it, one can claim it as property. It seems that for Locke the ability to own property is a natural right, that is, we are owed the right simply by being human. By now, this idea should sound familiar to you. Indeed, the idea that a human being is entitled to property just because one is a human being is similar to the ideas proposed by Kant and those who followed his philosophy. In this sense Locke is following the thinking of philosophers such as Kant when he states that ownership of property is something all humans are entitled to simply because they are humans. But as we all know the amount of physical space or the number of physical objects is always finite and limited and so there will always be a certain amount of competition when it comes to the ability to own things. How then do we decide who gets how much of what? A critical part of Locke's theory on property is called the *Lockean proviso*, which states that because the objects that can be owned through our labor are exclusive and limited in nature (exclusive meaning that only one person can be said to own a thing at any one time), no one person should ever be able to own all of any given object, regardless of how hard they work. So with the proviso, if we return to the forest example, we are fully within our right to cut down one tree and make the firewood that is subsequently owned, but one is not within one's right to cut down all the trees and call all the firewood one's own. In a similar way, you are well within your right to buy the CD of your choice, but you are not within your right to buy all copies of this particular CD, regardless of how much wealth you have earned. So for Locke, property is earned through toil and labor, with the stipulation that a person can't own everything or even all of one object.

The second theory of property stems from the utilitarian principle of maximizing the good. For a utilitarian if we protect personal property, then everyone in our society will benefit and this will result in an increase in happiness or pleasure for all. For a utilitarian, people who belong to a society in which they know that whatever they invent, create, or produce will be owned by them and protected in a way that is profitable to them will want to produce more and better objects and ideas and this will benefit society as a whole. Like all applications of the principle of utility, the idea of ownership is focused on the practical ways to promote happiness for as many beings as possible. As is so often the case with this theory, it is easy to apply and much easier to use than are other moral theories. If we were to discuss the CD, we could argue the utilitarian position in two ways. The first way would be to look at the CD itself, the object. Now it makes sense that being able to actually own an object means one is able to determine who uses it and this is to our economy. We buy things to own and everyone profits: we get what we want, the record company gets what they want, and the artist gets what he or she wants. This type of ownership encourages consumers to buy products, the economy grows, and everyone benefits. On the other hand, artists who see that success is rewarded monetarily would be encouraged to create even more music, and would also encourage others to create and invent knowing that the product that is produced is owned and will thus bring the creator reward in the form of money, fame, or other positive benefits.

The final theory of how one comes to own property is that presented by philosopher G.W.F. Hegel, a 19th-century follower of Kant. For Hegel, property ownership is not about your labor nor is it about maximizing societal happiness; rather, a person is entitled to an object if the object is an extension of the person's personality (or, in Hegel's words, their being or their soul). If a person creates an object that reflects him- or herself in some way, that person owns that object and it should be left up to the person as to how the object is viewed, distributed, or used. Returning to the CD example, this creates an interesting split between owning a physical thing (the disc) and owning the songs on the disc. There is no doubt that because you paid money for the CD that you own this particular object. However, according to this theory, you do not own the content. You may be able to listen to the songs as often as you like, but you do not have the right to manipulate the song to create your own song, to claim that the song on the CD is yours, or to use the song for profit without express permission of the author.

Physical Property versus Intellectual Property

A good example of this split can be illustrated by looking at the late 1980s practice of music sampling. Sampling involves an artist taking one or more musical elements from another artist and incorporating this into his or her music. This had gone on for many years in clubs and the street music known as rap, but it became a legal issue when those who had sampled music were now creating albums where the sampled music was making a substantial sum of money, not for the original composer but for the sampler. One of the most famous examples of this was when the artist Vanilla Ice created the song "Ice, Ice Baby." This song contained the bass line from Queen's song "Under Pressure," and used it without the express permission of that band. Now, although the writers and producers for Vanilla Ice had access to that song via CD or LP, and although they may have even legitimately purchased the song or the sheet music for the song, the bass line was not a product of their own creation, that is, it was the expression of the personality of Freddie Mercury and Queen, not of Vanilla Ice. In this example, Hegel's distinction is made clear as the physical object is not the object in question but the bass line that was an extension of one person being used without express permission by another person.

A discussion about the seemingly split ownership between physical and nonphysical property that seems to be emphasized in the Vanilla Ice example is a good way to start a discussion about the differences between a physical object and what has been referred to as an *intellectual object*. An intellectual object or intellectual property consists of something that is nonphysical or nontangible in its nature. Intellectual objects are usually creative works or inventions that are expressions of ideas, such as the bass line in the Queen song. So while the CD is a physical, tangible object, the lyrical content of that CD is a nonphysical, nontangible expression by an individual. It is clear that physical objects differ in their nature from intellectual objects in that one is tangible and the other is not but there are additional ways in which these objects are distinct. Where there seems to be a limit to the number of physical objects that can be produced or owned, intellectual objects tend to be unlimited or what is known as *nonexclusionary*.

Images © Shutterstock, Inc. Modified by the author.

The idea that there are limits within the physical world creates a powerful case for ownership; after all, if I own an iPod, no one else can also own that iPod. My ownership of the iPod makes this item exclusionary, that is, two persons can't own it at once. Likewise, although the supply seems limitless, in reality there are only so many iPods to go around. This is not to say that they are scarce or that demand cannot eventually be met, but it means that there will always be competition and rivalry surrounding these particular physical objects. Now consider the music contained on the iPod. If someone has added a Lady Gaga song to their iPod, this does not mean that there is one less song on the Internet for someone else to purchase. In fact, there is technically an unlimited supply of that same Lady Gaga song available for download from iTunes. When we look at intellectual property, especially property that exists in part due to emerging technologies, we do not have the same limitations as we do with physical property either in terms of availability or in terms of practical limitation. One can own hundreds, thousands, or even millions of MP3 files without being troubled by thoughts of loss of physical space. Additionally, one need not worry about having to compete with others to buy Gaga's next album; there is no competition or rivalry since there is always another digital copy readily available.

The second distinction between an intellectual object and a physical object is that intellectual objects such as an idea or other abstraction cannot be owned in the same way that a physical object can be owned. Certainly you can have a unique idea, but what distinguishes this idea from other ideas? In order for any idea of abstract physical entity such as an invention to be owned, it would seem that one must somehow create a physical manifestation of the object. For artists and authors that tangible object could be the painting or the book and for inventors that object could be tangible drawings and descriptions of a functional object. So it would seem that an intellectual object needs to somehow be made manifest as a tangible object in order for it to be owned or declared property. Again, if we were to return to the MP3 file of Lady Gaga's music it would seem that we could call the song she sings an intellectual object manifest physically since it is her idea that was recorded, which technically makes it more tangible than an idea, correct? Well, again, this is where the digital technologies make a concrete response to this question difficult. After all, computer files such as MP3 files are not physical, tangible objects. The software is essentially lines of programming code, which itself is not expressed or fixed in any tangible way in any tangible medium. Unlike a book or a painting, the song that is expressed through code is not a physical entity. This holds true for any software material that is available to individuals for purchase. Video games, movies, and even programming software such as Microsoft Office are all programmed lines of code. The inclusion of computer software into the debate surrounding intellectual property becomes even more complicated when one understands that computer software is not one single code consisting of 0s and 1s. Software requires an object code, a source code, and an executable code in order to work properly. So when we try to determine ownership of an MP3 file containing a song by Lady Gaga, we are looking at a nontangible object that was created by an artist, recorded by a record label, purchased by a consumer, and translated by one program into data that needs one, two, or more additional data codes to upload, download, and transfer the information to a listening device. Since the song is nonexclusionary in nature it can be uploaded and downloaded an infinite number of times and those who paid for the song at a pay-per-song site are now in some sense owners of the song. It would seem that the very nature of digital information precludes it from ever being owned as there are so many potential owners and too few ways to determine who in fact should be awarded this title.

If we were to look at the Lockean view, the idea that one owns what one toils and sweats for would not seem to apply directly to intellectual materials because these materials cannot be thought of as physical property and the toil that is usually involved in making such items is not the sort of toil that results in the sweat of physical labor, that is, not the kind Locke had in mind. Moreover, the objects that are being created or produced are not exclusionary in nature, that is, there is an endless supply of the object so there is no need for competition. That said, it would seem that Locke's proviso is an unnecessary element in our ownership discussions in that one can never take all of the software files in the same way one could take all of the trees or all of the land.

Looking at the issue of property from the stance of a utilitarian, one could certainly come up with a number of social reasons why intellectual property should be protected. If individuals who create software or other virtual products do not have their investments protected, there may be little incentive for individuals to spend their time and energy creating new products. If this were true society would certainly be worse off as innovations would simply not happen. So if it could be shown that the wealth that comes from creating an intellectual object is the sole or the largest contributing factor to innovation and creation, it would follow that it is important to a society to have all intellectual objects protected than to make it free for everyone to use or to own. Again the utilitarian view has the advantage of being practical with many of the assumptions it makes measurable in some way. For example, all we would need to do on this view would be to supply evidence that money is one of the most important motivations behind creation and innovation. If we could do this, then we could create a strong case for protecting certain kinds of intellectual property. Other kinds of intellectual property, however, may not have been produced with money or tangible gains in mind. For example, many people who create music or a poem or artwork may be motived by the creative process itself, so the idea of protecting them because there is economic gain to be had may not work as well. So although the utilitarian model may do a better job explaining why we should protect intellectual property, it seems that it too has some limitations.

It would seem that the third alternative, the personality theory, stands a good chance at being a theory that can articulate meaningfully why intellectual property should be protected. If people who create the property are expressing their personality through their work, then it stands to reason that they should own it. But in that case who owns the MP3 file? The recording artist or the programmer who created a program that would digitally hold the information being accessed? Both could argue that their creation is an expression of their personality. So who can actually lay claim to the file? Again it would seem that the complexity of the technology and the abstract nature of the product create difficulties for this particular theory.

Thus far in our discussion of intellectual property we have discussed reasons why digital information of certain kinds or types should be considered owned by a particular group or individual. We have also discussed some ways in which philosophers have attempted to justify ownership of objects. To end our discussion on intellectual property it may be interesting to discuss at least one reason why digital information should not be privatized, that is, a reason to allow unrestricted distribution and modification of digital information. A final alternative that has been proposed regarding ownership of intellectual property comes from an unlikely place. The ancient philosopher Aristotle has been used by some contemporary thinkers to attempt to solve the ownership problems that certain kinds of intellectual property create. The theory has been applied to computer software in particular, but for some this is only the beginning of a more widespread application. As we discussed in Chapter One, Aristotle believed that every being and every object has a *telos* or a goal (purpose) and every being or object that meets that goal exhibits an excellence. Recall that when Aristotle asked what a human being does well or what the goal of a human being is he responded by saying that a one's purpose or goal is to reason well. Now if we were to apply the very same question to digital information as philosopher Michael MacFarland did in his article, "Intellectual Property, Information and the Common Good,"[6] one would need to ask in an Aristotelian fashion, "What is the goal or purpose of digital information?" Although digital information can be understood in terms of expression and also as something socially functional, information itself seems to have an even more fundamental purpose and that is to communicate these expressions and to share ideas with others. If MacFarland is right and this is the ultimate goal or purpose of information, then it would seem that arguing for ownership or regulation of virtual information is in essence creating a barrier in the flow of information and is thus not allowing information to fulfill its purpose, which is to be shared. Information should be allowed to fulfill its purpose by being available uninhibitedly to as many individuals as possible so a focus on the ease with which information can be obtained as opposed to the ease with which it can be controlled would be an Aristotelian solution to intellectual property and ownership.

Nanotechnology and Nano Ethics

A look at the ethical issues surrounding technology in the 21st century wouldn't be complete without a look at one of the most bizarre and controversial types of technology to be developed in the first half of the 21st century: nanotechnology. Nanotechnology covers a broad range of disciplines and materials, from biological organisms to mechanical robots. With this field being so diverse it is a challenge to create a definition that encompasses all aspects of it, but in general an innovation is thought to be nanotechnology if it manipulates studies or designs artificial, natural, or technological objects at the nanometer scale. A *nanometer* is a unit of measure used at the atomic level, so when we say something is "nanotechnology," what we are saying is that the object or some critical aspects of that object is being manipulated, studied, or created at about one billionth of a meter. It is difficult for most of us to understand just how small one billionth of a meter actually is, so let's think of it in terms of an object we are all familiar with: the human hair. If you were to look at the diameter of an average human hair you would be looking at an object that is about 60,000 nanometers in size. So when we talk about nanotechnology we are generally talking about functional technology that cannot be seen without the use of a powerful electron microscope. Although the technology of the very small is still in its infancy, there are many places where it is currently being used. One of the most common uses of this technology is in computers and cell phones. The development of nanotechnology has allowed us to create smaller processors, amplifiers, and circuitry that gives us devices that are smaller, more lightweight, and more durable than their predecessors. Another way that nanotechnology extends the life of our electronics is through the creation of nano coatings, which are protective coatings developed to protect electronic equipment. Called Liquipel, this coating is 1,000 times thinner than a human hair but can protect our electronic devices from damage by liquid spills or accidental immersion.[7]

Though most commonly thought of as being connected with electronics and computers, nanotechnology is being used in medicine and criminal forensics work as well. We have already seen an example of nanotechnology in our chapter on bioethics, where we discussed the use of viruses that have been manipulated to act as vectors for DNA therapies. Along similar lines, stem cells referred to as nano ghosts are being programmed to target and destroy certain cancer tumors with a good deal of success, leading some researchers to speculate that nano ghosts will one day be as routine a medical procedure to cure cancer as chemotherapy is a routine procedure today.[8]

Of course, with this technology still being so new there are many more speculations about its future use than there are uses at the present time. Some speculation for future use has included the manufacturing of nano machines or nanites that could be programmed for a variety of tasks, including clean-up of toxic chemical spills, the creation of food at the molecular level, the creation of computers the size of a sugar cube, or the creation of undetectable surveillance equipment for military purposes. Probably the most interesting idea in nanotechnology is the creation of self-replicating nanobots who will be capable of doing many of the tasks just mentioned by replicating the exact number and type of bots specific to the particular task or problem.

Like the areas of bioethics that include genetic enhancements and cloning, much of the ethical issues we face when exploring nanotechnology have more to do with what we don't know and can't predict as opposed to what we do know and can predict. As you may recall in the last chapter, the nature of risk is an important concept to understand when thinking about the possible consequences as opposed to known consequences. This holds true with our use of emerging technologies as well. With nanotechnology, both the traditional and precautionary models can be used as a means to determine whether or not a particular nanotechnology should be created or used.

Apart and aside from the risk issues created by a myriad of unknowns in the area of nanotechnology, two specific concerns have been explored by philosophers with regard to these technologies. The first is concern over privacy and control issues and the second had to do with the potential problems created by runaway nanobots.

The first issue should be quite familiar to you at this point as issues of privacy and control have been the focus of many of our discussions regarding technologies thus far, with privacy issues being related to different types of available data gathering and control being related to not only the distribution of personal information but also the distribution of intellectual property.

Nanotechnology, like many other technologies, can be used for good or ill. The positive advances in technologies that fight cancer or fix genetic defects are examples of this technology being used in ways that will only improve our quality of life. But some philosophers are skeptical about nanotechnology as it also holds the ability to be used to monitor or manipulate behaviors. Some are concerned that the small size of this technology will be used to hide intelligence-gathering nanobots in everyday items, allowing individuals to pinpoint our locations, monitor our vital signs, or even send back personal data without our knowledge. What's more, this technology need not be mechanical, and could consist of organic organisms, making it impossible to detect. The privacy issues that we discussed in the first part of this chapter could all be easily applied to potential problems with nanotechnology, although certainly you would need to add risk factors to these discussions in addition to discussions of privacy since it is not yet possible to do many of the things that philosophers and skeptics are fearful may occur.

Lastly, some scientists and philosophers have speculated about the potential problem of runaway nanobots, sometimes referred to as the "gray-goo scenario" or "gray-goo problem." The scenario occurs in the far-flung future where nanotechnology has progressed in such a way that we are now able to create self-programming and self-replicating nanobots. In this scenario nanobots either escape from a lab or something goes wrong with their programming that makes them deadly not only to humans but to all life on earth. In one variation of this scenario, scientists create a nanobot called a *biological assembler*. This nanobot has been programmed to take human garbage and transform it into food. This process takes place at the molecular level and through rearranging one molecule at a time (e.g., a rotten banana peel transformed by a nanobot into a fresh watermelon). Of course, these "assemblers" have been programmed to do only this specific task and have also been programmed to break down and "die" if their programming goes awry. But imagine that something goes horribly wrong with the programming and this nanobot's program tells it to turn all living organic matter into rotten banana peels. Now also assume that our secondary system to kill the nanobot fails. What then? Since the nanobot is self-replicating, it will start to replicate this damaged program, creating other nanobots that are reprogrammed to turn us all into rotten banana peels and since there is no backup program to prevent it from replicating, this means that on a molecular level we would be assaulted by tiny beings that would take us apart molecule by molecule and then reassemble us. The gray goo mentioned earlier is actually referring to what would be left behind once these tiny bots did their job. In our scenario what would be left over are piles and piles of rotten banana peels, not exactly gray goo but not a more pleasant way to meet our end either. This scenario really hinges not so much on any general principle we have discussed thus far, but really comes down to looking at the potential risks and harms caused by this technology.

We looked at harm in an earlier chapter with regard to animals and how they can be harmed. Recall that harm is simply when something bad happens to a being. This certainly explains the gray-goo scenario as we are harmed when turned into a rotting banana. Although we have defined harm in a previous chapter, here we should look at the nature of harm and how we can weigh the risks of harm more efficiently if we understand certain distinctions in how any particular harm comes about. The gray-goo scenario is just one of many ways that nanotechnology can potentially harm us, two of which have been discussed in this chapter. It can be used by people with bad intent to monitor or spy on us and it can escape or not work correctly due to human error. These two categories are referred to as *harm by misuse* and *harm by mistake*. The third category of harm that was not covered in detail in this chapter is *direct or intentional harm.*

Looking at harm through these different lenses can allow us to pinpoint exactly what is at issue morally and perhaps separate the technology itself from the human intent or human nature involved in particular scenarios. If something is described as a direct harm that means that it has been shown to be likely to cause a harm or that it indeed does cause a harm. So if we were to show that nanotechnology is directly harmful, we would need to show that by creating the technology or the organism we are fairly certain that *X* number of people are likely to be harmed. This type of harm seems connected to the development of technology itself and it would be at this level of risk assessment that we would indeed need to employ either the traditional or the predictive risk assessment models to determine whether or not we should proceed with this kind of technology. If we do this, it seems that the technology by itself has not been shown to be harmful or to have any directly harmful effects associated with it.

But what about the second and third types of harms, the harms from which we get our two moral concerns about this technology? In the gray-goo scenario it would seem that we are clearly looking at a case of human error or a mistake. Either there were not enough precautions taken in the lab or with regard to the programming. Either way the gray-goo scenario is not created by the technology itself but rather from human nature, that is, the nature of our fallibility. Humans are flawed and mistakes can be made despite all the precautions we take. It would be difficult to place direct blame on nanotechnology in the gray-goo situation as the nanobots were just executing the programs they were given and the lab techs were just going about their business. Everyone involved was certainly well meaning and well intentioned, just an unfortunate mistake occurred.

In the first case, the case of nanotechnology being used to monitor or control people without their knowledge again doesn't seem to be a direct result of the technology but a direct result of the misuse of that technology. Personal privacy issues surrounding nanotechnology are really issues of misconduct by other humans and are only indirectly related to technological advances. This should lead us to question of who has access to this technology and what is its intended use, but from this we cannot conclude that nanotechnology in itself is directly harmful to human beings, nor could we argue that this technology can be shown to be directly harmful. These questions may lead us to moral issues such as returns to issues of privacy or other issues that are related but are not directly a product of nanotechnology itself.

Notes

1. Tavani, Herman, *Ethics and Technology* (Hoboken, NJ: Wiley, 2011), 137.
2. James Moor, "Towards a Theory of Privacy for the Information Age," *Cyberethics: Moral, Social, and Legal Issues in the Computer Age*, eds. R.M. Baird, R. Ramsower, and S. E. Rosenbaum (New York: Promethus Books, 2000), 207.
3. Ibid., 200–212.
4. Helen Nissenbaum, "Privacy as contextual Integrity," *Washington Law Review* 79, 1, 2004 119–57.
5. Lee, Timothy, "Everything you need to know about the NSAs phone record scandal," *Washington Post*, June 6, 2013. http://www.washingtonpost.com/blogs/wonkblog/wp/2013/06/06/everything-you-need-to-know-about-the-nsa-scandal/.
6. Michael C, Macfarland, "Intellectual Property, Information and the Common Good," *Readings in CyberEthics,* eds. R. A. Spinello and H.T. Tavani (Sudbury, MA: Jones and Bartlett, 2004), 294–304.
7. Nanotechnology Now, "Liquipel." http://www.nanotech-now.com/news.cgi?story_id=44324.
8. Nanowerk, "Highly Effective Tumor Targeting Platform with Nanoghosts." July 26, 2013. http://www.nanowerk.com/spotlight/spotid=31548.php.
9. Rundel, Michael, "3D Microprinter Builds Spaceship Thinner than a Human Hair in 50 seconds," *The Huffington Post.* March 18, 2013. http://www.huffingtonpost.co.uk/2013/03/18/3d-microprinter-builds-spacecraft-nanoscribe_n_2899301.html.
10. Kelly, Heather, "Facebook Home, Privacy and You," *CNN TECH.* April 5, 2013. http://www.cnn.com/2013/04/05/tech/social-media/facebook-home-privacy.

Name:____ Date:__________________

Review Questions

1. What invention is credited with spawning the first questions about privacy?

2. What makes technologies today more problematic than historical technology when it comes to issues of privacy?

3. Is privacy important to everyone? Explain.

4. Is personal privacy intrinsically or instrumentally valuable?

5. What is the Panopticon?

6. Name the three types of privacy.

7. What is a sphere of life and how does this help us determine if our privacy has been violated?

8. What is a cookie?

9. What is data mining?

10. What are three ways property can be defined?

Name:____ Date:__________________

For Further Discussion

1. How important is personal privacy to you? What technologies (if any) would you be willing to go without to make sure you have direct control over your personal information?
2. Do you download music and other media? Would you download it for free if you knew you would never get caught? Why or why not?
3. How plausible do you feel the "gray-goo scenario" really is? Do a risk assessment using one of the two models to see if you can support your view.

Name:____ Date:_________________

Case Studies

Build Your Own Spaceship in 50 Seconds[9]

It seems farfetched but it's true, you too can build your own spaceship in less than 60 seconds. So what's the catch? Well, to begin with the spaceship is what could be referred to as a nano ship. Thinner than a human hair, this little ship can be created using a technique referred to as *two-photon lithographic printing*, where lasers are fired at light-sensitive materials, which eventually solidifies into an actual three-dimensional model. Not impressed? How about printing a new heart, liver, or even lungs? Using a similar process, medical researchers are getting closer to this reality. Currently, human veins and other small pieces of tissue have been created by layering cell after cell of tissue in a process similar to what is being done with laser light. So in the not-so-distant future, it may be possible to create ships tiny enough to carry cargo into your cells or hearts for your heart transplant while you wait.

1. Thinking about these advancements with regard to risk and harm, what potential risks might these nanotechnologies pose and why?
2. Would these risks outweigh potential benefits? How might we assess this?
3. What do you foresee might be three potentially beneficial uses for a nano ship? What might be three risks or harms? Attempt to weigh these out using a utilitarian framework.

More than just friends: What Facebook Collects, Knows, and Can Sell About You

Many Facebook users have mixed emotions about the site. They love the fact that they can keep in touch with friends and family, post their vacation pictures, and play candy crush at work instead of, well, working. But increasingly, Facebook is collecting more data about users without their consent and distributing this data without their knowledge. In early 2013, Facebook offered Android users an application called "Home" that acts like a skin, updating Facebook users right on their phones, replacing their homepage with their Facebook information.[10] For heavy Facebook users, this app offers just one more way to quickly and easily update their accounts or see what their friends are doing. But there is a downside, as this latest app also allows Facebook to potentially collect more information and advertisers more opportunities to hock their wares. Since Facebook makes a large majority of its profits from advertising, this new outlet may provide them with more money but it may come at the expense of privacy. Some have argued that the moment you install this app, Facebook is capable of monitoring your every move, literally. They could get information about who you call, how long you talk to them, where you are calling from, what apps are installed on your phone, and other personal information about you. Many who already post much of their personal life to the site are not worried, but there are others who see a distinct difference between a person actively posting information and a company passively running in the background of your life, taking information, storing it, or potentially selling it.

1. Do you see a distinction between actively posting your personal information and a company passively collecting it? Explain.
2. How should we view our digital information? Is it our private property? Can we own a digital photograph that has been uploaded to a company site? Explain using concepts from the text.
3. Is personal privacy important? Does Facebook violate this privacy? Explain.

CHAPTER SEVEN

Global Distributive Justice

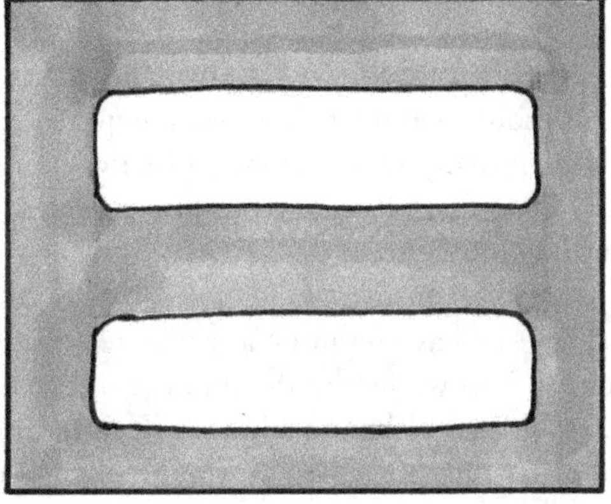

In our first chapter we met Richard Verone, a man who after finding out he had a cancerous tumor in his chest decided to rob a bank in hopes of going to prison and getting the health benefits that he could not otherwise afford. The question surrounding this scenario was whether or not Verone's action was morally wrong. In this our final chapter let's keep the Verone case in mind; however, instead of focusing our attention on Verone's actions, let's turn our attention to the society in which Verone lives and ask ourselves what, if anything, is owed to him. Did he deserve medical treatment despite the fact that he was out of work? Should medicines and other goods be available to everyone regardless of their financial situation? If not, should economic status determine who gets what? What should we use to determine who is deserving of goods? Race, religion, country of origin, or something more familiar to us like merit or need? Exactly how do we distribute our rare and valuable resources in such a way that justice is served? These are the kinds of questions that are raised when we discuss issues of justice and fairness, in particular when we discuss what is known as *distributive justice*.

Although cases like Verone's are quite rare the situation that he found himself in certainly is not. In many ways Verone's situation is not only reflective of life in the United States for quite a number of people, but also reflective of life for the majority of people in our modern world.

A poll taken in 2012 revealed that between 45 and 47 million Americans had no health insurance and as a result no access to reasonably priced healthcare.[1] Although this is quite a large number, it's dwarfed by the number of people worldwide who don't have access to even basic health services or basic sanitation. That number is estimated to be approximately 1.8 million if you count only the children who are living in poverty, stricken with disease or dying each year from illnesses that are easily cured through sanitation and readily available medicine. Many countries simply can't provide basic services such as clean water for their citizens and as a result millions die each year while others live well below the poverty line. The focus of this final chapter involves looking at some of the ways goods and services such as medical care and clean water are currently distributed around the world and then asking critical questions about the justice and fairness of these distributions.

You have already been introduced to the concept of distributive justice as it concerns distribution of gene therapies and genetic enhancements throughout our society and you are aware that what counts as a just distribution depends on what relevant facts we are using to determine who is equal and what treatment these equals deserve. There are merit-based systems, need-based systems, and contribution-based systems, to name just a few of the ways it is possible to distribute goods, all of which can be used in a variety of situations. But when we think of ideas of justice it isn't only the idea of equality that needs to be discussed but also the idea of obligation. Although philosophers cite many ways to distribute goods and services, they have yet to decide upon the best way. That said, there is no doubt that when goods and services are distributed, what is entailed in this distribution is a moral obligation of some kind on the part of the distributors. Since goods and services will always be in limited supply, we need to figure out the most just way to distribute them. Just distribution may require that some people who are more well off will have to give up their claims to some goods, distributing them to other people who are in need. It also may require us to give up some of our freedoms or other intangible benefits so that others may prosper too.

When discussing distributive justice the two most critical questions that need to be answered involve first deciding where our moral obligations lie and then determining exactly what those moral obligations are. To understand how philosophers have responded to the first question we look at two ways we may be obligated to other people: the *relational approach* to moral obligation and the *nonrelational approach* to moral obligation. Let's begin by looking at the relational approach.

Why Global Justice?

As the name suggests, the relational approach focuses on the relationships that exist both globally and between individuals. For a philosopher who takes the relational approach to distributive justice, the most relevant factor to consider are those relationships that are developed and maintained between people and institutions. These relationships may take a variety of forms and can exist between individual people, communities, and the citizens of specific countries or even between global communities or global citizens. What it means to exist in a relationship can be quite vague, so for our purposes it would be a good idea to explore some ways that the term "relationship" has been used with regard to just distribution of goods. The first kind of relationship is one in which people can impact or potentially affect the lives of other people and vice versa. A good example of this kind of relationship can be seen in our Chapter Three discussions of global climate change and the impact we are having on increasing global temperatures. When we think in terms of carbon dioxide emissions and global warming, it could easily be argued that our individual consumption patterns in the United States can and do impact those who live hundreds or even thousands of miles away. As we in the United States consume more goods and create more carbon dioxide and waste products, we are slowly adding to the temperature increases felt across the globe. As the earth continues to heat up, weather patterns will become more unpredictable and more violent. So it is not out of the question to argue that our consumption habits in the United States are creating a potential for more violent and deadly typhoons for the people who live in areas such as Bangladesh. That being the case, according to the relationship theory, when a U.S. citizen consumes an excessive amount of goods and creates an excessive amount of waste, they should be taking into account how their actions are affecting those who live in Bangladesh. If it turns out that overconsuming is taking away substantial opportunities for those people with whom we are related through the environment, we should change what we are doing and how we are acting.

Certainly this seems like a fairly concrete example of how one group of people can directly affect the well-being of another group of people. In most cases, however, the relationships that are forged globally are not so concrete since they are not forged between groups of individuals; rather, they are forged between global institutions such as corporations or banks.

This fact has led some philosophers to advocate for an institutional model of global justice which tends to focus on shared global economic, social, or political institutions as opposed to individuals or groups of individuals. In addition to corporations and banks, those who hold an institutional model also recognize organizations such as United Nations and the World Trade Organization as influential institutions. What seems to be a fundamental truth about global institutions like these is that they are not organizations that stand as direct representations of people.

These institutions in some respects are entities in their own right and instead of asking for consent from people, their policies are generally imposed on people who have little or no say in what they do or how they interact with other organizations. It's for this reason that most philosophers focus almost exclusively on global institutions when discussing relevant moral relationships. Though one certainly could choose to focus on individual people, this focus would offer a much more limited view than the global institution view.

Contrasting with the relationship model is the nonrelationship model. This model has components that will seem quite familiar to you by now. Fundamentally, philosophers who take this approach argue that the reasons for social or global justice have nothing to do with tangible empirical facts about the world or our relationships to others. What matters is that we are all fundamentally human and this similar humanity or universal humanness is all we need to see why we are obligated to work toward a global system that promotes the just distribution of goods. Human rationality and autonomy play the most important role in this approach and any discussion about country of origin, ethnicity, or economic circumstances is irrelevant to discussions of just distribution of goods on this model. The nonrelationship model argues that all humans deserve both tangible and intangible commodities such as equal rights, employment opportunities, and food and shelter regardless of where they reside or what your relationship to them may be. Unlike the relationship view, we don't have to have any direct or indirect relationships to a group of people in order for us to judge that they deserve to be treated justly and in turn that we are obligated to promote justice.

One example of how the nonrelationship model works is illustrated through a thought experiment offered to us by philosopher Chris Armstrong.[2] In his example, Armstrong asks us to imagine two distinct and separate civilizations. These civilizations are different economically, socially, and with regard to natural resources. The first civilization lives in a place with bountiful resources that are easily accessible. The people of this civilization don't have to work or compete for anything. The economic situation is stable and no one goes without the basic necessities. Quite the opposite can be said about the second civilization. The citizens of this society are constantly struggling to produce even the most basic necessities. Their water supplies are naturally polluted and the people suffer from constant hunger and thirst. As a result, the economic situation is dire and lack of resources has led to the maldistribution of resources so only a handful of people are fortunate enough to get by while the rest have next to nothing. Now let's imagine further that neither civilization is aware of the existence of the other. Not only that but there is also no way for people in one civilization to communicate with, visit, or affect the other civilization in any way.

With our imaginary civilizations in mind, Armstrong wants us to think about them both from a relationship model point of view and a nonrelationship model point of view. If we were to encounter these two civilizations under the relationship model, our first task would be to determine what relationships if any existed between the two. Since we can't find any relationship whatsoever we can conclude that even though one group of people is better off than the other group, there is no distributional injustice taking place because there are no relationships between those who have everything and those who have nothing. So with this model we could certainly say that the distribution of goods between the two countries is unfortunate but it is not unjust.

However, a philosopher who holds the nonrelationship model would not see the situation in this way. Since the nonrelationship model sees human rationality and autonomy as the relevant reason why goods and services should be distributed fairly, they would argue that both communities are deserving of stability, opportunity, and the basic necessities of life. In the case of the nonrelationship model, even though the two cultures don't know each other and don't have any relationship at all, the unequal distribution of essential goods is unjust. So, on the nonrelationship model, even if we are faced with a situation where we're unaware or unable to do something to help a person or a group of persons obtain basic goods, the injustice that results from an inequitable distribution of such good remains an injustice.

This idea of injustice resembles the moral ideas proposed by Immanuel Kant. As you may recall Kant felt that all persons deserve special consideration simply because they are rational and autonomous. For Kant, where you live, what political system you belong to, or how much money you make does not detract from your rationality and autonomy in any way. For him, despite our differences every person deserves to be treated as an end and never as a means to an end. So in the case of our two distinct civilizations: even if they don't interact, affect one another, or aren't even aware of one another doesn't diminish their personhood. For Kant the situation in which the second society finds itself is unfit for rational autonomous beings. In other words, it is unjust whenever people are treated unequally without relevant justification.

What Needs to be Distributed: Rights and Resources

Now that we have looked at a relationship-based reason and a non-relationship-based reason to assert that we need to recognize global justice or just distribution on a global scale, we need to turn to the question of what kinds of benefits, services, or burdens we should distribute justly and why. To begin this conversation we need to say something about the predominate language of distributional justice and that is the language of rights. Most of us are familiar with what it means to say that someone has a right. When a person says they have a right they are basically saying that they have an entitlement to something. This something can be as simple as a right to be left alone or it can be as complex as a right to have certain opportunities available to them. Now what makes asserting that you have a right seem like such strong and forceful language is that rights are thought of as stringent entitlements, that is, entitlements that are not only firm but that are also protected by others. The protection of a right is what is known as a *duty*. Because the terms "rights" and "duties" tend to go together, we can think of them in some sense as being correlatives, that is, in order to have one, you need to have the other. Take, for example, a right to listen to the music of your choice. If you have a right to do this, that means that others around you have a duty to respect that right and refrain from reaching into your pocket and turning off your iPod. Moreover, if others also have a right to listen to the music of their choice, you have an obligation to do the same (refrain from reaching into their pockets as well as protecting them from others who may want to do this too). So having a right or asserting that there is a right to some action is a way to make a very strong statement about what a person is owed.

There are two types of rights that are recognized not only by philosophers but also by many legal and political systems: negative rights and positive rights. Interestingly, the rights we are probably most familiar with are the negative rights, although you may not see them that way because they are framed in a positive language. A negative right by definition is a right that essentially prevents harm from being done to you. For instance, if we return to the music example above, "the right to listen to the music you choose" is really a positive way to phrase the negative right it reflects, which is "No one can interfere with your listening to the music of your choice."

Certainly the most well-known negative rights are those that can be found in the United States Bill of Rights, which include familiar legislation like the right to free speech, the right to worship freely, and the right to bear arms. Each of these rights embodies legislation instructing the government about what they cannot do to its citizens. For example, the government cannot prevent me from saying what I like, cannot prevent me from worshipping the way I choose, and cannot deny me my right to own a firearm.

On the other hand, positive rights are those rights that entitle a person to receive a benefit or a portion of some good or service. Unlike a negative right, positive rights do not tell others what can't be done to them but what they should receive. For example, one of the positive rights we are granted in the United States is an unemployment compensation. If you find yourself unemployed through no fault of your own (let's say the corporation that you used to work for closed the branch operating in your town), our government steps in and pays you a certain percentage of your former wages for many months until you find alternative employment. In this case the government gives you something, that is, they are not refraining from doing something but are proactively granting you a benefit. In countries such as Canada your positive rights not only consist of unemployment benefits but also include free healthcare and housing assistance.

If you're still confused as to what counts as a negative right and what counts as a positive right, a simple mind exercise may help. The next time you hear someone talking about rights try to imagine whether that right is something you could put into an imaginary "rights basket" or whether this right surrounds you like a bubble, keeping you safe from others. To try this consider the following familiar right, the right to an education. If someone says to you "Everyone should have a right to an education," are they asserting that there is someone that we need to be protected from, someone who is trying to do us harm? Or is this something that is a benefit given to us by someone? If you imagine this right as a tangible thing, is it the kind of thing you could place in a basket or is it the kind of thing that creates a barrier between you and those around you? If you envision it as an item in a basket you are correct. The right to an education is something that is a benefit given to us. To have a right to an education is a positive right. A right to an education does not protect us from others harming us in any way, so it could not fit the bubble model as well as it does the basket model. Conversely, if we were to say that we have the right to privacy, is this a positive or negative right? If I have a right to keep my personal life my own, am I preventing someone from harming me (forming a protective bubble) or am I reaping a benefit (to put in a basket)? Although there may be benefits to privacy, this is a right that tells others to "stay away" from my stuff; it prevents others from seeing things I do not give my permission to them to see. In that sense it is a negative right and acts as a bubble around my information, keeping it safe from harm. Granted, all rights are not so easily categorized by the bubble/basket thought experiment, but it can work for many of them, hopefully clearing up any confusion these terms may initially cause you.

If we were to look at positive and negative rights and relate these to the models we previously discussed regarding obligations based on relationships and obligations based on personhood or the nonrelationship model, we would find that those who favor the relationships model to describe our obligations are more inclined to recognize a need to create institutional and personal relationships that favor negative rights over positive rights. In contrast, the nonrelationship model tends to promote both negative and positive rights equally. Let's take a moment now to discuss the reasons why this is the case and what the implications are for using rights to promote the just distribution of goods globally.

If we look at just distribution of goods through the lens of the relationship model we see that because we are obligated to others through our relationships, our obligations are not really all that demanding. Relying on the relationships that currently exist between our global institutions we could resolve many inequalities by simply making them a bit fairer economically or politically. This could amount to little more than making sure that trade and banking institutions are not coercive or that they don't intentionally put people at a disadvantage. To achieve this institutions would only need to enact rules and regulations to protect more vulnerable groups from harm. Promoting benefits would not be as effective a tool for these types of changes and as a result it is unlikely that one who holds the relationship model would advocate for them in the form of positive rights.

Not only does the relationship model require only minimal obligations when it comes to rights and just distribution of goods, but it can also be used to argue against global justice and global rights altogether. The reason that it can argue effectively either for global justice and negative rights or against global justice entirely rests on the fact that the term "relationship" is vague. The vague nature of the term helps philosophers use it to support their own theories of justice, which may or may not include global justice. Since we've spent some time discussing how the relationship model works to promote moral obligations at the global level, we should look at the model as it's used to argue against both global obligations and global justice. Philosophers who argue against the existence of global obligations make their case by looking at the differences between the relationships that are found within countries and those that exist across borders.

Relationships between citizens, they argue, are fundamental and concrete, that is, they are relationships where the actions of one person can directly affect the well-being of another. This is not the case with relationships that exist between countries and between the citizens of different countries. In fact, most of the relationships between countries and their citizens are not direct but are mediated through global institutions, making them less concrete and less obvious. So if we are to think about our moral obligations as relying on actual relationships it would seem that there are concrete and tangible obligations between citizens of individual countries and the less concrete and somewhat intangible international relationships that are for some too vague to count as actual relationships. That said, philosophers who translate relationships in this way see the international community as one that functions amorally, that is, there are no moral obligations that can or should be applied to international interactions. It's only between citizens of countries where the relationships are strong enough to promote moral obligations.

Can the same be said about international obligations on the nonrelationship model? Is it possible to discount the idea of global obligations to be more just? Unlike the relationships model, if you follow the nonrelationship model you have no choice but to commit yourself to the idea of global justice as an obligation. You are also committing yourself to a more demanding moral ideal that will require the promotion of equality and rights in more ways than would be recognized by a person who held the relationships model. We discussed the reason for this earlier in the chapter but recall that it has to do with the idea that empirical facts above and beyond our humanity have no bearing on what a person deserves. People in general deserve freedom, education, food, shelter, and other basics. So when working with the nonrelationship model one must be committed not only to global justice but also to the moral obligation of promoting equality in the form of the positive and the negative rights previously mentioned.

This split between the relationships model and the nonrelationships model represents the first fundamental split in how individuals respond to the questions surrounding our global moral obligations. The second fundamental split involves answering questions about what goods and services need to be distributed across the globe.

Egalitarianism

The first response to the question of what goods and services should be distributed justly is an egalitarian one. The second response is inegalitarian in nature and is referred to as the *minimalist approach.* The term "egalitarian" is one we have encountered many times now throughout the book and have seen that in any application it generally refers to either the promotion of equality or the distribution of a good equally among those who are being considered to receive it. So it's easy to see how this term could be used to express how we should distribute both tangible and intangible goods. At the very least we know that whatever the good being discussed it should according to this model be distributed among people as equally as possible. Only then can we say that a good or service has been distributed justly.

Just distribution based on equal distribution seems like a very tall order when we look at how goods and services are currently distributed throughout the world. Just a quick glance at world events shows us that immense inequalities exist, whether they are in educational opportunities, natural resources, political freedoms, or even average lifespan. Recognizing this fact, egalitarians state that it is this maldistribution of fundamental goods that creates an unjust global situation. For them, justice can only be insured when the most important goods and services are distributed equally among all individuals. This of course highlights their egalitarian way of thinking but fails to answer the question about which items or goods are important enough that they should be possessed by everyone equally. Philosophers have offered a variety of responses regarding what is most important and their responses have ranged from natural resources to basic life opportunities.

Let's have a look at what some philosophers identify as the most important goods and then how they suggest we should redistribute these goods to rectify the immense global inequalities that we currently face. The first view we look at is one proposed by philosopher Charles Beitz.[3] Beitz suggests not one but two goods that are important enough to be distributed equally among all people. The first are the earth's natural resources and the second are the fundamental ideas of equality and justice.

Before looking at Beitz's first good, let's look at an example of the current natural resource distribution and explore why Beitz finds natural resources so important. When we look at countries such as the United States we see a place that consists not only of huge tracts of land but also of fertile soil, natural harbors, and a range of readily available minerals and metals. Contrast this with a country such as Afghanistan. This country is small and land locked, with poor soil and a harsh climate. There is mineral wealth to be had, but most individuals must spend their time subsistence farming and have little time to explore the innovations necessary to tap this resource. The country has little in the way of exports and assets (except opium, which is both a thriving and illegal export). Given this one example we can see that the United States is by chance better positioned to thrive politically, socially, and economically while Afghanistan must constantly struggle to ensure its people have the basics. Now the presence of natural resources does not simply ensure U.S. success and stability for the short term but ensures that we will always be in a better position than those who inhabit Afghanistan and similar countries.

Of course, natural resources are distributed through geological events and the fact that one country just happens to be in the appropriate geographical place on the map to enjoy them is based on sheer luck. The citizens of the United States didn't earn their natural resources, build their resources, or even ask for their resources, they just happened upon them. If we were to quickly return to some of the acceptable ways to distribute goods and services we've already encountered, we would quickly see that a distribution through sheer luck is not a just distribution. Beitz recognizes this and notes that a wealth of natural resources can guarantee a country's success almost endlessly while a lack of resources can condemn a country to perpetual hardship and instability.

For Beitz the only way to rectify the current unjust distribution of natural resources is to create a system that will allow for the redistribution of global resources that reflects equality. For him, natural resources should be redistributed in a way that allows every person to have an entitlement or right to the resource. So what exactly would such a redistribution of natural resources look like if put into practice? Beitz himself states that it would require the naturally wealthy countries to somehow redistribute their wealth to the less advantaged countries. This would require us to rethink our current political situations and perhaps force us as global citizens to realign our ideas about countries and nation-states. Beitz certainly realizes that a redistribution of this sort is difficult to imagine and probably even more difficult to put into practice, so he suggests this as something we should move toward as an ideal more than a reality. At the same time he does suggest that even if we are unable to redistribute wealth in this way, we should at a minimum advocate for a redistribution principle that would allow every society to develop just social institutions and an economy that can sustain and support their citizens at a basic level. In other words, just redistribution of natural resources would require that all countries be able to meet the needs of their people at the basic subsistence level and the basic human rights level. Certainly the redistribution of natural resources would go a long way to further his first goal of basic subsistence but in order to meet his second goal we need to discuss the distribution of his second most important good, the ideas of equality and justice.

The second of Beitz's ideas has to do with the promotion of the principles of equality and justice. We have seen that equality can be defined as equal treatment for equals and for Beitz this will certainly hold true. But how do we ensure that the equal treatment that a person gets is also a just treatment that reflects what they deserve? For egalitarians such as Beitz, the best-case scenario and the ultimate goal would be to create global systems that ensure that all people get the same important goods equally. But again he recognizes the practical difficulties involved in attempting to create systems that could do this. So, Beitz proposes a "what-if" scenario in an attempt to make more practical advances toward equality. His question was, "What if we could show that some inequalities actually did more to benefit the least advantaged than would absolute equality, could we as egalitarians be satisfied with this scenario and allow for some inequalities to remain?" Although it's not the ideal situation an egalitarian would hope for, this seems like a sufficient justification for allowing the existence of some inequalities. But what exactly would an inequality that benefitted the least advantaged actually look like? Let's look at an example that involves a system we are already quite familiar with in the United States. Let's have a look at capitalism. We've all heard that the reason why capitalism works well is that it rewards innovation and hard work with money. We can see examples of this, with people such as Bill Gates or Steve Jobs. Currently in our capitalist society we have some individuals who are very wealthy, some who have moderate wealth and those who have next to nothing. This is a clear case of inequality, but is it the kind of justified inequality that Beitz suggests is better than absolute equality? In order to show that this inequality is justified, one would need to show that the inequalities we experience here in the United States are inequalities that benefit those who have next to nothing better than a system that consists of absolute equality.

Arguments could be made that suggest this unequal distribution of goods does benefit the poorer classes. Arguments that they are better off stem from the fact that because more of us have an incentive to work harder in hopes of being one of the wealthy few, this hard work helps to fuel more creativity and that creativity opens new markets and creates new jobs. New jobs become available both to people in the middle and to the poorest among us. As more people benefit, make money, and go on to innovate, this leads to the creation of more jobs, giving the poor even more opportunities to rise up out of poverty than they would have had, had there been no incentives to work hard. So if we were to reason in this way, the income disparity we see in the United States might actually be acceptable for egalitarians such as Beitz, but only if we could show that the benefits to the poor were substantial.

A more contemporary egalitarian approach to global justice has been that of Simon Caney.[4] Caney advocates both for the egalitarian approach and the nonrelationship approach to global justice. He agrees with Beitz that there are substantial inequalities in the world that need to be rectified and the only way to do this is to equally redistribute the goods that are most important. Unlike Beitz, Caney is not looking at a tangible resource such as trees or minerals to distribute; rather, he is going to look at opportunities and then suggest that it is certain opportunities that need to be redistributed in order to create global justice.

So what exactly does it mean to redistribute an opportunity? Caney's definition of what constitutes an opportunity is very broad and can refer to opportunities for employment, education, food, shelter, or any number of other goods we as human beings desire. To distribute them means to make them available to anyone who has talent, ability, willingness, or drive, regardless of ethnicity, religion, race, gender, or country of origin. The opportunities Caney suggest are global in scope and though equal opportunity doesn't imply equal treatment it does mean that your nationality will be just as irrelevant to your success as would your gender or ethnicity. Looking at opportunity in this way it would be equally unjust to deny someone a job because of their nationality, as it would be to deny them a job because of their gender. For Caney, whether you come from the Ukraine or the United States, you should have an equal opportunity to live a full life. Like the equality proposed by Beitz, this is another tall order because it too would require substantial changes in the way we distribute resources and view national borders. In order for most of the world's inhabitants to compete equally there would need to be radical chances to education systems, technological infrastructures, and even the belief systems of many people. Again much of the burden would be on wealthy nations who would have to fund projects in the less-developed nations to create better education systems, and access to technologies such as the Internet. But the most challenging part of our redistribution of opportunity would come when we attempted to promote this idea in countries and in cultures who don't currently accept even the most basic ideas of equality. Countries where the status of men and women or natives and non-natives have been fundamentally recognized as unequal would need to be changed at fundamental levels in order for equal opportunity to be achieved.

Given the enormous challenges to an egalitarian distribution of important goods, it's not surprising that many philosophers have rejected this approach for both practical and philosophical reasons. These philosophers prefer to advocate for what is called the *minimalist* position on global justice and it's to this position we now turn our attention. Those who hold the minimalist position don't recognize equality as either a primary goal or a moral obligation when trying to distribute global goods justly. A minimalist's goal is to close the extreme gaps between those who have vast resources and those who have none. They will see our moral obligation as one in which we should make sure that everyone has access to at least a minimum number of goods and rights. Once everyone obtains this minimum any additional inequalities in goods and services are acceptable.

Minimalism

One of the most famous minimalists philosophers is John Rawls. Although you may have not heard of him there is no doubt that some of the ways you think about political organizations and justice have been highly influenced by his work. In fact, he is so influential that even those who disagree with him still rely on the basic principles of justice he proposed to support their views. You've seen two examples of this in our previous discussion of egalitarianism. Both Beitz and Caney have used two of Rawls's most famous principles of justice to support their own ideas of what should count as an important good even though Rawls would not only disagree with their egalitarian approach but also with their global outlook.

Rawls's writings focus almost exclusively on justice within societies and he has little to say about the idea of global justice. According to Rawls,[5] the principles he outlines should be used as a way to obtain justice within societies and were never meant to be applied globally. This certainly doesn't mean that he felt there should be no global justice at all, but it means that the way he envisions justice on a global scale will not be as formal or create the binding obligations that justice within a society does. Before we take a look at Rawls's assessment of global justice it's a good idea to sketch his theory of justice as it applies to individual societies and understand how he arrived at his ideas of what constitutes a just society. From this starting point we will be able to see more clearly why he felt that many of the ideas he thought were practical on a social scale would not function properly on a global scale.

The first Rawlsian principle you have already seen is the difference principle. Used by Beitz to justify inequalities in an egalitarian theory, this principle states that in order for a society to be just, any inequalities that exist within that society should always favor and promote the best interests of those who are worst off in that society. Rawls was well aware that we are all self- interested beings and that the only way to establish a truly just society would be to not only acknowledge that we are self-interested but to use this tendency to everyone's advantage. In order to justify the validity of the difference principle using our own rational self-interest, he created a thought experiment where a hypothetical group of people gathered together with the task of creating just laws for their society. He called this group the Original Position. Now to this thought experiment he added the fact that each participant in this group was covered in a veil of ignorance. As the name suggests, this veil of ignorance served to keep the participants in this group ignorant of any accidental features they would have when placed in the society they were creating. An accidental feature is anything that makes you what you are as an individual. It can be your gender, socioeconomic class, political affiliation, disability, religion, or ethnicity. By not knowing these accidental features about yourself, Rawls argued that the group of people would enact laws that would work to benefit the worst off in their society, just in case they happened to belong to that group once they left the room and joined the society they had created. So working in this room was like working in a magic room where everyone was stripped of all their features but their rationality and self-interest. Rawls argued that anyone who was to perform this experiment or imagine such a magic room would be compelled through reason to see that the difference principle was the most reasonable and rational way to ensure that a society's laws would be just.

Another interesting insight that this experiment can give us is that although there may be many things that are distributed unequally in a just society, there seem to be a handful of things that can never be distributed unequally if a society is to be considered just. Rawls proposed two things in particular, and you can see these two items represented in Carney's definition of opportunity. They are the ability to participate fully and freely in the most extensive basic liberties and also to have offices and positions that are open to everyone under equal opportunity. Rawls refers to this as the principle of equal opportunity and asserts that for any society to be truly, just both this principle and the difference principle must be in place. Keep in mind that both of these principles are set out so that any rational person would be willing to support a society that advocated them. We certainly don't need to be members of the original position to see that any social institutions that advocate

these two principles would be supported not only by the wealthiest but also by the poorest since all inequalities in wealth would have to work to favor the poor as opposed to favoring the rich.

Looking at the difference principle and the equal opportunity principle it's easy to see why this way of thinking can be easily applied to individual societies, as our relationships with other citizens are such that we can promote these principles effectively. But Rawls is adamant that these principles do not apply to relationships between individuals in different countries. Clearly there are philosophers who disagree with this assessment as they are willing to apply these principles on a global scale, so why did Rawls reject this application? He rejects it on the basis that the kinds of relationships we have with our fellow citizens are vastly different from those we can form with people from other countries. Let's look at an example of how relationships between citizens of a country differ from relationships between citizens of two different nations.

To begin with the idea of being citizens of a particular country means that individuals will be governed by a centralized government and that government will have a great deal of power over their individual fates. Additionally, in democratic republics it's not only the centralized government that has power over its citizens but the citizens themselves can direct this power to influence their own lives and the lives of their fellow citizens.

Let's take an example that revolves around educational opportunities. There are three individuals who want to attend college: Rachel, Raymond, and Raj. Rachel and Raymond live in the United States and Raj lives in India. Rachel comes from a very wealthy family, all of whom have attended college at an Ivy League institution. She has had all the advantages of both wealth and superior education and college is a certainty. Raymond, on the other hand, is from an inner-city family, none of whom have attended college. He has attended poorly funded schools with few resources and no technologies. Raymond works full time but still does not make enough to pay for college. Although Raymond does qualify for financial aid, he will not be able to get the time off work to attend the community college of his choice. Raj comes from Goa, India, and hopes to travel to a bigger city to attend college. He has five younger siblings and he, his mother, and his father all work to make ends meet. Although he did well in school, Raj attended a school with no technology and no resources. He has never used a computer. There are no financial aid opportunities for Raj, so he hopes that one of his more wealthy relatives will help.

A couple things should strike us about these scenarios. First is that we have one person who is quite well off and two others who are doing poorly. Rachel has all the advantages and will be in an even greater position of advantage once she graduates. Both Raymond and Raj are both hardworking individuals that are disadvantaged, with little hope of changing their situation. Now Rachel and Raymond live in a democratic country and as such they can use their votes to correct injustices. That said, both Rachel and Raymond have a responsibility to one another to correct any injustices that may occur in the United States by pushing for reforms that would bring about more just situations for all those who desire an education.

The relationship between Rachel and Raj and even Raymond and Raj is very different. Unlike Raymond and Rachel, the relationships between Raj and Rachel are not basic institutional structures that can be used to change Raj's circumstances. Whereas Rachel and Raymond can call on state and federal institutions to help them equalize the resource of education, there are no institutions available to either Rachel or Raymond to help them create direct changes for Raj. So in one case it would seem that there exist real and tangible relationships that can be used to create more just situations. In the other case these relationships don't exist and that makes direct action leading to change nearly impossible. To attempt to promote either the difference principle or the principle of equal opportunity between Rachel and Raj would not seem possible as they don't have the relationship mechanisms in place to do this.

So if we can't apply either of Rawls's fundamental principles on a global scale, what if anything do we owe the people living in other countries? As a minimalist Rawls is going to argue that although global justice is not a possibility, we do owe other less-fortunate countries what he refers to as a "duty of assistance." What this comes down to is that when we find certain societies who are simply unable to operate as well as other societies, that is, they are not thriving, but they are not aggressive toward other countries nor do they violate their citizen's human rights, we have a duty to help them improve themselves by helping them to become self-sufficient. This amounts to helping them develop social and political institutions, allowing them to address fundamental inequalities, and providing them with technological support and material assistance they need to help them function better.

In the end it's clear that the ideas that Rawls lays out for the international community are very modest. For him global justice is about nothing more than nations coexisting peacefully with societies who are better off and assisting societies until they are stable and self-sufficient. Anything above and beyond this would be the responsibility of individual governments. So as a minimalist Rawls is not interested in redistribution of resources or granting assistance beyond what is needed for a country to remain stable. Apart and aside from these minimal goals, he feels we aren't obligated to reallocate resources in any way.

We've seen that the minimalist approach especially as it relates to the work of John Rawls means an almost full-on rejection of the idea of global justice. But does it have to follow that if you're a minimalist you must reject the ideas of global obligations and global justice mostly or entirely? Not necessarily. Remember that if you advocate for the minimalist position you are simply rejecting equality as the ultimate goal and obligation. A person could certainly accept the fact that inequalities exist and that they probably always will and from this we should choose another more obtainable goal. They may argue that it's not the inequality between individuals in different countries that makes us feel that the global distribution of goods is unjust. The reality, some argue, may be that the only time it seems to bother us that inequalities exist is when those inequalities are stark, that is, when one group of individuals suffers from a great deal of poverty while another group of individuals enjoy a vast amount of wealth and prosperity. A good example that supports this minimalist observation is one in which we can compare the standard of living between the United States and Norway on the one hand and the United States and Uganda on the other.

As far as wealth and opportunity, the U.S. surpasses both of these nations, so we can say with confidence that none of these countries is equal in relevant distribution of goods. Now consider how troubled you are that those who live in Norway aren't quite as prosperous as those who live in the United States. For most of us, the modest gap in prosperity that exists between these two countries is probably not something that is disconcerting at all. Now consider the gap in prosperity that exists between the average U.S. citizen and an average citizen of Uganda. The gap here is quite large. The government of Uganda is unable to provide what we would consider even the minimal amount of basic necessities of food, shelter, and healthcare to its citizens. This is a situation where most people are troubled by the inequalities between the two countries. Unlike the comparison between the U.S. and Norway, the comparison between the U.S. and Uganda points to a situation where the gaps are vast and one of the two countries is unable to provide even the basics while the other lives in a constant state of excess.

Our moral intuition tells us that one of these situations is wrong while the other is quite acceptable. This leads us to one of the most important points made by philosophers who adhere to the minimalist approach to justice and that is we are morally troubled by inequality not because we feel that all humans deserve the exact same amount of goods; rather, we are troubled when the gap involves those who have a lot and those who can't even get the basics. It is a lack of the bare essentials that we find troubling, not the idea that some goods are distributed unequally. So for the minimalist our primary responsibility should reflect our moral intuition and we should work to provide help to those who don't have the basics and as a result suffer the most. The minimalist position does not obligate us to anything above and beyond ensuring that everyone gets their basic needs met through both the distribution of basic resources and also basic human rights. After these have been met either within particular societies or globally, our obligations are fulfilled and any inequalities that exist after this are justified and in no way affect the fact that just distribution of goods has been achieved.

Now that we've seen the minimalist and egalitarian responses along with the relationship and nonrelationship models, one question may still need to be answered and that is where these approaches intersect. It seems clear that the nonrelationship approach is quite compatible with the egalitarian approach and the relationship model works well with the minimalist model, but does one need to hold the relationship model in order to be a minimalist and vice versa? The answer to this question is complex. These theories are not mutually exclusive, meaning that you could certainly be a minimalist and hold either the relationship model or the nonrelationship model. Likewise, you could be an egalitarian and hold either model.

The issue of global justice is a complicated one, with very few clear-cut answers that all philosophers can agree upon. That said, understanding the different approaches to global justice can go a long way in helping us to look at some of the contemporary issues we face when discussing the problems surrounding the just distribution of goods, benefits, and human rights. In the next section we look at issues involving human rights, natural resources, international trade, and climate change. Our focus is on some of the concerns these issues raise with regard to global justice and some of the possible solutions that have been proposed by contemporary philosophers.

Contemporary Concerns with Global Distributive Justice

Human Rights

The first issue is that of human rights. Remember that human rights are those strict entitlements that can be split into two different types or kinds: the positive rights where a person can make claims on goods and services and the negative rights or those where others have a duty to refrain from harming us. Recall also that both egalitarians and minimalists use rights language to emphasize those pressing claims that should demand our immediate attention. Whether it be advocating for food, shelter, natural resources, or equal opportunity, these claims are all more or less grounded in the idea that what is really morally wrong about someone lacking these things is that they have a fundamental right to them and since their claims on these items are not being met, an injustice occurred. This is the reason why rights language is so strong and also so important to a discussion of global justice. Although the use of strong rights language seems to compel us to action, questions about which claims are actually entitlements and who should get these entitlements is something that warrants further discussion.

For most Western societies the idea that there are human rights and that they are universal has formed the bedrock of our social and political consciousness for the last several hundred years. Although a mainstay in Western cultures, many other cultures either don't recognize universal human rights or they view what is owed to a person or how a person can be treated very differently from the way we do. Additionally, in many cultures including our own the idea that basic human needs constitute basic human rights is a controversial one. This can be easily seen in the ongoing debates over universal healthcare in the United States. Where some understand access to basic healthcare as a human right, others see it as a benefit of employment. With so many different views on human rights coexisting in one culture it would seem that those who wish to promote human rights globally have a difficult task ahead of them. Two prominent approaches to human rights have been suggested as a way to begin this difficult conversation: the *personhood/autonomy approach* and the *basic needs/interests approach.*

The personhood/autonomy approach should sound familiar by now. Personhood as you now know was asserted and used by Immanuel Kant to emphasize our inherent value and to put constraints on those who want to use us as tools. The personhood/autonomy approach to global human rights uses Kant's idea of the universality of the inherent value of all humans to ground rights. Our personhood grounds the idea that we deserve certain treatment regardless of our origin or nationality, religion or socioeconomic status and our ability to make independent life choices determines what relevant characteristics need to be protected. The idea behind the personhood/autonomy approach is that by universalizing the kinds of rights that guarantee our autonomy and our continued ability to reason freely, we are in fact protecting the very attributes that make us human.

The other approach to human rights is similar in that it also focuses on specific aspects of our human nature. The basic needs/interests approach looks at how the idea of universal human rights can serve the basic needs and interests of all human beings. Despite cultural differences there are many basic needs that all human beings have: adequate food and water and opportunities to make a decent living, obtain an education, and live securely and freely with others. This list of basic human needs reflects not only what humans need to merely survive but also what they need to flourish. By understanding what humans need to flourish and then attempting to codify laws that support fulfillment of these needs lead philosophers who hold this view to propose a handful of rights that they see as critical to human existence. These critical rights can easily be seen as universal, they argue, because all humans regardless of their geographical location need them in order to thrive and flourish.

This last paragraph brings up another interesting question: How do we determine which rights are basic or critical and which rights are not? Some rights seem uncontestable, like a right to food, shelter, and water, but other rights seem to be less basic since they don't express physical or tangible necessity. Rights such as a right to job opportunities or a right to vote are not as obviously basic as a right to food and water. One of the most influential philosophers to address this issue is Henry Shue.[6] He argues that a basic right can be distinguished from other rights based on the fact that without a basic right one cannot enjoy other rights. For example, a person could not enjoy the freedom to vote for a particular political candidate if she were starving or didn't have any clean drinking water. Likewise, if she always feared for her life, it would seem quite absurd to offer her the right to an education. So it would seem if we categorized a basic right as a right that needs to be in place in order for a person to enjoy other rights, we can see that our initial list that included food, water, shelter, and freedom from fear is a good start. But not all issues about what a person is entitled to are as clear cut as determining that they need to eat and drink. Earlier in this chapter we looked at how the maldistribution of natural resources was of concern to some philosophers who were trying to advocate for global justice and it's to the global distribution of resources that we now turn our attention.

International Trade

We've already seen that egalitarians such as Charles Beitz are concerned about the arbitrary distribution of natural resources on this planet and the implications to global justice these distributions bring. But not everyone agrees that global injustices are a direct result of the maldistribution of natural resources. For philosophers such as Thomas Pogge and Leif Wenar,[7] it's not the geological distribution of natural resources that creates injustices but the systems that coordinate the ownership and sale of these resources globally.

Pogge asserts that there are reasons above and beyond simply having abundant resources available to you that explains why so many economic and social inequalities exist globally. Pogge refers to a concept he calls the *resource privilege*,[8] which is simply the web of international systems that allow any person or group of persons holding effective power in a region to sell the resources of that country on the international market. This is a problem in many resource-rich regions because the people who are in charge of the resources may not be legitimate governments but insurgent groups, guerillas, or oppressive regimes. If these illegitimate groups know that there will be no sanctions on the sale of resources even though their ownership of these resources is questionable, this creates strong incentives for groups to take control of national resources through force, creating social unrest and bloodshed for many developing nations. But the armed, violent, and power-hungry groups are only part of this problem. Multinational corporations who do business with these groups are equally responsible for bringing about the inequality, poverty, and injustice that is often the result of these transactions. In fact, Pogge argues that anyone including the citizens of wealthy, stable countries that buy these products is complicit in continuing to impoverish the native populations and create a global atmosphere that breeds human rights violations.

A second concept is adopted by Pogge from economists. This concept, called the "resource curse," is a term used to refer to the phenomenon that often occurs when a developing country is rich in resources. These countries are "cursed" because their wealth tends to increase the chances that there will be civil wars and violent coups. So contrary to Beitz's assumption that resource wealth brings fundamental equality, it would seem that countries that are most rich in natural resources are actually more likely to be at a greater disadvantage in some respects than their poorer counterparts since this wealth can be seen as "up for grabs" and encourage power-hungry factions or resource-hungry corporations to terrorize anyone who gets in their way.

It would seem that these two concepts are related to one another in that resources can be traded internationally by anyone who possesses them, regardless of how they were obtained, which encourages groups to seize resources for profit, even if those profits come at the expense of the country or the legitimate citizens. Once a group has been rewarded for trading resources, this creates an unending cycle of power acquisition and expansion. Oil fields, diamond mines, and other natural resources are held, exploited, disputed, and fought over again and again, with the general population suffering the consequences of violence and instability.

This has clearly been the case in some of the most resource-rich countries in Africa where civil wars can rage for decades and total collapse of governmental institutions and basic infrastructures are fairly common. In the Democratic Republic of the Congo, for example, civil war and social unrest have crippled the country. Conflicts over a multitude of natural resources including water, diamonds, copper, coltan (used to make cell phone components), and tin have been waged by warring factions for decades, fueled by a number of multinational corporations fighting to obtain these precious commodities. Since 1995 over 5.4 million people have died as a result of these ongoing conflicts in the DRC, with some 1.5 million living as displaced refugees and over 45,000 more dying each month. As one news article stated: "These shocking figures are usually more than enough to get media attention . . . . Yet, perhaps as a cruel irony, influential nations of the world benefit from the vast resources coming from the DRC for which people are dying over."[9]

Like Pogge, Wenar believes that it's the systems through which the resources are traded and not the resources themselves that create the majority of injustices we observe. For him, if we really wanted to promote global justice we in the wealthier countries would need to recognize our responsibility to identify resources that come from illegitimate groups or regimes and refuse to do business with them. If we don't, he agrees with Pogge's assessment that we are complicit in the human rights violations and injustices that occur in these countries. For Wenar the natural resources of a country belong to its citizens and when they are taken from the citizenry by force or fear and traded without consent and knowledge it is nothing short of stealing. So if we as a country knowingly purchase goods from a group or dictator that has taken them from the citizenry without permission, we are complicit in the buying of stolen goods. Not many people will argue against the fact that buying of stolen goods is wrong and would therefore by Wenar's reasoning have no justifiable way to say that purchasing goods from these individuals wasn't immoral global injustice or not.

One recent example of global complicity in the stealing of resources can be found in the global export and sale of diamonds from Sierra Leone through much of the first part of the decade. It's a well-known fact that the rebel group Revolutionary United Front (RUF) has seized many of the diamond mine operations. They are using profits from these mines for a number of activities including the purchasing of weapons and supplying of their troops. The RUF has been connected to many terrible human rights violations including the amputation of limbs and the maiming of civilians. They are also famous for recruiting child soldiers, forcing boys as young as 9 to rape and murder members of their own family.

In as early as 2001, the United Nations Security Council placed an 18-month ban on the sale and purchase of diamonds from this region. Since that time the ban has been knowingly violated by a number of international diamond companies and the diamonds that are fueling this war are knowingly being purchased by consumers around the world, including consumers in the United States.[10] It is clear that the more we consume these products the stronger the RUF becomes and the more the citizens of Sierra Leone suffer. It certainly seems that one could argue Wenar's point quite well, at least in this instance. As you can see, we can either take Beitz's view of maldistribution of natural resources as the core cause of so much global injustice or you can look to the systems that foster practices that lead to the exploitation of resources as the cause. Or if you like there is no reason why the inequality that surrounds natural resources couldn't be attributed to both of these proposed reasons. The only thing that we know for certain is that the wealthier countries may need to rethink how we obtain our resources and the impact it may have on other citizens of the world.

Images © Shutterstock, Inc. Modified by the author.

International trade in general has always been fiercely scrutinized and criticized for a variety of reasons, whether it's concerns about trading diamonds from war-torn countries or simply trading plastic toys from China, trading goods internationally has always raised issues of justice and equality.

One of the problems that we can face when attempting to discuss justice and fairness with regard to international trade is that it's a world that few of us have any direct contact with. From the acronyms to the distinct language of international contracts, attempting to understand how trade and trade agreements work can be a daunting task. That said, for our purposes here we focus on international trade in its most general sense and use some hopefully familiar examples as an attempt to make the complex ideas that surround international trade manageable enough to give us a better view of the potential concerns that are raised by this practice.

When thinking about international trade, we can safely say that many of the topics we have already covered in this chapter are intimately connected to this idea. Our discussions of natural resources and human rights, for example, can both be seen as two familiar subjects that are tied into international trade. Even our discussion of relationships can be seen as tied directly to the idea of international trade as one of the institutional relationships that is recognized by that model.

If many of the topics we've already covered are directly related to international trade, why cover it as an individual topic at all? To begin with, international trade in general is one of many international institutions that when functioning properly is supposed to be mutually beneficial to all those involved. The idea behind international trade is that one country may desire a product they can't easily produce and another country is able to produce this product quite easily. An agreement can be reached where both countries get what they want and need at a price and with an effort that is reasonable to both involved. Consider as a simple example the buying and selling of coffee. It's well known that a country such as Japan lacks both the space and the climate to grow coffee effectively, but there is a demand in Japan for this commodity. What can the Japanese do to obtain what they want? If they turn to a country such as Sumatra, who is capable of coffee production, they may be able to trade coffee for a product that they can easily produce to sell to the island of Sumatra. It would seem that there are few ethical questions raised by this transaction. Both countries benefit, getting what they want and need when they cannot produce the goods themselves. But it seems that the way trade is currently conducted brings up a number of ethical questions regarding the reality of these supposed beneficial relationships. It would seem that although we would like to think in terms of mutual benefits, there are a number of common trading practices that create situations that are not beneficial to both trade partners. For example, sometimes producers of high-value goods subsidize those goods, making it difficult for poorer nations whose products are not subsidized to break into certain markets. A subsidy is a sum of money paid to certain industries by the government as a way to assist in the production of that item. One of the most subsidized items in the United States is dairy products. The government spends billions of dollars each year subsidizing the production of dairy cows. It was noted in a United Nations report that in 2003 the average dairy cow in the United States received a subsidy of almost $1,000 per year. With this kind of wealth supporting an industry, American farmers can produce more milk, cheese, and yogurt for less, discouraging the importing of dairy products from other countries. In effect, our wealth prevents smaller countries from being able to trade with us, or with anyone else for that matter, since we can export our milk and cheese for less as well.

Even when countries are not competing against wealthier, subsidized nations it may still be difficult for them to break into international markets because an immense amount of start-up investments or a good deal of money to spend on technologies is necessary to effectively manufacture goods. Finally, there is the practice known as *dumping*, which is when a wealthy country is able to maintain their hold in a market through selling their goods at a loss for a substantial amount of time, thus running any global competition (who is too poor to sell goods at a loss) into the ground.

All of these practices exist in our current trading system and they all should lead us to question the idea that trade is based on mutually beneficial agreements that are fair for all those involved. It would seem that there are benefits to be had through trade, but these benefits don't seem to be spread evenly across the globe. Another reason for this inequality may be that there is such a disparity of wealth and power among nations that poorer nations are hard pressed to bring anything of value to the trading table. If one has nothing or very little to offer, it would seem that those who have the most will not only set the trade rules but will also force the less powerful nations into agreements that may not benefit them much if at all. It would seem that if we were to adopt trade agreements that were truly just, then we couldn't rely on wealth, power, or even the amount and kinds of goods that are to be traded. What we would need are systems that can look beyond those factors and somehow create systematic or institutional justice from the ground up.

Philosopher Darrel Moellendorf[11] creates a case for just such an arrangement. He feels that we should not look to an equality of goods as a way to assess whether or not justice has been served through an international trade agreements; rather, we should look to see whether or not the terms of the trade agreements are such that any inequalities that are produced by the agreement would be acceptable to anyone entering into the agreement. This sounds suspiciously like Rawls's difference principle and in a way it mirrors the idea closely in that even those who stand to be the worst off in any one international trade transaction should, without pressure, fear, or coercion, see the trade agreement as beneficial if it is indeed just.

A very concrete example of trade organizations that highlights some of the issues and concerns we have discussed regarding international trade is the World Trade Organization (WTO). Probably known less for its actual policies and more for the protests and riots that plague WTO meetings, it is one of the most influential trade organizations in the world. Formed in 1995, the WTO is currently comprised of 159 member countries from all over the world. According to its mission statement, it is an organizational body that negotiates trade agreements internationally, with its main purpose being to act as a forum where governments can convene to negotiate agreements, settle disputes, and discuss ways to eliminate trade barriers. Its primary goal is ". . . to open trade for the benefit of all."[12] With such noble-sounding intentions it's curious that whenever this organization meets, protests from outraged citizens tend to follow.

In 1999, about 50,000 citizens in Seattle, Washington, protesting globalization of trade took to the streets to protest the arrival of WTO participants. The protest turned violent as riots broke out in many areas of the city. Across the United States and throughout other parts of the world protests in support of the Seattle riot were formed and hundreds of thousands of people worldwide took to the streets to express their discontent with this organization. So what exactly was it about the "globalization" of trade that made people so upset? Many people express their outrage at what they see as an organization that placed profits over people, allowed for the destruction of natural resources, and did nothing more than increase profits for corporations. Some of the specific charges protesters cited against the WTO were its decisions to allow Venezuelan oil companies to sell products filled with banned chemicals, its refusal to protect small banana farmers from large corporations, and its dismissal of legislation that would have protected endangered sea life. Though many of these allegations remain disputed, there is no doubt that some people are worried about the consequences that are direct results of WTO decisions.

Although the WTO touts its democratic processes and decision-making matrix, many are convinced that critical decisions are not discussed up-front with all members. Many fear that there are a number of behind-the-scenes dealings between wealthy nations and corporations that predecide trade agreements before they are brought to the table. Others fear that many of the poorer countries simply don't have the expertise and qualifications needed to understand and negotiate trade agreements that would be truly beneficial. The inability of some to represent their own interests may lead to intended or unintended coercion of the less powerful by the more powerful.

For many, the overwhelming evidence that outcomes of the agreements made through the WTO are clearly unjust rests on the fact that as an organization the WTO has done little to stop or discourage the use of some of the very practices that lead to unjust trading conditions, such as the wealthy subsidizing products, dumping, and creating surpluses in global availability of products. With these scenarios being the reality of our current international trading climate it's of little wonder that the viability of the WTO as an organization for good is hotly contested and will likely continue to be as long as inequalities in the distribution of benefits from trade remain unreconciled.

Global Climate Change

Thus far our discussion involving global justice has focused on the challenges we face when attempting to distribute goods justly. But there are also burdens and harms that need to be considered for distribution when looking at the global picture. To end this chapter, we turn our attention to the distribution of a harm, namely the harmful effects of global climate change. As we saw in Chapter Three, there are many concerns surrounding the fact that the weather is getting warmer. There is no doubt that this warming trend can be directly linked in some ways to man-made carbon emissions. As you may recall, as these emissions heat up the atmosphere they will cause more unstable and violent weather, rising oceans, and the loss of habitable land due to increased desertification. It will probably not surprise you that on the global stage the United States is the number-one producer of carbon emissions in the world. In fact, we produce more metric tons of carbon per person per year than does China, Denmark, India, and Sierra Leone combined. On average, one U.S. citizen will produce approximately 20.6 metric tons of carbon dioxide where one person from Sierra Leone only produces .2 metric tons per year. With the negative effect of excess carbon dioxide a scientific certainty, it stands to reason that we are all going to suffer the ill effects of a warmer climate. But with such a disparity between producers and so many negative effects on the way, it stands to reason that we should ask how best to justly distribute the costs of cleaning up our air and saving the planet, that is, how best to distribute the burden of managing global temperatures in addition to distributing the negative effects of a warmer planet.

One of the most practical solutions offered to solve this distribution problem has been proposed by Peter Singer. In addition to offering us solutions regarding our treatment of humans and

animals, Singer offers us the following approach to cleaning up the environment. He refers to it as the "principle of equal per capita emissions." Basically he suggests that every country that emits carbon dioxide should be allowed to emit an agreed-upon amount each year. Each country will be allotted the same metric tons of carbon emissions and each can use it in any way they choose. So in the case of a wealthy country like the U.S., it is likely that we would be asked to lower our current emissions where a country like Kenya would very likely be allowed to increase emissions in order to meet those of the United States. Singer does not give us the agreed-upon level as he admits that these calculations would be best left up to scientists and not philosophers. What he does know is that the level we finally agree upon would have to be one that scientists determined was an amount that allowed us to sustain a level of climate change that is acceptable to all of us. Now, with every country being allotted an equal number of emissions, there will be those countries that will use them all within the year and some who will not.

It is interesting to note that the idea behind Singer's emissions principle is that we all have an equal allotment of carbon emissions to use as we see fit. An equal allotment of resources, even if they are carbon emissions, is clearly an egalitarian way to manage the growing climate crisis. As you can probably guess this also falls directly in line with the utilitarian principal of equality since we all share the air. So by instituting this principle we're not only allowing everyone to share something valuable in common, we are also distributing the burden of keeping it clean equally. But what if there were some countries who need to emit more carbon over and above their allowance? Could this need be met through Singer's proposal? For this contingency Singer offers us the idea of emissions trading. Emissions trading could occur between any country who was not using their full amount and those who knew they were going to exceed their amount. So if wealthy countries need to increase their emissions, they can "buy" emissions from the developing nations that are not currently using them. That is, if each country were allotted 10 tons of emissions per year and Georgia only has emissions equaling 6 tons, they would be free to sell the additional 4 tons to the highest bidder. Singer and others assert that this would be fair for a number of reasons. First, we could continue to maintain our current and agreed-upon levels of carbon dioxide ensuring that everyone has access to clean air. Second, those countries that are worse off have a very valuable commodity to sell to the wealthy nations. Poorer, less-developed countries could use this money to improve life for their citizens. Moreover, if selling these emissions proved to be very economically valuable, countries that are developing will have further incentives to not create more carbon emissions; rather, they will want to develop clean energies so they can continue to make a profit by selling unused emissions. So it would seem that everyone is in a position to win.

Although this certainly will not solve the climate crisis nor will it resolve all global injustices involving the burdens of climate change, Singer's proposal may go a long way to creating alternatives to the way we live now and to the types of international relationships we currently foster.

Notes

1. Young, Jeffrey, "Uninsured Americans 2012: more than 45 Million Lacked Health Insurance Last Year, CDC Reports," *Huffington Post,* March 21, 2013. http://www.huffingtonpost.com/2013/03/21/uninsured-americans-2012_n_2918705.html.
2. Armstrong, Chris, *Global Distributive Justice: An Introduction* (New York: Cambridge University Press, 2012), 30–31.
3. Beitz Charles, *Political Theory and International Relations* (Princeton, NJ: Princeton University Press, 1979).
4. Caney, Simon, *Justice beyond Borders* (New York: Oxford University Press, 2005).
5. Rawls, John, *A Theory of Justice* (Cambridge, MA: Harvard University Press, 1979).
6. Shue, Henry, *Basic Rights: Subsistence, Affluence and US Foreign Policy* (Princeton, NJ: Princeton University Press, 1980).
7. L. Wenar, "Why Rawls is not a cosmopolitan egalitarian," *Rawl's Law of People's: A Realistic Utopia?,* eds. R. Martin and D. Rediy (New York: Oxford University Press, 2006).
8. Pogge, Thomas, *World Poverty and Human Rights* (Cambridge, UK: Cambridge University Press, 2002).
9. Shah, Anup. "The Democratic Republic of the Congo." Global Issues. August 21, 2010. http://www.globalissues.org/article/87/the-democratic-republic-of-congo.
10. Ibid., http://www.globalissues.org/article/88/sierra-leone.
11. Moellendorf, D., *Global Inequality Matters* (Basingstoke, UK: Palgrave-Macmillan, 2009).

12. WTO Website. 2013. http://www.wto.org/english/thewto_e/whatis_e/wto_dg_stat_e.htm.
13. Fihlani, Pumza, "Marikana: 'My Husband Died In Vain," *BBC News Africa*. August 15, 2013. http;//www.bbc.co.uk/news/world-africa-23710613.
14. Biswas, Soutik, "How India treats it's women," *BBC News India*. December 29, 2012. http://www.bbc.co.uk/news/world-asia-india-20863860.

Name:________________________________ Date:_______________

Review Questions

1. What is a negative right?

2. What is the nonrelationships model of global justice?

3. According to Shue, how can we tell if a right is a basic right?

4. What is the personhood/autonomy model?

5. According to Beitz, what is unjust about our current global situation?

6. What does Caney mean by equal opportunities?

7. What is the resource curse?

8. How can the resource curse be avoided?

9. What is the minimalist approach to global justice?

10. What are the two principles advocated by John Rawls?

Name:______________________________ Date:______________

For Further Discussion

1. Given what you now know about basic human rights, in your opinion should healthcare be labeled a basic human right? If so, why and what kinds of healthcare? If not, why not?
2. In your opinion, is there anything that we as consumers in the United States can do to make international trade agreements more just? Explain.
3. When considering our moral obligations, which theory do you find more plausible, the relationships model or the nonrelationships model? Explain the reason for your choice.

Name:_______________________________________ Date:__________________

Case Studies

Mining for a Living Wage: South African Miners Strike for Improvements

Another mining strike in late 2013 marks at least a decade of similar strikes in South Africa. The National Union of Mineworkers has been urging members to strike, asking for a 60% pay raise to compensate for the rise in the cost of living. They are also calling for better working conditions and benefits for miners and their families. Mining represents about 10% of South Africa's gross national product and employs over 500,000 people. South Africa is by far one of the richest countries in terms of mineral and metal wealth, with over 50% of the world's gold and 80% of the world's platinum. But their mine workers are some of the world's poorest, with many being paid less than the equivalent of $600 a month despite years of difficult and dangerous work. Many of the miners live in substandard shacks with broken sewer pipes that run out into the streets. In addition to substandard living conditions there are hints that the old apartheid system has been slow to die in the mining industry as the majority of the dirty and dangerous work is done by black miners while the management and supervisory jobs are exclusively had by white workers. Last year following an unofficial mining strike over 30 miners were killed by riot police and more than 70 were injured. Everyone who is currently striking wants to avoid bloodshed but miners are unsure if they can trust police to simply keep the peace. It is ironic to think that a nation who exports so much mineral and metal wealth also has one of the most unequal societies in the world, with their poor getting poorer and their wealthy getting wealthier.[13]

1. How might the situation in South Africa reflect injustices within the international trade system?
2. If we were to use the minimalist model to attempt to help South Africa become more, just what might we need to do?
3. If we were to look at the South African miners through the nonrelationships model, why might we owe them assistance to improve their situation?

And the Winner is . . . . India, for Worst Place to be Born a Woman

In 2013 a new study reported that of all the G20 countries, India was ranked the worst country in which to be a woman. In addition to female fetuses being aborted and newborn baby girls being killed, women who do survive into adulthood face a lifetime of discrimination, violence, and neglect. In 2011 more than 24,000 cases of rape were reported with more than 95% of those cases involving someone the victim knew. India faces the serious problem of what is referred to as "missing women," that is, those women who would have been around had they not "disappeared" at birth, in childhood, at reproductive age, or older ages. These missing women are having an impact on India's birthrates as there are currently many more men than there are women in the country. But it isn't just concerns about rape or the women who are no longer here that is prompting some to demand action. The torture of women is up by over 5% and sex-slave trafficking is up an alarming 122%.

Despite promises of improving the lives of women, many political leaders in India have done little or nothing to protect them. This should not come as a surprise since over the last 5 years various political parties have fielded over 27 candidates who have been knowingly charged with rape.

Long-held attitudes about women have been blamed for the slow and almost nonexistent change in the treatment of women and many argue that nothing can or will be done on the political or legal level until these long-standing prejudices can be overcome.[14]

1. What challenges might we face if we were to try to promote universal human rights in a place like India?
2. Do you think it would be more plausible to advocate for positive or negative rights in a place like this? Explain.
3. If you were to attempt to bring about more just conditions to the people living in India, do you think it would be better to use an egalitarian approach or a minimalist approach? Explain your response.

Selected References

Many of the texts cited here were used as resources for this book. They may provide further insight into the particular topics presented in addition to providing strong primary resources if instructors are interested in adding primary texts to their course content. The journal articles listed may be the most useful as they have been selected specifically for this purpose and many of them can be accessed directly from the Internet or through common university and college databases such as EBSCO Host and JSTOR.

Allhoff, F., Lin, P., Moor, J., Weckert, J., & Roco, M. C. (2007). *Nanoethics: The ethical and social implications of nanotechnology.* Hoboken, NJ: Wiley.

Annas, G. J. (2010). *Worst case bioethics: Death, disaster and public health.* New York: Oxford University Press.

Armstrong, C. (2012). *Global distributive justice: An introduction.* Cambridge, UK: Cambridge University Press.

Armstrong, S. H., & Botzler, R. G. (Eds.). (2003). *The animal ethics reader.* New York: Routledge.

Arnim, W., Foley, R. W., Guston, D. H. (2012). What does nanotechnology offer to address complex sustainability problems? *Journal of Nanoparticle Research, 14,* 1093. EBSCO Host (80730994).

Arora, N. (2013). On eating animals. *The Humanist, 4,* 26–31.

Ates, A. E. (2012). The feasibility of global justice: A discussion on John Rawls' ideas. *Trakya University Journal of Social Science, 2,* 23–32. EBSCO Host (84566837).

Attfield, R. (2011). Schmidtz on species egalitarianism. *Ethics, Policy and Environment, 2,* 139–141. EBSCO Host (65453649).

Beauchamp, T. L., Waters, L., Khan, J. P., & Mastroianni, A. C. (2008). *Contemporary issues in bioethics.* Boston: Wadsworth.

Boylan, M. (Ed.). (2011). *The morality and global justice reader.* Boulder, CO: Westview Press.

Brooks, T. (Ed.). (2008). *The global justice reader.* Malden, MA: Blackwell.

Brooks, T. (2011). Respect for nature: The capabilities approach. *Ethics, Policy and Environment, 2,* 143–146. EBSCO Host (65453667).

Fenton, Andrew. "Neuroscience and the Problem of Other Animal Minds: Why It May not Matter So Much for Neuroethics." *Monist.* no. 3 (2012): 463-485. EBSCO Host (78154973).

Floridi, L. (Ed.). (2010). *The Cambridge handbook of information and computer ethics.* Cambridge, UK: Cambridge University Press.

Freeman, C. P. (2010). Framing animals rights in the "go veg" campaigns of U.S. animal rights organizations. *Society and Animals, 2,* 163–182. EBSCO Host (48846748).

Freeman, L., & Peace, G. (2005). *Information ethics: Privacy and intellectual property.* Hershey, PA: Idea Group.

Garrett, J. R. (Ed.). (2012). *The ethics of animal research: Exploring the controversy.* Cambridge, MA: MIT Press.

Hartzog, W., & Stutzman, F. (2013). Obscurity by design. *Washington Law Review, 2,* 386–418. EBSCO Host (88775639).

Hayward, T. (2006). Global justice and the distribution of natural resources. *Political Studies, 2,* 341–472. EBSCO Host (20858151).

Hursthouse, R. (1999). *On virtue ethics.* New York: Oxford University Press.

Jamieson, D. (2002). *Morality's progress.* Oxford, UK: Oxford University Press.

Jamieson, D. (2008). *Ethics and the environment.* New York: Cambridge University Press.

Jefferson, V. (2006). The ethical dilemma of genetically modified food. *Journal of Environmental Health,* 1, 33–34. EBSCO Host (21646210).

Jones, D. A. (2012). The ethics of creating chimeras and other admixed organisms. *Ethics of Medicine: An International Journal of Bioethics, 3,* 81–93. EBSCO Host (82234460).

Keller, D. R. (Ed.). (2010). *Environmental ethics: The big questions.* West Sussex, UK: Wiley.

Kesan, J. P., Hayes, C. M., & Bashir, M. N. (2013). Information privacy and data control in cloud computing: Consumers, privacy, preferences and market-efficiency. *Washington Law Review, 1,* 341–472. EBSCO Host (87120174).

Korsgaard, C. M. (1996). *Creating the kingdom of ends.* Cambridge, UK: Cambridge University Press.

Korsgaard, C. M. (2012). *A Kantian case for animal rights* (M. Michel, D. Kühne, & J. Hänni, Eds.). Zürich: Gallen.

Kuhse, H., & Singer, P. (Eds.). (2006). *Bioethics: An anthology.* Malden, MA: Blackwell.

Lane, R. (2006). Safety, identity and consent: A limited defense of reproductive human cloning. *Bioethics,* 3, 125–135. EBSCO Host (20672385).

Liao, M. S., Sandberg, A., & Roache, R. (2012). Human engineering and climate change. *Ethics, Policy and the Environment, 2,* 206–221. EBSCO Host (78084357)

Lombord, B. (2001). *The skeptical environmentalist: Measuring the real state of the world.* New York: Cambridge University Press.

Lunney, D. (2012). Wildlife management and the debate on the ethics of animal use: II. A challenge for the animal protection movement. *Pacific Conservation Biology, 2,* 81–99. EBSCO Host (79815862).

Mappes, T. A., Zembaty, J. S., & Degrazia, D. (2007). *Social ethics: Morality and social policy.* New York: McGraw-Hill.

Matthews, F. (2012). The anguish of wildlife ethics. *New Formations, 76,* 114–131. EBSCO Host (86040690).

McGinn, R. E. (2010). What's different ethically about nanotechnology? *Nanoethics, 2,* 115–128. EBSCO Host (53465343).

Morell, V. (2013). *Animal wise.* New York: Crown.

Regan, T. (2004). *The case for animal rights.* Berkeley: University of California Press.

Rogers, B. (2000). The Nature of Value and the Value of Nature. *International Affairs, 2,* 315–323.

Sachdev, Y., & Veena, S. (2011). Human cloning: Perspectives, ethical issues and legal implications. *International Journal of Pharmacology and Biosciences, 1,* B28–B41. EBSCO Host (60147168).

Schmidtz, D. (2011). Respect for everything. *Ethics, Policy and Environment, 2*, 127–138. EBSCO Host (65453650).
Sen, A. (2012). The global reach of human rights. *Journal of Applied Philosophy, 2*, 91–100. EBSCO Host (75232706).
Silva, F. G. (2002). Ethics of the new biology and genetic medicine (molecular ethics): (Re)view from the USA. *Pathology International*, 9, 555–562. EBSCO Host (7606364).
Singer, P. (1990). *Animal liberation.* New York: Avon Books.
Sterba, J. P. (2011). Biocentrism defended. *Ethics, Policy and Environment, 2*, 167–169. EBSCO Host (65453661).
Sunstein, C. R., & Nussbaum, M. C. (2004). *Animal rights: Current debates and new directions.* New York: Oxford University Press.
Taddeo, M., & Vaccaro, A. (2011). Analyzing peer-to-peer technology using information ethics. *Information Society, 2*, 105–112. EBSCO Host (59132061).
Talbot, M. (2012). *Bioethics: An introduction.* Cambridge, UK: Cambridge University Press.
Tansey, G. (2008). For good or greed. *The Ecologist, 9*, 26–29. EBSCO Host (35287788).
Tavani, H. T. (2011). *Ethics and technology: Controversies, questions, and strategies for ethical computing.* Hoboken, NJ: Wiley.
Varner, G. E. (1998). *In nature's interests?: Interests, animals rights and environmental ethics.* New York: Oxford University Press.
Varner, G. E. (2011). Speciesism and reverse speciesism. *Ethics, Policy and Environment, 2*, 171–173. EBSCO Host (65453660).
Walker, Rebecca L. and Philip Ivanhoe J. (eds.) *Working Virtue: Virtue Ethics and Contemporary Moral Problems.* (2007) New York: Oxford University Press
Weidel, T. A. (2011). Are human rights wrong?: A human language ethic approach to global poverty. *Perspectives on Global Development and Technology, 1*, 213–223. EBSCO Host (59144193).
Welchman, J. (Ed.). (2006). *The practice of virtue.* Indianapolis, IN: Hackett.

Index

A

B

H

I

J

K

T

U

V

W

Z